Multinational Federations

This is the first comparative volume focusing on multinational federations, bringing together an international range of expert scholars on federalism.

Multinational federations reflect the increasing contemporary global trend towards social differentiation. The new millennium has coincided with the unleashing of powerful forces of cultural-ideological differentiation that have acquired a dramatic constitutional and political salience across the world. Today we allude to this in broad terms as 'identity politics'.

Multinational federations are federal states whose principal purpose is to accommodate, manage and resolve some of the most intractable political conflicts of our time that emerge from identity politics: those that stem largely from competing national visions, whether within or between established states. Nationalism and national identities in their many forms have not disappeared. Indeed, they have been revitalised and rekindled in many established states. Consequently this unique book draws on a wide range of country studies including Canada, Belgium, Malaysia, India, Spain, Russia, Cyprus, Switzerland and the European Union (EU) in order to show the pivotal relationship between federalism and nationalism. In so doing it addresses the practical relevance of federalism to the new political recognition of difference and diversity in the specific form of national minoritarianism.

This book will be of strong interest to students and researchers of federalism, democracy and nationalism.

Michael Burgess is Professor and Director of the Centre for Federal Studies in the Department of Politics and International Relations at the University of Kent, UK. **John Pinder** is former Professor at the College of Europe, Bruges, Chairman of the Federal Trust, London, UK and Chairman of the James Madison Trust, London, UK.

Routledge series in regional and federal studies
(formerly the Cass series in regional and federal studies)

Series editor: Michael Burgess
University of Kent
Formerly edited by John Loughlin, Cardiff University

This series brings together some of the foremost academics and theorists to examine the timely subject of regional and federal studies, which since the mid-1980s have become key questions in political analysis and practice.

Multinational Federations

Edited by Michael Burgess and
John Pinder

Routledge
Taylor & Francis Group

LONDON AND NEW YORK

First published 2007
by Routledge
2 Park Square, Milton Park, Abingdon, Oxon OX14 4RN

Simultaneously published in the USA and Canada
by Routledge
270 Madison Ave, New York, NY 10016

Routledge is an imprint of the Taylor & Francis Group, an informa business

© 2007 Selection and editorial matter Michael Burgess and John
Pinder; individual chapters, the contributors

Typeset in Garamond by Wearset Ltd, Boldon, Tyne and Wear
Printed and bound in Great Britain by TJI Digital, Padstow, Cornwall

British Library Cataloguing in Publication Data
A catalogue record for this book is available from the British Library

Library of Congress Cataloging in Publication Data
A catalog record for this book has been requested

ISBN10: 0-415-41490-3 (hbk)
ISBN10: 0-203-96451-9 (ebk)

ISBN13: 978-0-415-41490-6 (hbk)
ISBN13: 978-0-203-96451-4 (ebk)

Contents

Contributors

Ismail Bakar is Senior Principal Assistant Secretary, Ministry of Finance, Kuala Lumpur, Malaysia.

Harihar Bhattacharyya is Reader in Political Science in the Department of Political Science at the University of Burdwan, West Bengal, India.

Michael Burgess is Professor of Federal Studies and Director of the Centre for Federal Studies (CFS) at the University of Kent in Canterbury, UK.

Murray Forsyth is Emeritus Professor of Politics, University of Leicester, UK.

Alain-G. Gagnon is Canada Research Chair in Quebec and Canadian Studies at the Université du Québec à Montréal, Canada.

John McGarry is Professor of Political Studies and Canada Research Chair in Nationalism and Democracy at Queen's University, Kingston, Canada.

Luis Moreno is a Senior Research Fellow at the Spanish National Research Council (CSIC), Madrid, Spain.

Brendan O'Leary is Professor of Political Science in the Department of Political Science at the University of Pennsylvania, USA.

Patrick Peeters is Associate Professor of Law in the Faculty of Law at the University of Leuven (KUL) and the Université Catholique de Louvain, Belgium.

John Pinder is former Professor at the College of Europe, Chairman of the James Madison Trust and Chairman of the Federal Trust, London, UK.

Cameron Ross is Reader in Politics in the Department of Politics at the University of Dundee, Scotland, UK.

Ronald L. Watts is Principal Emeritus, Professor Emeritus of Political Studies and Fellow of the Institute of Intergovernmental Relations at Queen's University, Kingston, Ontario, Canada.

Preface

The origin of this volume of essays dates back to an international research workshop on 'Multinational Federations' held in April 2003 at Tickton Grange Hotel in the rolling countryside just outside the market town of Beverley, East Yorkshire, England. The workshop was generously funded by the James Madison Trust (JMT), London and the participants were invited to contribute papers on the specific problem of multinationalism in federal states. The papers presented at that meeting were subsequently revised, updated and resubmitted in 2004, and then subjected in 2005 to the editorial pens of Michael Burgess and John Pinder. The result of this lengthy but thorough process has been the collation of the following 12 chapters that constitutes the first edited collection of essays on multinational federations.

Clearly there remains to this day a conceptual problem with the term 'multinational', but terminological precision was to some extent subordinated to the collaborative pursuit of comparative insights and perspectives. It was deemed on balance worthwhile to commit ourselves to empirical analysis even while the conceptual territory remained disputed. Consequently the choice of federations was limited to those that the editors believed to be good examples of the federal idea grounded in the practical circumstances of competing conceptions of nation and nationalism. This flexible approach led us to include not only Canada, Belgium, Russia, India and Malaysia in the case studies but it also enabled us to incorporate both Spain (multinational but not formally a federation) and Cyprus (a largely bicommunal federal arrangement in the remaking) in the first part of the survey. The second part of the volume, however, brings into focus the larger overarching picture with four chapters that include first the European Union (EU) and then the three comparative surveys on India and Switzerland, ethnic nations and a wide-ranging overview that serves as the conclusion to the book.

It is intended that this sharp focus upon multinational federations will stimulate further research into this most complex and challenging of contemporary problems of the modern state in the twenty-first century. The provision of detailed case studies is the first step towards a reconceptualisation of the term 'multinational' and more insightful comparative explorations. It is with this purpose uppermost in mind that we encourage others to follow our first tentative steps in the broad direction of the comparative politics of identity, difference and diversity.

Michael Burgess
John Pinder

1 Multinational federations

Introduction

John Pinder

Multinational federations are intended to provide a framework that can accommodate and as far as possible resolve some of the most intractable political conflicts of our time: those that stem from competing national visions, whether within or between established states. Yet although experience of the working of relevant political systems has accumulated in recent decades, it has not been the subject of comparative study that the importance of the subject requires. The aim of this book is to respond to this need.

One reason for the lack of attention paid to the subject may be the intellectual, institutional and emotional capital invested in the nation state and the idea of its sovereignty. That has deep roots: in France, from Bodin, through the Jacobins' 'nation une et indivisible' and with strong influence to the present day; in Britain, from Hobbes' absolute monarchical sovereignty through Austin's, then Dicey's, doctrine of indivisible parliamentary and national sovereignty, likewise influential up to the present. In the nineteenth century the doctrine was supported by many internationalist liberals, because of their sympathy with the Greek, Hungarian, Italian and Polish struggles for national independence. John Stuart Mill, in his essay on nationality published in 1861, was not untypical in preferring a unitary national state;[1] and the frontiers drawn under President Wilson's influence in Central and Eastern Europe after the First World War followed in that tradition. The doctrine became embedded in the language with terms such as nation state and national sovereignty.

Intellectual traditions of federalism: Hamiltonian and Proudhonian

While the doctrine of the centralised unitary and sovereign state became particularly deep-rooted among the British and the French, events in the past century have pressed them towards a new view of sovereignty and its indivisibility: in France, following the Second World War, with its leading role in the establishment and development of the European Union (EU) and the accompanying constraints on national sovereignty; in the United

Kingdom, with its participation, albeit reluctantly, in the EU, then the creation of the Scottish Parliament and the Welsh Assembly. Such political developments too had their intellectual antecedents, from Althusius and Locke in the seventeenth century, through Montesquieu in the eighteenth, from whom the American Founding Fathers drew intellectual sustenance for their remarkable innovation of democratic government at two levels, of both the federation and the states. The US constitution in turn gave rise to the Hamiltonian tradition of federalist thought, named after the most politically influential of the authors of *The Federalist*,[2] which emphasises the institutional requirements for the establishment of a federation of states.

Almost concurrently with Mill's essay, the liberal historian Acton expressed an opposing view of federation, seeing it as 'the most efficacious and the most congenial of all the checks on centralised oppression of minorities', with the 'coexistence of several nations under the same state' as 'the best security of its freedom';[3] and he was to take issue with Mill over the idea that the state must be congruent with the 'national unity which is the ideal of modern liberalism'.[4] Acton's view was not without influence. He was Gladstone's adviser over the question of Irish home rule in the 1880s and 1890s; and the concept of a federal Britain attracted considerable support as a way of treating the running sore of Irish discontent in the United Kingdom until the issue was resolved by Irish secession after the First World War.[5] Acton's federalism extended to relations among, as well as within, existing states, enabling 'different nationalities ... to exist in harmony side by side', and as such, he envisaged it would be capable of 'unlimited extension'.[6]

Other distinguished British scholars who, like Acton, wrote favourably in the second half of the nineteenth century about the federal principle were James Bryce, Edward A. Freeman, J.R. Seeley and Henry Sidgwick; indeed, among those who gave their attention to it, only A.V. Dicey was hostile.[7] Spurred by the European and world crisis of the 1930s, this tradition was revived in a literature by authors of the stature of William Beveridge, Ivor Jennings, Lord Lothian and Lionel Robbins; and the horrors of the Second World War led Beveridge to return to the subject in 1945, while K.C. Wheare's classic study of federal government was published in the following year.[8] But subsequent rejection by the British political class of the idea of a federal Europe, together with entrenched opposition to formal systems of devolution, was reflected until the latter part of the twentieth century in the scant academic attention paid to the subject in Britain. Meanwhile English-language literature on the subject was to come mainly from Canada and the United States.

Following the influence of Montesquieu on the American Founding Fathers and French support for American independence, the US Constitution in turn influenced French thinking in the period up to 1791. But the Jacobins who then seized power regarded the federalism of their opponents, the Girondins, as akin to treason and treated them accordingly, thus establishing a remarkably durable tradition of unitary centralisation. Alexis de

Tocqueville's great book on American democracy was nevertheless the first influential study of the American federal system.[9] But it was not until Proudhon's *du Principe Fédératif* was published that a specifically French tradition of federalism emerged. The date of Acton's first published work on the subject was not the only similarity, for Proudhon's main interest in federalism was likewise its decentralising aspect.[10] Whereas Acton had, however, like most other English-speaking writers, concentrated on the dimension of political institutions, Proudhon cast his net wider, to embrace decentralised economic institutions in particular. His ideas, which inspired the Proudhonian tradition of federalism, strongly influenced the French labour unions until displaced by Marxism in the early twentieth century. But interest in them was to revive in the personalist movement, which was subsequently to influence Jacques Delors.[11]

It was, however, in order to set in train an incremental process of constructing a European federation on Hamiltonian lines that Jean Monnet in 1950 drafted the Schuman declaration which launched the establishment of the European Coal and Steel Community designed to 'build the first concrete foundation of a European federation which is essential to the preservation of peace'.[12] The result has been the creation of a federal political system through a series of steps over the past half-century, which has, as Monnet envisaged, gone far towards becoming a federation.

The EU is a particularly interesting example of the integration of a group of states into a federal system through a series of steps which may well lead to a federation and from which lessons can be drawn for other groups of states that may wish to embark on a similar course. Some scholars have indeed defined federalism as a process rather than relating it to a completed state.[13] As the federations studied in this book demonstrate, there is also a process of development in the relations between the centre and the states inside existing federations, particularly to accommodate the demands of nations within them, which may be of particular interest with respect to newly established federal systems such as Belgium and Spain, or to states such as the United Kingdom that may be moving in that direction.

Discussion of federations and federal systems is, however, so bedevilled by misunderstandings about words, that before passing on to the studies of particular cases, we need to consider the meaning of relevant concepts such as nations, sovereignty, federal political systems, federal states and multinational federations.

Nations, sovereignty, federations, federal political systems, multinational federations

Nations and sovereignty

Ernest Gellner famously defined a nation as people who 'share the same culture, where culture in turn means a system of ideas and signs and associations and ways of behaving and communicating' and who 'recognise each other as belonging to the same nation ... nations are the artefacts of men's convictions and loyalties and solidarities'.[14] He warned against paying too much attention to definition on the grounds that neither the cultural nor the voluntaristic criterion is adequate and that definitions of culture are themselves difficult and unsatisfactory. Given this wise advice, we shall not probe deeper into definitions, save to note that various combinations of linguistic, cultural and ethnic characteristics as well as shared history are to be found in the 'nations' which are the subjects of succeeding chapters, and that they 'see themselves as distinct societies and demand various forms of autonomy or self-government to ensure their survival as distinct societies' (see Chapter 12 by Ronald L. Watts, 'Multinational federations in comparative perspective', p. 357).

Where groups that share such characteristics are not geographically concentrated, they may form part of a multi-ethnic rather than a multinational state. Austria-Hungary before the First World War was an example of such a state, which though hardly a democracy devised some means to satisfy the desire of ethnic minorities for autonomy through measures of self-government in fields such as education and culture;[15] and the Belgian federal constitution has applied a similar principle in providing for an allocation of powers for the 'communities' of the Dutch-, French- and German-speakers, with respect to linguistic, cultural and educational functions, separate from that for the territorial regions.

These arrangements are relevant, if peripheral, to the theme of this book, which concerns nations that relate to a particular territory and which demand autonomy or self-government within a state, or take part in a federalising process among independent states, thus causing tension or conflict regarding sovereignty, in the sense of 'legal or political freedom from external control'.[16] In principle, sovereignty is usually regarded as legally absolute, even if limits are in practice accepted. But the terms national sovereignty and nation state often carry the connotation that such limits are aberrant and should as far as possible be avoided, which raises a semantic problem regarding national component parts of a multinational state. Switzerland, where the citizens of the cantons, though not comprising nations, are likewise extremely sensitive about their sovereignty, has dealt with it by affirming in Article 3 of the Constitution that 'the Cantons are sovereign in so far as their sovereignty is not limited by the Federal Constitution and, as such, they exercise all rights which are not transferred to the Federal power'. Thus sovereignty has been divided between the cantons and the federation, each being sovereign within its own fields of competence; and this can be seen as generally valid in a federation, although the delineation between the fields of competence can be changed by constitutional amendment, usually by a qualified majority of states or citizens or both. The ultimate test of whether the system was federal or confederal was resolved in the USA only at the enormous human and economic cost of the Civil War.

In 1998, however, the Supreme Court of Canada issued a judgment that secession could be legitimate if negotiated respecting procedures which, however, remain subject to political definition.[17] It is surely reasonable for practical purposes to regard sovereignty as divided between a federal centre and its constituent parts, recognising that whatever the definition of sovereignty, it remains possible that the circumstances which the word reflects may not endure for ever.

Federations and federal political systems

That article in the Swiss Constitution reflects the desire to establish shared rule for some purposes while retaining the historic self-rule of the cantons for others. Following a brief and almost bloodless civil war, the Swiss had in 1848, drawing on the example of the USA, reformed what had hitherto been a confederal association into a federal state. They thus created a federation in the sense defined by Ronald L. Watts as 'a compound polity combining constituent units of government and a general government, each possessing specific powers delegated to it by the citizens through a constitution' (p. 226, Chapter 12).

Watts explains the concept more fully in Chapter 12. Here we need only note that a federation has government at two (or more) levels, each with a direct relationship with the citizens, including through elections of their representatives. The distribution of powers between the centre and the states[18] has to be guaranteed by the constitution, each having a sufficient proportion of the legislative, administrative and taxing powers to give it the capacity to be a viable polity. Thus the effective operation of the states is not dependent on the centre, so there is a 'shield for minority groups that would otherwise feel threatened';[19] nor, in order that there can be effective shared rule, is the centre dependent on the individual states. The constitution is defended by an 'umpire', usually a federal judiciary, to rule on disputes between governments, often with respect to the division of powers between the centre and the states. Constitutional amendment is not usually majoritarian, in the sense of being decided by a simple majority of the citizens or the states, but nor is it usually subject to veto by a single state, though the Canadian parliament resolved in the late 1990s that the constitution would not be amended against the will of the province of Quebec; and the Supreme Court's judgment on the possibility of negotiated secession also indicates a remedy should a state be unwilling to tolerate an amended constitution.

While this definition is, we hope, clear and useful, discussion of federations is often confused by variable terminology. Thus Switzerland has an explicitly 'Federal Constitution' which provides for a federal state, although its French title is Confédération Suisse (owing mainly to the problem, in the mid-nineteenth century, of translating the German word 'Bund' into French). Malaysia, though named a federation, has in fact many of the attributes of a unitary state. The Spanish Constitution, though establishing a polity with many federal features and a process whereby these features are being steadily strengthened, deliberately eschews the 'f' word. The question also arises whether the term federation is identical with federal state. If a key attribute of a federal state is its general responsibility for the deployment of armed force, the above definition could apply to federal systems that are not federal states, provided that the powers of the centre appear sufficient to enable it to maintain its autonomy over the long run. As Murray Forsyth argues in Chapter 9, however, the stability of a federal system will remain in question for as long as its states may part company over issues concerning the use of armed force.

Forms of association among states that fall short of being federations may nevertheless contain significant federal elements. Daniel Elazar included confederations, federacies, associated statehood, condominions, leagues, joint financial authorities and asymmetrical federal arrangements among what he called 'federal political systems'; and Watts adds 'hybrids of these'.[20]

Forsyth, in his study of confederations, concluded that they often develop sooner or later into federations:[21] five and a half centuries later than the first emergence of a 'federal political system' within Switzerland, but only 12 years later in the USA. Belgium took its first step of constitutional reform from a unitary towards a federal state in 1973 and with its fourth, in 1993, became an explicitly federal state. In 2001 there was a fifth step in what seems likely to be a continuing process of constitutional reform, demonstrating that institutions are adjusted in response to problems in federations as well as in federal systems. Luis Moreno describes Spain as 'a latent federation' (p. 86 of Chapter 6) because it has, within the framework of the Constitution, been incrementally accumulating the characteristics of a federal state.

Multinational federations

Australia, Austria, Germany and the USA may be called single-nation federations, within which none of the component states, with the exception perhaps of Bavaria, has a particularly enhanced sensitivity regarding its sovereignty, whether on linguistic, cultural or ethnic grounds or because of a heightened sense of its history as an independent state. For them federation is a good way of ensuring sufficiently decentralised government rather than defending a unique national culture. We use the term multinational federation to denote a federal state among whose component states there is at least one such distinct nation. Thus in Canada the Québécois are a nation as defined by Gellner, while the term has been extended to cover numerous, mostly very small, Aboriginal Nations, sometimes called First Nations; and these are all nations within what is generally construed as the Canadian nationality. In Belgium the Dutch-speaking Flemish and the French-speaking peoples have similar national claims, whether or not they are called nations. The Spanish Constitution terms the Basque, Catalan and Galician peoples 'nationalities', with the right to autonomy 'within the indissoluble Spanish nation'. The boundaries of Indian states have, since the federation's Constitution was inaugurated in 1950, been redrawn on linguistic lines, which also correspond to cultural, historic and in a number of cases ethnic distinctions; and national concepts are increasingly used to underline their claims to autonomy within the federation. In Malaysia the main linguistic, cultural and ethnic groups, comprising the Malay majority, the large Chinese and the smaller Indian minority, are largely dispersed around the federation, which therefore has more of the characteristics of a multi-ethnic than of a multinational state. The Russian Federation includes many states containing national minorities as well as those comprising territorial divisions of the Russian majority.

None of the citizens of the Swiss cantons would regard themselves as a nation within the Swiss nation, nor indeed do any of the four linguistic groups. But the cantons have such a deep-rooted history of autonomy that their sensitivity to infringement of their sovereignty is as acute as that of nations with pronounced linguistic, cultural or ethnic distinctions. Gellner's warning against being too absolute about definition of nations applies with added force to multinational federations. States within them that are congruent with nations are apt to insist on self-government with particular intensity, which may conflict with effective federal shared rule. But as the Swiss example shows, similar intensity may exist in cantons whose citizens would not see themselves, or be described by others, as nations. Study of such cases can contribute much to understanding of the particular problems of multinational federal states, or of forms of devolution embodying federal elements within multinational states.

Thus the study of existing multinational federations is relevant to a wider range of polities which are located in the spectrum of federal political systems. This applies to associations among existing independent nation states as well as to the development of devolution within states. The EU has, since the initial launching of the first European Community, added enough federal elements to its powers and institutions to become a hybrid between a federation and a confederation. So the experiences of multinational federations are germane to the understanding of its present condition and prospects for further development. It may be seen as the realisation of Acton's vision that the federal principle would be capable of 'unlimited extension'. While conditions may not be ripe for such extension in the wider world, the study of multinational federations and federal systems is likely to be a useful preparation for dealing with the intensifying problems of international and global interdependence.

Conditions that enable multinational federations to work

Many of the conditions that underlie nations' acceptance of shared rule are similar to those that apply to single-nation federations.[22] Expectations of security, economic and environmental benefits are particularly important. For independent states jealous of their sovereignty, satisfaction with a prior political association that has federal elements may be added; and previous measures of devolution that have been regarded as useful by nations within hitherto unitary multinational states can likewise be important. Enduring strength of such motives is a necessary condition for enabling multinational federations to work effectively. But it is not sufficient.

Democratic political institutions in the governments of both the constituent states and the federation are also essential, because authoritarian regimes are not able to share their power. If the centre is authoritarian, it will not tolerate effective self-rule in the states; and if states have authoritarian regimes, they will not accept effective shared rule – or, if they may to some extent accept it, the federal government which is influenced by those states and the citizens they control will not be regarded as democratically legitimate either.[23] This has been illustrated by failure of federal constitutions in Latin America, modelled on that of the USA, in states which have been subject to dictatorship, as well as by subsequent difficulties during the course of establishing effective democracies. It has also been shown by the fate of most federal constitutions in Africa and of some in Asia, though here India is a notably important exception. States in the former Soviet Union were federal in name alone, because the reality was rule by the fiercely centralised authoritarian party. While most of the Central and East European states that were within the former Soviet bloc have made remarkable strides in establishing effective democracies, the democratic consolidation of some of them must remain a preoccupation for the EU for some time to come.

Even among democratic states within a federation, a state so big as to be a hegemon can present great difficulty. Either it will dominate the other states, which they are not likely to accept for any length of time, particularly if they include nations; or it will defer to them to an extent that its citizens are not likely to tolerate. This was one of the causes of the failure of the Federation of the West Indies, in which Jamaica contained the majority of the population, as well as of the Central African Federation and of the Nigerian federal constitution of 1960, which were dominated by the then southern Rhodesia and northern Nigeria respectively. Nor is a binational federation likely to be stable. If one of the two states is likely to be a hegemon, as with the proposed Cypriot federation, the problems associated with hegemony are likely to be compounded; or if they are of fairly equal size, constant deadlock may stand in the way of effective shared rule. If on the other hand the states are all small in relation to the federal whole, the imbalance between their human and financial resources and those of the federal government will undermine the effectiveness of their self-rule in the face of federal dominance. A combination of at least two, and preferably more, states that are big enough to defend their self-government against encroachment from the centre, together with a number of smaller states, offers the best structure for success in both shared rule and self-rule.

While liberal democracy is a fundamental requirement for the government of federations and their states, similarity of social institutions does not appear to be necessary, except in so far as is essential for the civil society that is a fundamental basis of democracy. Differences in such matters as the nature and scope of the welfare state are a natural concomitant of the coexistence of different national cultures within a federation, and at least some of them are best handled in the field of self-rule. The same applies to questions of language, culture and education, as well as police, which are particularly sensitive fields for nations within a federal system. Along with these goes the need for the states within a federation to have the assurance of enough fiscal and financial resources to carry out their responsibilities in these and other matters; and this, together with the institutions and powers for effective self-government, has to be constitutionally entrenched and guaranteed.

Consensus democracy through consociational arrangements

National minorities, and indeed other minority groups, are not well protected within a political system based on the principle that 51 per cent of the votes cast are enough and that until the next election the winner takes all. Multinational federations therefore resort to various consociational arrangements, i.e. institutions and procedures that encourage consensus rather than allowing the will of those who represent a simple majority of the population to prevail.

Thus in the legislatures of federal systems the smaller states are usually over-represented relative to population in the federal house of the states, for example with equal representation of each state in Switzerland, following the example of the United States, and with substantial weighting in their favour in the Council of Ministers of the EU. Qualified majority voting, requiring a majority of usually between two-thirds and three-quarters of the total, is normal for votes in legislatures or referendums on matters as important as amendment of a federal constitution and, in the EU, for the Council's approval of most legislation. At the limit there may be a constitutional requirement for a unanimous vote, in other words a right to veto. This could in effect apply in Belgium to decisions that are challenged by three-quarters or more of the representatives of either the Flemish-speaking or the French-speaking community; and the EU's member states have a right to veto decisions on a number of subjects. It has been promised to Quebec by the resolution of the Canadian federal parliament with respect to constitutional amendment, while Swiss custom and practice, which has powerful status in that political culture, requires unanimity among the cantons with respect to certain particularly sensitive questions. While voting by simple majority generally applies in a federal house of the people, an absolute majority rather than a majority of those voting is quite often required in the European Parliament, and for some purposes a qualified majority. Consensus in the legislatures of most federations is also fostered by electoral systems of proportional representation rather than first-past-the-post.

There is usually a power-sharing structure in the federal executive, which stems more readily from the European system of a parliamentary, rather than the American system of a presidential, executive, though power-sharing can be built into the latter by provision for the distribution of other senior posts. In Switzerland's modified parliamentary executive, the seven posts that the constitution stipulates for the principal executive body, the Federal Council, are distributed according to a customarily agreed formula among the linguistic, religious, regional and party groups, and the post of Swiss president rotates annually among them. The posts in the EU's Commission are distributed among the states on a more-or-less equal basis stipulated in the EU Treaty. Multinational federal systems normally have arrangements for distributing appointments in the federal civil service and other public bodies among the citizens of the different states, either in proportion to population or with over-representation of the smaller states.

There are also systems for states' representation in federal judiciaries. The Belgian Constitution, for example, provides for six Dutch-speaking and six French-speaking judges in the Supreme Court together with a president alternating annually between the two; and the EU Treaty requires the Court of Justice to comprise one judge from each state, who together choose its president from among their number.

A special status for national minorities is recognised in some federations by means of asymmetrical provisions designed to cater for their particular problems. The Canadian federal parliament's decision to allow Quebec to veto constitutional amendments is one example.

The question arises as to how far these procedures which favour consensus inhibit the capacities of politicians and the citizens they represent to choose solutions to a multinational federation's problems. Thus there are fears that deadlock may empty the Belgian federal institutions of meaningful content. The EU, with its highly consensual system, has succeeded, among other things, in enacting the bulk of its massive programme of single market legislation, even if it is less certain how far the system ensures that the laws are effectively applied within the states. But there is concern whether the consensual arrangements will work well enough in a European Union of 27 or more states, or whether they will be capable of producing the hard decisions that may be required to resolve problems which may arise in future, arising perhaps from macroeconomic crises, urgent demands for a radical increase in the Union's fiscal and financial resources to deal with critical under-performance of the economies of some of the newer member states, or a need for a more effective Union foreign policy, particularly in matters relating to security. One view is that the Union has done well enough in bringing peace, stability and some other benefits to its citizens and should not try to do more. Another is that this is not likely to suffice to meet the future needs of its citizens; and there are similar concerns in some other multinational federal polities. How to ensure that there is enough desire and capacity to make shared rule effective remains an essential question for multinational federations.

The desire and capacity for effective shared rule

A measure of cultural compatibility is necessary to make shared rule possible. The presence of nations within a multinational federation makes for more cultural diversity than is to be found in single-nation federations. But can we identify an essential minimum of compatibility?

The minimum of common civic and political culture must clearly include what is necessary to sustain a system of liberal democracy. Beyond that, the Swiss federal state is based on other shared political characteristics which include, in addition to direct democracy, a profound respect for local autonomy which underlies self-rule, and a deeply entrenched practice of accommodating divergent interests through compromise, which is cement for effective shared rule.

A culture of democracy has become rooted in the Indian federation too, though, given the relatively short period of India's experience of liberal democracy, it naturally has shallower roots than in Switzerland. There is at least as much ethnic diversity among the states as is to be found in Europe; there is also linguistic diversity, moderated by the roles of Hindi as the mother tongue, though with various dialects, of two-fifths of the population, mainly in northern states, and of English as a lingua franca, particularly in the south. The four-fifths of the population who are Hindus, however, despite Hinduism's religious diversity, share characteristics which doubtless help to underpin shared rule. But these may well be no more significant than the religious, cultural and social affinities among the Swiss. Using the terms 'thick' and 'thin' nations, which Harihar Bhattacharyya has applied in Chapter 11 to distinguish between those with more linguistic, religious, ethnic and cultural homogeneity and those whose union is based rather on shared political values, it seems reasonable to locate both India and Switzerland towards the thinner end of the spectrum.

Jürgen Habermas's theory of what may be seen as constitutional patriotism addresses this question. Starting from the search for a rationale for citizens' commitment to the Constitution of the Federal Republic within a 'thick' German nation that was divided between its democratic western and Soviet eastern parts, he moved on to the more general question of commitment to a multinational federal political system in the form of the 'thinner' European Union and of the potential for sustaining citizens' commitment to its constitution in the absence of a 'thick' European nation.[24]

The EU is committed to liberal democratic values including the rule of law based on human rights and representative government; its states are liberal democracies and its system of shared rule has been more or less adequate for the powers that it has exercised hitherto. But the principles of representative government have been only partially applied to the institutions of the Union itself and there is contention as to whether this attribute of a federation should be completed, as well as how far the competences of the Union should be further extended, particularly in the field of security. It is frequently argued that in the absence of a coherent European demos, the development of a European liberal democracy is not possible. But not only have the Union's citizens shown the capacity to fulfil their roles as citizens within their own member states, even if some doubts may remain regarding the citizens of some of the newer states; they also appear to have as much in common ethnically, culturally, socially and with respect to religion as do the peoples of the Indian federation, and linguistically not much less. It seems unduly sceptical to assume that Europeans are inherently incapable of achieving effective democratic shared rule. The pertinent question is, rather, through what stages they may be able to develop their capacity to do so.

John McGarry and Brendan O'Leary suggest in Chapter 10 that, in addition to the consociational arrangements necessary to ensure sufficient consensus in a multinational federation, a 'Staatsvolk', defined as 'a national or ethnic people, who are demographically and electorally dominant' though not necessarily an absolute majority of the population, can provide the necessary cohesion within a multinational federation.[25]

Canada, with its English-speaking (though by now far from ethnically British) majority and Québécois minority is one relevant case. The English speakers, who generally regard their national identity as identical with that of Canada, are seen by francophone Québécois as dominating the Canadian political culture. Both groups have the necessary democratic political and civic culture; there are divergences among the English-speaking provinces which usually cause them not to vote as a unified bloc; and there are consociational arrangements aiming to achieve a necessary minimum of consensus. But the linguistic and historic distinctions have been sharp enough to enable the separatist Parti Québécois to form provincial governments and in 1995 to come within half a percentage point of winning a provincial referendum in favour of secession, thus demonstrating that neither the dominant English-speaking culture, nor the elements of political culture shared by the two groups, nor the consociational arrangements then prevailing, provided a truly solid basis for the federation's viability. Subsequent developments may, however, have contributed to its consolidation.

Spain's equivalent of Canada's English speakers is the Castilian-speaking majority, with the Basques, Catalans and Galicians as the national minorities. Here, too, while there are significant elements of a common political culture, the Castilian speakers are far from homogeneous and there are consociational arrangements. The Constitution provides, moreover, for much further development of regional self-rule. But a firm balance between the factors that support shared rule and those that emphasise self-rule remains to be achieved.

In the United Kingdom (UK) the English are the undoubted 'Staatsvolk'.

English is spoken by almost all the citizens, including half a million people whose first language is Welsh, and there is a high degree of common culture, though historic religious differences remain an acute problem in Northern Ireland. Four-fifths of the population is English, compared with one-tenth Scots and the remaining tenth in Wales and Northern Ireland. There has been a good deal of mutual accommodation between the English and the other nationalities, though not until relatively recently with the Irish nationalist Roman Catholics in Northern Ireland. But the possibility of Scottish secession remains and it is not clear whether the (re)creation of the Scottish Parliament with some significant powers will permanently satisfy the Scots that their future lies in the UK. There has been less separatist sentiment among Welsh nationalists and the relative weakness of the Welsh Assembly does not seem likely to provoke secession. But the agreement of 1998, which launched the peace process in Northern Ireland, devolving substantial powers to the province's Assembly and introducing a number of consociational procedures based on Belgian federal experience, was accompanied by an undertaking that the UK government would accept a decision by a majority in a Northern Ireland referendum to join the Irish Republic; and since the Roman Catholic minority already comprises some two-fifths of the population and average incomes are now higher in the Republic than in the UK, this is by no means impossible. Thus the English majority has still not managed to make the cohesion of the United Kingdom entirely secure, quite apart from the bloodshed that was involved in the secession of republican Ireland, with its repercussions enduring to this day.

Although the UK is beginning to assume the form of a federal political system, a federal state comprising four national states would, given the massive disproportion between the English majority and the other three nations, come too close to being in practice a unitary system to satisfy at least the Irish, and not improbably the Scottish, nationalists. Proposals were indeed put forward in the period up to 1914 for a federal UK comprising Ireland, Scotland, Wales and a number of English regions with comparable populations. One such proposal, envisaging seven such regions, was made in 1912 by the young Winston Churchill, then a member of the Liberal Cabinet, as an answer to the Irish question; and it was supported in the Cabinet by the future Prime Minister, Lloyd George.[26] The strength of English nationalism which stood in the way of that, or any other federal solution, was reflected in Dicey's reaction to what he saw, writing in 1914, as the current notion 'that federalism contains the solution of every constitutional problem that perplexes British statesmanship', in the form of his vehement assertion that 'this belief in a new-fangled federalism is . . . a delusion not only to England but to the whole British Empire' and a menace to 'that small country limited in size, but still of immense power, which is specifically known by the august name of England'.[27] But a federal structure could hardly have been less successful in accommodating Irish nationalism than was the unitary state influenced by such uncompromising English nationalism. England's power now is not what it was then, when Westminster ruled a quarter of the people in the world. But the English have still not fully come to terms with their status as the majority nation in a middle-sized European power; and one aspect of this is a failure to understand the theory and practice of federalism, despite the decisive impulse given to the federal idea by eighteenth century Britons in North America, followed in the United Kingdom by a significant contribution on the part of British scholars and politicians of the nineteenth century and again in the period leading up to and into the Second World War.

Federalism

Preston King defines federalism as an ideology, in the sense of 'a broad and reasonably coherent set of ideas which is invoked with a view to mobilising and directing political action in order to serve some relatively specific purpose', which has three different orientations, centralist, decentralist and balance, responding to 'opposed demands for the centralisation and decentralisation of power on a specifically territorial basis'.[28] More briefly, Michael Burgess takes federalism to mean 'the recommendation, and sometimes the active promotion, of support for federation'.[29]

King also observes that 'although there may be federalism without federation, there can be no federation without some matching variety of federalism';[30] and this is highly relevant to both definitions, for a viable federation will not be established without sufficient desire to create it and understanding of what is involved, including in particular the necessary powers and institutions for both the centre and the states, as outlined earlier in this chapter and explained in more detail by Watts in Chapter 12. Nor will a viable polity be delivered and maintained without commitment, on the part of the politicians and the citizens they represent, to both effective self-rule for the states and effective shared rule at the centre.

Some of the conditions that favour the success of a federation have been indicated in this introduction. A state big enough to be a hegemon is hard to accommodate; and if there is a hegemonial nation, its people are best divided among states representing its regions in such a way as to ensure that there is no single dominant state. Consociational arrangements are necessary to facilitate consensus, but without going so far as to prevent the taking of decisions required for effective shared rule.

Shared rule has to be based on a solid commitment among the states and citizens to liberal democracy, supported by an adequate civil society. Further elements of a common culture can be helpful but may not be essential, provided that there are adequate consociational arrangements and that sufficient powers are allocated to the states. Diversity of social institutions may be accommodated mainly by the allocation to self-rule of responsibilities in that field.

Shared rule should be confined to fields where there is a strong case that it is required to meet common needs; and the scope of self-rule should be extensive enough to ensure that states, and in particular those representing national minorities, have their own viable polities. There must be solid enough guarantees of the powers and institutions of states' self-rule.

Neither shared rule nor self-rule will function unless they are supported by patterns of behaviour that enable the institutions to wield their powers effectively, including the commitment of politicians and citizens to the proper working of the federal institutions, respect for the autonomy of the states and readiness to reach accommodation when there is conflict between the two.

Federation is not an easy option. But it addresses the difficult questions posed by relations between citizens, nations and states in an ever more inter-dependent world, in which citizens set store by local and national autonomy while the problems with which their parliaments and governments have to deal reach increasingly beyond national frontiers. We hope that this book will help readers to identify some of the answers.

Notes

1 J.S. Mill, 'Nationality', in *Considerations on Representative Government*, in *Collected Works: Essays on Politics and Society*, vol. 19 (Toronto and London: University of Toronto Press and Routledge and Kegan Paul, 1977, original essay 1861), pp. 547–9.

2 James Madison, Alexander Hamilton and John Jay, *The Federalist Papers*, edited by Isaac Kramnick (London: Penguin Books, 1987, first published in New York journals, 1787–88).

3 Sir John (later Lord) Acton, 'Nationality', in *Home and Foreign Review*, July 1862, reprinted in Lord Acton, *The History of Freedom and Other Essays* (London: Macmillan, 1907), pp. 285, 290.

4 Lord Acton, 'Sir Erskine May's Democracy in Europe', in *The Quarterly Review*, January 1878, reprinted in ibid., p. 98.

5 See Michael Burgess, *The British Tradition of Federalism* (London: Leicester University Press, 1995), ch. 4.

6 Cited, from notes in Acton's unpublished manuscripts, in G.E. Fasnacht, *Acton's Political Philosophy* (London: Hollis & Co., 1952), p. 243.

7 See John Pinder, 'Federalism and the British Liberal Tradition', in Andrea Bosco (ed.), *The Federal Idea* (London: Lothian Foundation Press, 1991), pp. 99–118.

8 See Sir William Beveridge, *Peace by Federation?* World Order Papers, First Series (London: Royal Insitutue of International Affairs, 1940) and *The Price of Peace* (London: Pilot Press, 1945); W. Ivor Jennings, *A Federation for Western Europe* (Cambridge: Cambridge University Press, 1940); Lord Lothian, *Pacifism is not Enough: nor Patriotism Either* (London: Oxford University Press, 1935); Lionel Robbins, *The Economic Causes of War* (London: Jonathan Cape, 1939); K.C. Wheare, *Federal Government* (London: Oxford University Press, 1946, second edition 1951).

9 Alexis de Tocqueville, *de la Démocratie en Amérique* (Paris: vol. 1, 1835; vol. 2, 1840); reprinted, with introduction by François Furet, (Paris: Garnier-Flammarion, 1981); in English, *Democracy in America* (Chicago: Chicago University Press, 2000).

10 P.-J. Proudhon, *du Principe Fédératif* (Paris, 1863), reprinted in *Oeuvres completes de P.-J. Proudhon*, vol. 16 (Paris: Librairie Marcel Rivière et Cie., 1959).

11 Charles Grant, *Delors: Inside the House that Jacques Built* (London: Nicholas Brearley Publishing, 1994), pp. 12–15, 277.

12 Statement by Robert Schuman, French foreign minister, on 9 May 1950.

13 For example Carl J. Friedrich, *Trends of Federalism in Theory and Practise* (London: Pall Mall Press, 1968).

14 Ernest Gellner, *Nations and Nationalism* (Oxford: Blackwell, 1983), p. 7.

15 See Otto Bauer, *Die Nationalitätenfrage und die Sozialdemokratie* (Vienna: Wiener Volksbuchhandling, 1907); Karl Renner, *Das Selbstbestimmungsrecht der Nationen* (Leipzig; Deuticke, 1918); Charles Taylor, 'Why do Nations Have to Become States?' in C. Taylor (ed.), *Reconciling the Solitudes: Essays on Canadian Federalism and Nationalism* (London: McGill-Queen's University Press, 1993), p. 58.

16 N. MacCormick, 'Sovereignty', in Vernon Bogdanor (ed.), *The Blackwell Encyclopaedia of Political Institutions* (Oxford: Blackwell, 1987), p. 583.

17 See James Tully, 'Introduction', in Alain-G. Gagnon and James Tully (eds), *Multinational Democracies* (Cambridge: Cambridge University Press, 2001), p. 7.

18 The constituent units in the federations studied in this book are variously called cantons, provinces, nationalities, regions and states. When referring to a particular federation its own word has been used, but when referring to federations in general the word states has been used for the units and federal state for the whole.

19 Alain-G. Gagnon, 'The Political Uses of Federalism', in Michael Burgess and Alain-G. Gagnon (eds), *Comparative Federalism and Federation: Competing Traditions and Future Directions* (Hemel Hempstead: Harvester Wheatsheaf, 1993), p. 15.

20 Daniel J. Elazar, *Exploring Federalism* (Tuscaloosa, AL: University of Alabama, 1987), ch. 2; Watts, p. 000.

21 Murray Forsyth, *Unions of States: the Theory and Practice of Confederations* (Leicester: Leicester University Press, 1981), p. 208.

22 The conditions are examined in Wheare, op. cit. in n. 7 (2nd edn), pp. 37–40, and in Ronald L. Watts, *New Federations: Experiments in the Commonwealth* (Oxford: Oxford University Press, 1966), p. 42.

23 See Wheare, ibid., pp. 46–8.

24 For example in J. Habermas, 'Citizenship and National Identity: Some Reflections on the Future of Europe', in *Praxis International*, 12.1, 1992, pp. 1–19.

25 See Brendan O'Leary, 'An Iron Law of Nationalism and Federation?: a (Neo-Diceyian) Theory of the Necessity of a Single Staatsvolk, and of Consociational Rescue', in *Nations and Nationalism* 7 (3), 2001, pp. 273–96, citation from pp. 284–5; and John McGarry and Brendan O'Leary, 'Federation as a method of ethnic conflict regulation', Chapter 10 in this volume.

26 See Michael Burgess, op. cit. in n. 5, pp. 100–1.

27 A.V. Dicey, *Introduction to the Study of the Law of the Constitution* (London: Macmillan, 1885), citation from 8th edn, 1915, pp. xxiv, xxxiii, xxxiv.

28 Preston King, *Federalism and Federation* (London: Croom Helm, 1982), pp. 1, 3.

29 Michael Burgess, 'Introduction', in M. Burgess (ed.), *Federalism and Federation in Western Europe* (London: Croom Helm, 1986), p. 20.

30 Op. cit., p. 76.

2 Democratic multinational federalism under scrutiny

Healthy tensions and unresolved issues in Canada[1]

Alain-G. Gagnon

Introduction

The concepts of multination, multinational democracies and multinational federations have gained prominence in academic circles during the last decade. Democratic multinational federations are characterised by a propensity to reflect deep diversity and stability even though significant strains do exist. Contrary to non-democratic multinational federations, these are capable to resist better the test of time through the proper management of politics and power sharing. Most democratic federal multinational federations, such as Belgium, Canada and Switzerland,[2] have faced different types of challenges over the years. All three have proven to be rather stable under different conditions of stress. Other types of democratic multinational federation exist as well. The United Kingdom and Spain, for example, offer an additional basis for comparison as "unions of states" to use Murray Forsyth's terminology.

The Canadian experiment is possibly one of the less stable of the cases that qualify as democratic multinational federations. I will argue, in this chapter, that this is largely due to a stronger identity quest on the part of Quebecers in response to misrepresentations by the central government and the other member states of the Canadian federation, who are unwilling to recognise Quebec on its own terms.

In the Canadian context, the concept of multinational federation has gained popularity following the Meech Lake debacle of 1990, the discussions leading to the failed Charlottetown Accord of 1992 and the Quebec referendum of 1995 and its aftermath. During such times of particularly high tensions, the notion of multinational federation has not been well received in most "federalist circles".

Canadian colleagues, such as John Meisel and Jean Laponce, have been among the scholars most at ease with the concept of multination to depict the Canadian political community and, above all, to defend it as a real option in the management of diversity. This is probably due to their broader exposure to Western Europe, which for these scholars has represented somewhat of a land of predilections. Other Canadian colleagues, such as Philip

Resnick and Alan Cairns, have also shown some receptiveness to the idea but have been quick to insist that if the concept was to be applied, it would be clear that political powers gained at the level of the nation (understand Quebec) will be lost at the central level (read Ottawa) of the country. Canadian nationalists[3] have considered the notion of multinational federation to be un-Canadian, divisive and detrimental to the future of the country, interpreting such an approach as providing the seeds for secession.

In English Canada and Quebec, members of the Research Group on Multinational Societies have been strong proponents of multinational federalism for Canada. They point out, however, that if Quebec were to secede the same issue would surface considering the presence of 11 Aboriginal nations on the territory.

Three bodies of literature are relevant to the present discussion of democratic multinational federations. More specifically, the literature can be grouped around three established authors: John Rawls' "cooperative scheme in perpetuity", Daniel Elazar's self and shared rules and Ernest Renan's "daily plebiscite".

I intend to assess the extent to which these authors provide theoretical insights for the management of diversity in Canada in light of the country's historical foundations and contemporary constitutional and political developments.

John Rawls' cooperative scheme in perpetuity

The first body of literature that inspires most policymakers concerned with the integrity of the Canadian state builds on the work of liberal philosopher John Rawls. Rawls was concerned with establishing a contractarian basis for the just distribution of wealth and authority in a liberal community. In the end, it is an abstract theory of pure distribution. Centralists that seek to deny multinational solutions to the problems of Canadian federalism thus invoke Rawls' defence of just liberal principles to legitimate a homogeneous view of the nation state, which Rawls himself describes as a "cooperative scheme in perpetuity". From this reading, the just liberal state is to be neutral with regards to "particularistic" group demands (i.e. national minorities). The only exceptions to the notion that individuals should be free to determine their own conceptions of the good involve instances where certain actions: (i) threaten liberal equality itself (preventing an individual from pursuing his/her ends in life); or (ii) result in a distribution of wealth that would leave the least-advantaged worse off than they would have been prior to such actions (the "difference principle").

It is clear from this brief sketch of Rawls' basic framework for a just liberal order that his understanding of politics applies more readily to unitary states and communities that are homogeneous, as well as to states that build on territorial federalism – the United States constituting his ideal type. Indeed, he establishes in his early writing "that the boundaries of these schemes are given by the notion of self-contained national community".[4] But this does not imply that Rawls might prescribe that states replicate the political structures of these real-world examples. Rather, it just so happens that such states are devoid of many of the political conflicts that occur *between* communities and are theoretically conducive to a Rawlsian justification for the distribution of power and wealth. Rawls simply took the confines of any community for granted in discussing just liberal principles. In other words, Rawls never answers questions about what determines the boundaries around communities to which his principles are to apply – his ideas operate prior to political conflict between nationalities

If one wishes to invoke Rawlsian principles to make a case for a liberal polity, it nonetheless remains a liberal or just exercise to question the boundaries of a political community if the subsequent configuration itself follows Rawls' basic framework concerning the distribution of wealth and authority. A community in perpetuity is not an independently existing object – although it may be conceptualised as such in the abstract. Canada should not be assumed to constitute the boundaries of a Rawlsian contractarian community that "lives in perpetuity" due to its commitment to a liberal political framework. Indeed, Rawls must commit to a harmonious and organic society to sustain his principles of justice because there is no provision in the initial abstract "contract" that assumes individuals would opt out in order to be "unfree" or "more disadvantaged". The logic of implicating Rawls in debates surrounding the value of multinationalism means that all national communities can be assumed to be fixed in perpetuity and are defined as nations simply because they are spanning over a given territory that is committed to liberal practices. If one liberal country subsumed another without the latter's consent, would we then talk about how this constituted a cooperative scheme in perpetuity? This is clearly not the implication that Rawls intended. Rawls provides a coherent framework for a just liberal society – which can be applied to Canadian or Quebec societies, or to some creative form of multinational arrangement.

Perhaps one attractive aspect for proponents of the status quo in centralised multinational states is that the notion of a "cooperative scheme in perpetuity" projects the image of containment more profoundly than a notion of free deliberation and open process. We contend, in contrast, that some open-endedness that would allow for political flexibility is necessary in plural societies in order for communities to feel and be free to determine their future without undue pressures.

An important number of Canadian political scientists have drawn upon Rawls' and his orthodox liberal followers' pattern of politics to deny Quebec's aspirations for a different status within the federation, and have argued that to say otherwise would lead to a slippery slope argument in favour of secession.[5] Jeremy Webber, a jurist by profession, has expressed his opposition to the slippery slope to secession argument, commenting that such a position leads to the impossibility of any discussions between political leaders. For Webber this type of argument is a non-starter in a democratic regime, whether it is federal or not.

> Those who resist all accommodation assume that political allegiance naturally tends to be single. They therefore refuse concessions to local allegiances and emphasise a single, central allegiance in order to maintain commitment to the whole. In doing so, however, they suggest, usually implicitly but sometimes explicitly, that minority communities have to be ready to weaken their commitment to their local communities in the interest of the whole – that Quebecers must be Canadians first, that they should choose between Quebec and Canada.[6]

Canadian nationalists have been ingenious at developing arguments that draw upon the "cooperative scheme in perpetuity". But why draw on this scheme in the first place? On what principles are such arguments based? How did such developments emerge and in order to serve and defend whose interests? And at the behest and on behalf of whom? All of these questions remained largely unanswered and need clarification.

From a very different perspective, one based on the principle of nationality, David Miller elaborates a typology of three forms of social division that can be identified within a political community, namely ethnic cleavages, rival nationalities and, his personal contribution, nested identities. Type 1, ethnic cleavages, are illustrative of segmentation within a given political community. In many ways, one can argue that Switzerland corresponds best to this category rather than to the "multinational pattern", in contrast to what Kymlicka has argued elsewhere. Type 2, rival nationalities, are catering to separate groups, inward-looking and exclusive. Coming easily to mind in this category are Cyprus, Israel and the former Czechoslovakia. Type 3, nested nationalities, are to be found when territorially-based political communities are encompassed within a single "nation", understood here as a "nation state". According to Miller, cases in point include the Basque country, Catalonia, Galicia, Scotland, Wales, Flanders, Wallonia, Quebec and many other small nations that often have a split identity.

Miller's typology is not naive. It is motivated by a desire to abandon the use of the term "nation" to describe nations without formal statehood. By his own admission

> the label matters because of the power of the idea of national self-determination. Once it is conceded that a territorial community genuinely constitutes a nation, we seem already to have shown that there is good reason for the community in question to be granted political autonomy.[7]

In reaction to this type of argument, I would stress that the power to name oneself is an act of power and an expression of political freedom that constitutive nations of given multinational democratic federations have a right to establish and to assert. For authors such as Miller, democratic multinational federations are antinomic and fall in his second categories of rival nationalities.

I would make the argument that, though Miller is sensitive to the presence of diverse ethno-cultural groups on a given territory and "nested identities", he simply continues the work of Rawls' cooperative scheme in perpetuity. Miller goes on to argue that Belgian, Canadian, Spanish and Swiss nationalities are singular because of their respective long-established cultural and political associations. Because of their coexistence with an encompassing nation it would be inconceivable, according to Miller, for them to see themselves as constituting something other than a subset of an established polity for three reasons: "cultural overlap", "mutual economic advantage" and an "interwoven history".[8] As such, according to Miller, no one can disentangle what has been interlocked over the years through exchanges of different kinds. Those communities are prisoners of each other – reminiscent of a cooperative scheme in perpetuity – and secession is simply a non-option for members of constitutive nations since their members are intertwined in an existing nation state.

Daniel Elazar's self-rule and shared rule

The second body of literature that I want to stress is composed of contributions surrounding the influential work of Daniel Elazar, and more pointedly to his depiction of "self-rule plus shared rule"[9] as a way forward to finding solutions to conflicts that undermine community relations in several multinational federations. Essentially, Elazar is speaking of the combined need for autonomy and the quest for solidarity as a way to manage diversity properly. With respect to potential conflict management in multinational federations, it is clear that the balance between self-rule and shared rule is central and necessitates our attention.

Elazar portrays the federal principle as a founding pillar of modern democratic states, as an insurance policy that allows communities to develop further their democratic practices. In *Exploring Federalism*, Elazar makes the point that the pursuit of the federal project is not about centralisation but rather about non-centralisation. Elazar consistently argues in his work for the need to diffuse powers between several centres so that no one can dominate the agenda and permanently impose its views on the others.[10] For Elazar, this condition is contractual and guarantees respect for all members in a federal compact.

Admittedly, Elazar has had a major influence on members of the Comparative Federalism and Federation Research Committee of the International Political Science Association. Robert Agranoff, Michael Burgess, John Kincaid and Ronald Watts and several others have benefited from his writings and further elaborated on his work.

In my case, I have defined federalism as a political device for establishing viable institutions and flexible relationships capable of facilitating interstate relations, intrastate linkages and inter-community relations. Inspired by Elazar, I have also warned against the dangers of nationalising central governments since they undermine federal practices. The issue at stake concerns power relationships and the extent to which the central government is sufficiently democratic so as not to act as a hegemon even in cases where it has the capacity to flex its muscles and display political strength.

The desire for additional powers by the central state apparatus in multinational federal settings has often led to a growing inclination on the part of the member states, especially when ethnic fragmentation corresponds to state boundaries, to opt out of the federation. This is the situation in which Quebec finds itself.

What this suggests is that, at the very least, central governments within democratic multinational federations need to exert a high level of restraint. Echoing Elazar, Robert Agranoff has very aptly described this phenomenon. "The federal idea," he argues, "is not a centralising principle, but a non-centralising one. While it may require a whole body of one people or the importance of the federation as a general commitment, an all-powerful centre is not the core idea."[11]

The desire to centralise on the part of majority nations within multinational federations has rarely led to the implementation of policies favouring diversity and has frequently been accompanied by political tensions. Opposition by member states are easy to understand, considering that such initiatives are meant to homogenise economic, political and social practices and to undermine the roles of member states in the federal pact. Historical legacy becomes a non-issue since what matters is the *hic et nunc* and, for central state managers, it is simply unfortunate if the member states of a given multinational federation see the original compact being eroded on a day-to-day basis, as long as the centre holds and can impose its will. But for how long, one may ask?

This leads me to the question: can the centre hold for the long term under strained conditions due to misrecognition? Charles Taylor is surely one of the most influential political philosophers who has tackled the issue. He argues that

> If a uniform model of citizenship fits better the American image of the liberal state, it is also true that this is a straitjacket for many political societies. The world needs other models to be legitimated, in order to allow for more humane and less constraining modes of political cohabitation.[12]

Other political philosophers have done just that. Will Kymlicka, for one, has opened up a major field of research by demarcating special representation rights from political rights, to be granted respectively to polyethnic communities and to national groups within existing nation states, be they multinational or not. This has contributed to the notion that there exist new ways in which political communities can reside in multinational federations.

Kymlicka makes the argument that polyethnic rights are meant

> to help ethnic groups and religious minorities express their cultural par-
> ticularity and pride without it hampering their success in the economic
> and political institutions of the dominant society. [. . .] Unlike self-
> government rights, polyethnic rights are usually intended to promote
> integration into the larger society, not self-government.[13]

He goes on to establish, and this is highly relevant to our discussion, that

> Multination federalism divides people into separate "peoples", each with
> its own historic rights, territories, and powers of self-government; and
> each, therefore with its own political community. They may view their
> own political community as primary, and the value and authority of the
> larger federation as derivative.[14]

Being characterised by societal diversity, federal societies constitute a propitious setting for multinationalism. To quote Kymlicka, "federalism can
provide meaningful self-government for a national minority, guaranteeing
its ability to make decisions in certain areas without being outvoted by the
larger society".[15] However, it should be mentioned that in the Canadian
case, Quebec's self-government capacity has been seriously eroded,[16] especially during the last decade. Indeed, many initiatives have been undertaken
by the central government to diminish or, at a minimum, to constrain the
power that national minorities can exercise, with a view to rallying allegiance of individuals towards the centre.

In the Canadian context, this can be illustrated by the multiplication of
federal programmes that fall under exclusive provincial jurisdictions.
Following the failed referendum of 1995, which proposed the establishment
of a new relationship between Quebec and the rest of Canada, the central
government has launched a series of initiatives in the fields of education,
health care, as well as municipal politics, to make its presence felt in those
provincial sectors.[17]

Quebec provincial parties of various stripes, stretching from Jean
Charest's Liberals (federalist), to Mario Dumont's Adéquistes (autonomists)
to the Bernard Landry's Péquistes (autonomists/secessionists), have all
denounced the central government intrusion in provincial policy fields.
Others, like Claude Ryan – a former leader of the Quebec Liberal Party –
argue that too often federal-provincial negotiations have failed due to unnecessary rigidities on the part of the central government. "This vision," Ryan
argues,

> contains an abstract and doctrinaire equality of individuals and
> provinces; it denies any form of asymmetry in our federal system. This
> vision was at the root of the failure of the Meech Lake Accord. It was

also present in discussions leading to the Framework Agreement [Canada's Social Union, 1999–2002]. Similar causes usually produce similar effects; no serious progress will ever be realized with Quebec as long as this vision prevails.[18]

Therefore, to borrow Ron Watts' terminology, is there in Canada "a supportive federal culture" that can contribute to ease the tensions between constitutive minority nations? With Ryan and several others, I am less enthusiastic than Watts on this subject. If "past Canadian experience confirms the importance of such a political culture",[19] current central government practices are tilting the balance in favour of a strong centralist trend. In Quebec, the Séguin Commission on fiscal imbalance has clearly demonstrated the extent to which Ottawa takes advantage of its position to force the member states to play to its tune, short of which money is not available for its own programmes and tax payers run the risk of paying twice for a given service.

Rather than pushing an imperialist agenda, as Guy Laforest portrays the federal government's project in Canada,[20] it would seem more appropriate to pursue a balance between self-rule and shared rule so that Canada's institutions are reflective of its societal make-up and more in tune with a covenant tradition.

Ernest Renan's daily plebiscite

A third body of literature pertaining to the management of diversity in multinational federations can be aggregated around Ernest Renan. Renan coined the notion of a "daily plebiscite" to portray the extent to which people need to be informed, consulted and involved in the elaboration of state policies. This notion paves the way towards democratic deliberation and constitutes a genuine commitment to an open process of negotiation for members of a federation built on multiple national groupings. In short, it is an issue of empowerment through the potential for resistance.

James Tully's theoretical work is highly relevant here as he actualises Renan's depiction of a political contract. Indeed, Tully seeks to identify ways to recognise national diversity in complex political settings. He believes that most important activities ought to be inter-subjective, continuous, agonic as well as multi-logical. In other words, the process of negotiation between member states has to be an open process – that is an "activity-oriented" process rather than an "end-state" process where all is fixed and relations of power are predetermined.[21] As with Renan's portrayal, peoples here are free to deliberate, and to decide their own future.

Examining the Supreme Court of Canada in Reference Re the Secession of Quebec of 20 August 1998, Tully concludes that it represents an open process for negotiation and that it contributes to attenuate the view of the Constitution Act, 1982 as a straitjacket that emerges from the written text of the constitution.[22] Tully's view of Canada is instructive:

a multinational democracy is free and legitimate, therefore, when its constitution treats the constituent nations as peoples with the right to self-determination in some appropriate constitutional form, such as the right to initiate constitutional change. This enables them to engage freely in negotiations of reciprocal disclosure and acknowledgement as they develop and amend their modes of recognition and cooperation, in conjunction with the fair reconciliation of other forms of diversity.[23]

In (multinational) federations, one witnesses from time to time state actors associated with a central government that see themselves as the only legitimate political actors. This contributes to undermining the legitimacy of federal practices and requires our attention. The danger is that the central state be viewed as the only state that matters, leading to what Ernest Renan equated in *Qu'est-ce qu'une nation* with the expression of "One state, one culture."

In multinational federations, the principle of divisible sovereignty[24] gains some ascendancy since it is conceivable to imagine that internal nations, let's say national communities such as Scotland, Catalonia or Quebec, be able to exercise increased powers almost as if they were quasi-independent states. Rainer Bauböck goes further when he argues that the concept of multinational federation "rejects the conservative realist approach that views claims to self-government rights of national minorities as a threat to the territorial integrity of existing states".[25] In a globalising world, this scenario gains support within nations whose boundaries fall along the lines of existing member states of federated units since the nearest government is often viewed as the one where citizens can exercise the strongest influence.

In addition, debates surrounding a theoretical push in favour of multinational federations also imply that culture matters and that it is essential to find ways to reflect deep societal diversity in institutions. For national and subnational minorities, it is

> a societal culture – that is, a culture which provides its members with meaningful ways of life across the full range of human activities, including social, educational, religious, recreational, and economic life, encompassing both public and private spheres. These cultures tend to be territorially concentrated, and based on a shared language. [. . .] for a culture to survive and develop in the modern world, given the pressures towards the creation of a single common culture in each country, it must be a societal culture. Given the enormous significance of social institutions in our lives, and in determining our options, any culture which is not a societal culture will be reduced to ever-decreasing marginalization.[26]

Clearly, "national cultures" are advantaged to the extent that they reflect the values of the dominant political community in any given (multi)national federal settings. In the Quebec context, the notion of "global society" has been utilised to depict the extent to which this region state is highly cohesive. It already constitutes a host society in its own right, possesses strong liberal corporatist structures in which state–business–labour work together and has a noted international presence.[27]

Creative politics: healthy tensions and unresolved issues

The prevailing visions in the literature suggest that there are many contending issues to be reckoned with and that further theoretical work is necessary. One thing that is sure, however, is that authors such as Rawls, Elazar and Renan have their followers. In my view, the objective to be pursued now is not to argue that one author is right while the other two are wrong but more to assess the extent to which their influential work has contributed to express healthy tensions with respect to the Westphalian model and take into account many unresolved issues in several multinational democratic federations.

For instance, Elazar warns us against the desire to centralise power excessively and stresses the need to find an appropriate balance between self-rule and shared rule, inviting state managers to be more inventive and open to a variety of models that can accommodate communities. This position is even more grounded at a time when, to use the phraseology of David Held, "All independent states may retain a legal claim to 'effective supremacy over what occurs within their territories', but this is significantly compromised by the growing enmeshment of 'the national' with transnational influences."[28]

The work of Rawls has often been utilised to discredit any serious questioning of dominant relationships in a given polity. Experts have often wrapped themselves in Rawls' procedural liberalism to deny the right of national minorities to exert their right of self-determination. As a result, the notion of a cooperative scheme in perpetuity has become a justification for non-recognition of (sub)national claims, in the name of an overarching majority nationalism, and contributes to circumventing the possibility for a national minority to guarantee "its ability to make decisions in certain areas without being outvoted by the larger society", to emphasise Kymlicka's point.[29]

With the creation of several new nation states since the late 1980s, it has become clear that we need to develop models that can further accommodate national minorities by legitimating new institutions, short of which several cases of secession might occur. The Westphalian model needs to be revamped and one way of doing so, I believe, is to give proper exposure to the concept of multinational federalism.[30]

The validation of the concept of multinational federalism becomes clear when one considers the added value to be gained by a refinement of our democratic practices. If federalism allows us, according to Reg Whitaker,[31] to have a more refined definition of sovereignty, the notion of multinational federalism contributes to give meaning to federal conceptions of citizenship. The establishment of multinational federalism, as an ideal type, constitutes a way forward to bring into the political equation more diverse societies that are experiencing a sense of alienation due to the fact that power appears to be escaping national minorities through a process of globalisation which, in turn, is accompanied by a further quest for centralisation on the part of existing nation states.

Multinational federalism allows us to enlarge our notion of citizenship and eventually develop a theory of genuinely differentiated citizenship. In the Canadian context, debates between proceduralists and communitarians with respect to Quebec's right of secession, as well as Aboriginal claims to self-government, have led to an enrichment of political attitudes and contributed to a legitimisation of these two liberal streams.

Such debates have also permitted liberals to consider new institutions that reflect "deep diversity"[32] in diverse (pluralist) democratic societies. With a view to avoid a secessionist trajectory, multinational federalism constitutes a way forward and should be considered as having healing potential for communities that share many values even though they may not share the same political and sociological profiles. In other words, what is wrong with the emergence of multinational federalism if the societal projects inspiring respective member states are founded on liberal premises?

Arguably, power alone can dictate how multinational federalism will be operating since it is the very essence of the problem, leading national minorities to ask for reappraisal of the operation of the existing nation state or to affirm their right to secede.

Indeed, Michael Ignatieff, a former adherent to cosmopolitanism, reminds us with regard to the case of Quebec–Canada relations that,

> At the moment, might lies with the majority and right with the minority. Mutual recognition must rebalance the relationship, with both power and legitimacy finding a new equilibrium. Then, and only then, will we be able to live together in peace in two countries at once, a community of rights-bearing equals and a community of self-governing nations.[33]

To get there, we need a constitutional sense of trust and respect of the type that can be found in the Supreme Court of Canada's Reference case with respect to Quebec's right of secession. In their decision, the nine chief justices establish four principles from which to enter into negotiation in a federal setting such as Canada; a democratic tradition, federal practices, constitutionalism and the rule of law, and respect for minority rights. Based on these principles, Quebec can freely enter into negotiation with Canada in order to be recognised on its own terms. In sum, mutual respect on the part of the communities involved and a sense of constitutional morality are necessary to enter into proper negotiation.[34]

Conclusion

I am of the view that in the Canadian context we are faced with three nations that aspire to govern themselves. We are also faced with two host societies (Quebec and Rest of Canada) that are capable of integrating citizens effectively in their respective communities. At a minimum, we need to find ways by which to accommodate those national communities. In some ways, Quebec has been able to achieve such arrangements with the Crees and the Inuit whereas Canada has been successful in doing the same with the Inuit of Nunavut. These are promising avenues and more needs to be accomplished on that front.[35]

I find myself in complete agreement with Martin Heisler when he states that "I don't think that federalism can resolve conflict. I don't think it can avoid conflict. I don't think it ought to. I think it ought to provide a context in which conflict can be approached, arbitrated and managed."[36] Multinational federalism is a more refined model of federalism and it has added potential for state managers to come to terms with political issues confronting diverse societies.

The purpose of multinational federalism should be obvious to anyone who believes in furthering democratic practices in liberal democratic states. It contributes to bringing power closer to citizens and invites majority nations to show solidarity toward their minorities while continuing their political associations. Multinational federalism, as with the politics of identity which, according to Stuart Hall, works with and through difference, is able to build those forms of solidarity and identification that make common struggle and resistance possible without suppressing the real heterogeneity of interests and identities, and which can effectively draw the political boundary lines (without which political contestation is impossible) without fixing those boundaries for eternity, is an essential component for contemporary states as it leads to a refinement of democratic practices.[37]

In closing, let me stress that multinational federalism constitutes a major advancement for the management of diversity as it initiates debate on recognition, assists in identifying defining moments as potentially empowering and constraining, and compensates for inadequate recognition by revisiting original compacts.

Notes

1 The research assistance of Raffaele Iacovino, associate researcher with the Canada Research Chair on Québec and Canadian Studies at the Université du Québec à Montréal is acknowledged and appreciated.
2 Though in the case of Switzerland it is easier to make the case that we are in the presence of a plurilingual federation.
3 See, Alain-G. Gagnon, "Undermining Federalism and Feeding Minority Nationalism: The Impact of Majority Nationalism in Canada", in Alain-G. Gagnon, Montserrat Guibernau and François Rocher (eds), *Conditions of Diversity in Multinational Democracies* (Montreal: Institute for Research on Public Policy, 2003).

4 John Rawls, *A Theory of Justice* (Cambridge, MA: Harvard University Press, 1971), p. 457.
5 For a similar argument, see Jeremy Webber, *Reimagining Canada: Language, Culture, Community, and the Canadian Constitution* (Montreal: McGill-Queen's University Press, 1994), p. 252.
6 Webber, op. cit., pp. 254–5.
7 David Miller, *Citizenship and National Identity* (Cambridge: Polity Press, 2000), p. 130. Miller makes a similar argument in "Nationality in Divided Societies", in Alain-G. Gagnon and James Tully (eds), *Multinational Democracies* (Cambridge: Cambridge University Press, 2001), pp. 299–318.
8 David Miller, *Citizenship and National Identity*, op. cit., p. 132.
9 See, Daniel Elazar, *Exploring Federalism* (Tuscaloosa, AL: University of Alabama Press, 1987), p. 12. Also, see Burgess, 1993, p. 5.
10 Elazar, op. cit., pp. 34–6.
11 Robert Agranoff, "Power Shifts, Diversity and Asymmetry", in Robert Agranoff (ed.), *Accommodating Diversity: Asymmetry in Federal States* (Baden-Baden: Nomos Verlagsgesellschaft, 1999), p. 15.
12 Charles Taylor, "The Deep Challenge of Dualism", in Alain-G. Gagnon (ed.), *Quebec: State and Society*, 2nd edition (Scarborough: Nelson Canada, 1993), p. 94.
13 Will Kymlicka, *Multicultural Citizenship* (Oxford: Clarendon Press, 1995), p. 31.
14 Will Kymlicka, *Politics in the Vernacular* (Oxford: Toronto, 2001), pp. 114–15.
15 Will Kymlicka, *Finding Our Way: Rethinking Ethnocultural Relations in Canada* (Toronto: Oxford University Press, 1998), p. 135.
16 See Gagnon, op. cit., footnote 2.
17 See, in the field of health care, Alain-G. Gagnon and Hugh Segal (eds), *The Canadian Social Union Without Quebec: Eight Critical Analyses* (Montreal: Institute of Research on Public Policy, 2000).
18 Claude Ryan, "The Agreement on the Canadian Social Union as Seen by a Quebec Federalist", in Alain-G. Gagnon and Hugh Segal (eds), op. cit., p. 222.
19 Ronald Watts, "Federalism and Diversity in Canada", in Yash Ghai (ed.), *Autonomy and Ethnicity: Negotiating Claims in Multi-Ethnic States* (Cambridge: Cambridge University Press, 2000), p. 49.
20 Guy Laforest, "Le ministre Dion, la Charte des droits et l'avenir du Québec", *Le Soleil*, 26 April 2002.
21 James Tully, *The Unattained Yet Attainable Democracy: Canada and Quebec Face the New Century*, Grandes conférences Desjardins, Québec Studies Programme, McGill University, 23 March 2000, pp. 4–5.
22 This point is made convincingly by James Tully in "Liberté et dévoilement dans les sociétés multinationales", *Globe. Revue internationale d'études québécoises*, vol. 2, no. 2, 1999, p. 30.
23 James Tully, "Introduction", in Alain-G. Gagnon and James Tully (eds), *Multinational Democracies* (Cambridge: Cambridge University Press, 2001), p. 33.
24 Rainer Bauböck, "Why Stay Together? A Pluralist Approach to Secession and Federation", in Will Kymlicka and Wayne Norman (ed.), *Citizenship in Divided Societies* (Oxford: Oxford University Press, 2000), p. 383.
25 Bauböck, op. cit., p. 383.
26 Will Kymlicka, *Multicultural Citizenship* (Oxford: Clarendon Press, 1995), pp. 76, 80.
27 I have made a similar argument in "Quebec: The Emergence of a Region-State?", in *Scottish Affairs*, Special Issue, "Stateless Nations in the 21st Century: Scotland, Catalonia and Quebec", 2001, pp. 14–27.
28 David Held, "The Changing Contours of Political Community: Rethinking Democracy in the Context of Globalization", B. Holden (ed.), *Global Democracy: Key Debates* (London: Routledge, 2001), 23.

29 For a similar line of argument, see Will Kymlicka, *Finding Our Way: Rethinking Ethnocultural Relations in Canada* (Toronto: Oxford University Press, 1998), p. 135.
30 See, Michel Seymour, colloquium 2000.
31 Reg Whitaker, *A Sovereign Idea: Essays on Canada as a Democratic Community* (Montreal: McGill-Queen's University Press, 1992), p. 193.
32 Charles Taylor, op. cit.
33 Michael Ignatieff, *The Rights Revolution* (Toronto: Anansi, 2000), p. 84.
34 I doubt the central government's initiative, named the Clarity Bill, contributes in any way to feed a sense of trust between Quebec and Canada, to the contrary. See, François Rocher and Nadia Verrelli (Ch. 10, pp. 207–37) as well as Stephen Tierney, "The Constitutional Accommodation of National Minorities in the UK and Canada: Judicial Approaches to Diversity" (Ch. 9, pp. 169–205), in *Conditions of Diversity in Multinational Democracies*, op. cit.
35 One may refer to Alain-G. Gagnon and Guy Rocher (eds), *Reflections on the James Bay and Northern Québec Agreement* (Montreal: Québec Amérique, 2002) to get a fuller sense of developments underway.
36 Martin Heisler's statement found in Daniel Elazar (ed.), *Self Rule/Shared Rule* (Lanham: University Press of America, 1984), pp. 158–9.
37 Stuart Hall, "New Ethnicities", in David Morley and Kuan-Hsing Chen (eds), *Stuart Hall: Critical Dialogues in Cultural Studies* (London: Routledge, 1996), p. 444.

3 Multinational Federations

Reflections on the Belgian federal state

Patrick Peeters

Introduction

The 2001 state reform[1] is the fifth and most recent, but certainly not the last step in the process of transforming the former Belgian unitary state to a federal state. During the preceding stages of this transformation process, three communities and three regions were constitutionally acknowledged, each with exclusive legislative and executive powers for the subject matters that were entrusted to them. This process resulted in the solemn proclamation in the 1993 state reform that "Belgium is a federal state, composed of communities and regions."[2] This immediately refers to one of the most typical characteristics of Belgian federalism, namely a federal state composed of two types of member states (communities and regions) that partly overlap territorially.[3] Much of the complexity the Belgian federal state is known for is due to this double-layered structure.

Belgium is also an example of a centrifugal, bipolar or dualistic federal state. This chapter will discuss some aspects of these characteristics and the institutional, partly asymmetrical solutions which were put in place to address the specific problems caused by the coexistence of two large (and one small) language communities within the same state.

A centrifugal federal state

The "Belgian fact" can be summarised as follows: about 5.8 million Dutch-speaking people live in the northern part of Belgium (Flanders). The southern part (Wallonia) is French-speaking and has approximately 3.2 million inhabitants. The Brussels-Capital Region is located in the centre. It has approximately one million inhabitants. It is officially bilingual (French and Dutch), although the French-speaking inhabitants are a clear majority. In the eastern part of Belgium, near Germany, there is also a small German-speaking community, with approximately 68,000 inhabitants. This results in the following distribution of the population: 57.85 per cent are living in the Dutch-language region; 32.03 per cent in the French-language region; 9.44 per cent in the bilingual Brussels-Capital Region and 0.68 per cent in the German-speaking region.

This already tells us something about the "Belgian problem": a majority of Dutch-speaking people against a substantial minority of French-speakers and a small minority of German-speakers at the national level; a majority of French-speakers in the Brussels-Capital Region, where the Dutch-speaking community is clearly in a minority position.

This problem could only be solved within the framework of one Belgian State through a progressive transformation in successive stages of the unitary state to a federal state structure.[4] The Belgian process of federalisation is therefore essentially *devolutionary*.[5] In most federal states, previously independent or confederally-related component entities transfer certain powers to a newly created central level (integrative federalism). In Belgium, on the contrary, the federalisation process started at the central level, transferring powers to the communities and regions. This centrifugal character of the federal state explains several typical aspects of Belgian federalism: the powers of the communities and the regions are (still) enumerated; the centre has the residuary powers; the powers of the federal state and the communities and regions are in principle exclusive; no hierarchy between federal and community or regional legislation; the regional and community institutions are in principle determined by the federal legislature only, although this legislation has to be enacted by a special majority vote necessitating the approval by the Dutch and French language groups in both Houses of the federal Parliament.

The territoriality principle: the division of the territory into four language regions

After secession from the United Kingdom of the Netherlands (1815–30), the French-speaking bourgeoisie created the Belgian State. The electoral system allowed only people paying a minimum amount of taxes to vote ("the property assessment franchise"). This enabled the French-speaking bourgeoisie to hold on to power for several decades.[6] The constitutionally guaranteed freedom of language was used to perpetuate the preponderance of the French language. (French) unilingualism was considered to be essential for the unity of the country.

Gradually, a "Flemish movement" emerged, demanding the equal treatment of Dutch and French as official languages. Bilingualism in Flanders would reduce social discrimination of the Dutch-speaking people. The growing linguistic–political consciousness thus also had an socio-economic dimension.[7] This resulted in a first series of language statutes in administrative matters (1878), in criminal matters (1873) and in educational matters (1883). These language statutes were based upon the principle of bilingualism (Dutch in addition to French) in Flanders, while the principle of unilingualism (French) was preserved in Wallonia.

The introduction of universal plural suffrage in the 1883 constitutional reform and universal single (male) suffrage in 1921 increased the electoral weight of the Flemish voter. A second series of language statutes were enacted in 1932 and 1935, introducing the *principle of territoriality*:[8] the authorities should use the language of the region in administrative matters, in education and in judicial matters. The 1962–63 language statutes would finally establish the linguistic border.[9] The national territory was divided into four *language regions*: three unilingual regions (the Dutch, the French and the German language regions), and one bilingual region of Brussels-Capital. In unilingual regions, all public institutions have to use in principle only the language of that region. In the bilingual region of Brussels-Capital, Dutch and French are on the same legal footing.

The division of Belgium into four language regions would become the territorial basis for the future federal state. This division into language regions was constitutionally enshrined in the 1970 constitutional reform, together with the recognition of three communities (the Flemish, the French and the German-speaking communities)[10] and three regions (the Flemish, the Walloon and the Brussels regions). The territorial division into language regions will determine the territorial competencies of the communities and the regions in the federal state.

The division into language regions reflects and has also contributed itself to significant homogeneous component entities. This phenomenon can be qualified as "incongruent federalism", with the population of the federated entities being more homogeneous than the population of the federation taken as a whole. According to A. Lijphart, Belgium, Canada and Switzerland are the only federations where such incongruent federalism exists, since elsewhere the federated entities are socio-ethnically relatively faithful reflections of the federation as a whole.[11]

Two types of member states (I): the division into three communities

The concept of the *communities* met the demands of the Flemish movement for linguistic, cultural and educational autonomy. The communities, being autonomous political entities as from 1971, have exclusive legislative powers in these matters. The Flemish and the French community parliaments were initially composed of members of the federal parliament belonging to the Dutch, respectively of the French language group of the national House of Representatives and the Senate (the so-called "double mandate"),[12] and it was only in the 1980 state reform that the communities got their own executive in addition to their parliament. At that time, they also became competent for so-called "person-related" matters: certain aspects of health policy and social aid to persons.

The Flemish community is competent in the Dutch language region; the French community is competent in the French language region and the German-speaking community in the German language region. The Flemish and the French communities are also competent in the bilingual region of

Brussels-Capital. In Brussels, however, the Flemish and French communities do not have any direct power vis-à-vis persons. This would indeed imply the recognition of sub-nationalities in Brussels which was politically felt to be unacceptable. The Flemish and French communities are therefore only competent in Brussels for the institutions which can clearly be considered as belonging to their community only. The Flemish community is therefore, for instance, competent for the schools in Brussels which are Dutch-speaking, whereas the French community is competent for the French-speaking schools.[13] On the other hand, cable networks situated in Brussels are considered not to belong exclusively to either the French or the Flemish community in Brussels. They fall under the residuary power of the federal authorities.

It is paradoxical to notice that the concept of the communities, which was constitutionally recognised at the insistence of the Flemish for the protection of their cultural identity, is now used by French-speaking political parties to claim powers of the French community beyond the language border vis-à-vis all persons who use the same (French) language. However, according to well-established case law of the Belgian constitutional court ("Court of Arbitration"), the principle of territoriality is the foundation of the Belgian federal state structure. This principle also applies to the communities. They too are subject to "the system of an exclusive territorial division of powers".[14] The European Court for Human Rights has itself recognised that the protection of the linguistic homogeneity of a language region constitutes a legitimate goal justifying a different treatment with regard to the enjoyment of fundamental rights and liberties.[15]

Two types of member states (II): the division into three regions

Although the *regions* have been constitutionally recognised in the 1970 state reform, for the Flemish and Walloon regions it would take until the 1980 state reform, and for the region of Brussels-Capital until the 1988 state reform, before they became fully operational, with their own parliament and executive. The institutions of the Brussels-Capital Region could only be created in 1988 because a solution first had to be found to the long-lasting disputes regarding the borders of the Brussels region and about the question as to whether or not the Brussels region could become a region in its own right, equal to the Flemish and Walloon regions. The Flemish feared that, although they constitute a majority at the national level, the (French-speaking) Walloon and (predominantly French-speaking) Brussels regions would outnumber them. Finally, a complex institutional compromise was found for the co-existence in Brussels of the two linguistic communities. Just as the French-speaking minority in Belgium as a whole is protected at the federal level, the Dutch-speaking minority in Brussels-Capital is protected at the Brussels regional level.

The regions should be clearly distinguished from the language regions. As for the communities, the territorial division in language regions also determines the territorial competence of the regions. The Flemish region exercises its powers in the Dutch language region; the Walloon region exercises its powers in the French and German language regions; the Brussels region exercises its powers in the bilingual region of Brussels-Capital.

The concept of regions was introduced as a result of the efforts made by the Walloon people to attain autonomy at the social and economic level. These attempts were inspired by divergent economic developments of the northern and southern parts of the country, with a manifest economic recession in Wallonia as compared with Flanders as from the 1960s. The Walloons feared that, within a Belgian state in which the Flemish numerical majority would progressively also appear to be a political majority, they would permanently be pushed into the minority. They then wished to obtain the levers of economic policy in the Walloon region. On the occasion of the 1970 state reform, the concept of regions was indeed set out in the Constitution, although the implementation thereof remained uncertain, contrary to that of communities. Initially these regions were conceived as merely decentralised institutions functioning within a unitary Belgian state. Subsequently, in 1980, they were, in addition to the division into communities, transformed into autonomous political entities within the Belgian federal state. The regions obtained legislative and executive powers relating to "place-related" matters: rural and town planning; protection of the environment; housing; economy; supervision of subordinate administrations and employment policy. In the subsequent 1988, 1993 and 2001 state reforms, the powers of the regions were even further extended, more specifically concerning public works and transportation and vis-à-vis decentralised territorial authorities (provinces and municipalities).

The protective mechanisms at the federal level of authority

The transformation of the unitary state into a federal state comprising communities and regions was accompanied by significant reforms of the federal institutions. Finally, the joint administration of the federal state was reached. In order to mitigate the Walloons' fear of being permanently pushed into the minority at the federal level, a series of measures have been worked out in order to neutralise, from a political point of view, the Flemish majority at the federal level. Belgium is thus a clear example of the suggestion made by B. O'Leary that in the absence of a national or ethnic people who are demographically and electorally dominant (the so-called "Staatsvolk"), majoritarian federalism is not enough to sustain stability; in such circumstances, a stable federation requires consociational rather than majoritarian institutions if it is to survive.[16] This has been certainly the case in Belgium where, as will be seen below, several consociational techniques have been developed, both at the level of the federal legislature and executive, in order to establish a balance of power among the two large linguistic groups.

Pursuant to the Constitution, the federal Council of Ministers is composed of an equal number of Dutch-speaking ministers and French-speaking ministers, with the exception, if need be, of the Prime Minister who is in any case supposed to act as a "community a-sexual". Moreover, according to well-established constitutional practice, the decision making within the Council of Ministers does not take place by means of a vote but by means of a "consensus": concertation leads to a decision with which everybody can agree. If such consensus finally appears to be impossible, the ministers still having objections towards a decision supported by the vast majority of the Council of Ministers, will have the choice between two options: either accept the decision for the sake of the required solidarity, or tender their resignation. The rule of consensus guarantees the effective participation of the French-speaking minority in federal policy, even more than the rule of parity.

The French-speaking minority not only has a guaranteed equal representation within the federal executive, it is also protected at the level of the federal legislature. The division of the federal Members of Parliament into a Dutch and a French language group makes it possible that no special majority legislation may be enacted without the consent of the French-speaking minority. The greater part of legislation relating to institutional reforms must, according to the Constitution, be adopted by a special majority vote. The same applies to the creation, the powers and the functioning of the Court of Arbitration. This court, as a constitutional court, supervises notably the observance of the distribution of legislative powers between the federal state, the communities and the regions. The Dutch language group in Parliament consists of the members elected in the constituencies of the Dutch language region and of those members elected in the bilingual region of Brussels-Capital who took the oath of office exclusively, or first, in Dutch. The French language group consists of members elected in the constituencies located in the French language region and of those members elected in the region of Brussels-Capital who took the oath of office only, or first, in French. The members elected in the German language region belong by right to the French language group. The special majority requires that in each House the majority of the members of the Dutch and French language groups be present and that in each language group a majority approves the proposed legislation, while at the same time the total number of votes in favour (of the two language groups taken together) amounts to two-thirds of the votes cast.

The division into language groups also forms the basis for the so-called "Alarm Bell Procedure", another protection mechanism in favour of the French-speaking minority in both Houses of the federal parliament. Whenever a language group is of the opinion that a government bill or a private member's bill (except budgets and special majority legislation however) is likely to seriously impair relations between the two large, i.e. Flemish and French communities, it can start the Alarm Bell Procedure by means of a reasoned motion signed by at least three-quarters of the members of this language group. This motion results in the immediate suspension of the parliamentary procedure. The Council of Ministers must then submit its well-reasoned findings on the motion and invite the House to reach a decision either on those findings or on the bill as it may have been amended. Any dispute between the communities on the federal level is therefore either resolved in the Cabinet, where the communities are equally represented, or results in the resignation of the federal government.

Since it was introduced in 1970, the protective mechanism of the "Alarm Bell" was used only once, i.e. in 1985 regarding a rather minor bill concerning university education. This illustrates the effective dissuasive character of the procedure. Any dispute between the communities is either solved in the Cabinet where the communities are equally represented, or the motion results in the resignation of the government.

A bi-polar federal state

It may be concluded from the above that although the Belgian federal state is composed of three communities and three regions, the co-existence of two major ethnic communities makes it in essence "bi-ethnic",[17] "dualistic"[18] or "bi-polar".[19]

Bi-polar federations are more vulnerable than others because there are not sufficient possibilities for "tension-reducing coalitions"[20] or, as expressed by I.D. Duchachek, "Either the common interest is discovered or the negative attitude of one group opposing the other implies a threat of a veto or secession."[21] In the same way, R. Watts correctly points out that

> the problem within two-unit federations generally has been that insistence upon parity in all matters between the two units has usually tended to produce impasses and deadlocks. This is because there is no opportunity for shifting alliances and coalitions among the constituent units which is one of the ways in which multi-unit federations are able to resolve issues[22]

and, "The existence of mutual vetoes where there are only two units is likely to be a recipe for repeated impasses and deadlocks contributing to cumulatively sharpening frustrations."[23]

These observations are very much applicable to the Belgian reality as well.[24] State reform is functioning as a way out of what has been called the Belgian version of the "Baron Von Munchhausen-dilemma": large groups hinder themselves, small groups hinder other groups and are often much too powerful.[25] Belgian state reform means essentially withdrawing as many powers and financial resources as possible from the parity-based national decision-making entities. The exercise of federal powers is reduced to a continuous search for compromise between the two large communities – a search for the largest common denominator in the personal interests of the two major communities. This increasingly appears to be an insufficient justification for national policy making.[26]

These dynamics are reinforced in Belgium by the splitting up of the political parties along community lines. Together with the federalisation process, the Catholic (1968), the Liberal (1972) and the Socialist (1978) national parties have broken into separate Flemish- and French-speaking political parties. Even the Green political movement has split into a Flemish- (AGALEV) and a French-speaking party (ECOLO). Today, only "regional" political parties are operating at the federal level. Belgium no longer has any significant national political parties that could play a stabilising centripetal role. Dewachter refers to "party confederalism".[27]

An increasingly asymmetrical federal state

According to C.D. Tarlton "an ideal symmetrical federal system would be one composed of political units comprised of equal territory and population, similar economic features, climatic conditions, cultural patterns, social groupings, and political institutions".[28] In such a symmetrical model, each of the federated states would maintain essentially the same relationship to the central authority. The division of powers between central and state governments would be nearly the same in every case and representation in the central government would be equal for each component polity.

The concept of asymmetry, on the contrary, refers to a differentiation as to the status and powers of the component entities of the federal state. This differentiation reflects their historical, geographical, political, economic and cultural diversity: "each component unit would have about it a unique feature or set of features which would separate in important ways, its interests from those of any other state or the system considered as a whole".[29]

The transformation of Belgium from a unitary decentralised state to a federal state resulted from the beginning in important asymmetrical structures. The "double-layered" structure with communities and regions is probably the most typical (asymmetrical) characteristic of the Belgian federal model.

Asymmetries in the relationship between the communities and the regions

Despite the fact that regional and community competencies were initially attributed to regional and community institutions respectively, the possibility was created from the beginning, and also made use of, to have community institutions also exercise regional competencies and conversely. This has taken place in an asymmetric manner however. As far as the Flemish are concerned, the regional competencies are exercised by community institutions, whereas, as far as the French-speaking community is concerned, community competencies are partly exercised by regional institutions. In addition, the German-speaking community also exercises certain regional competencies.

A *"merger" between the Flemish community and the flemish region*

Pursuant to the Constitution, the possibility was created to have the parliaments and governments of the Flemish community and the French-speaking community exercise the competencies of the Flemish region and the Walloon region respectively.[30] The conditions of this exercise and the manner in which this should take place must be determined by means of special majority laws.

According to a special majority law, the parliament and government of the Flemish community exercise the competencies of the Flemish region.[31] The special majority legislator did not establish the same "merger" concerning the French community and the Walloon region. Initially, it was only provided that the institutions of the French community would be able to exercise the competencies of the Walloon region in so far as this would be decided by a two-thirds majority by the parliament of the Walloon region and the parliament of the French community. This has never taken place however. This possibility was finally removed by the state reform of 1993. A merger of these institutions appeared to be impossible due to the fact that the Walloon region embraces two language regions (the French and German language regions) and because of the sociological and political independence of the Brussels francophones with regard to the Walloon region.[32] After the 1993 state reform, the institutions on the francophone side have even evolved in the opposite direction, i.e. a transfer of powers from the French community to the Walloon region ("dismantling of the French Community", see *infra*).

Although on the Flemish side only one parliament and one government exist, there is no "merger" between the Flemish community and the Flemish region in the legal sense of the word. The Flemish community and the Flemish region remain separate legal entities. The Flemish region has no institutions of its own. Its competencies are exercised by the institutions of the Flemish community: the Flemish parliament and the Flemish government. The "Flemish parliament" is composed of 118 representatives who are directly elected in the Flemish region. Moreover, the six members are directly elected to the Flemish parliament by the electorate in the Brussels region. This brings the total number of seats in the Flemish parliament to 124. In order to avoid that the "Brussels" members of parliament would vote on Flemish regional matters, these members do not participate in the voting of Flemish regional statutes. They only have voting rights with respect to community matters. A strict distinction is therefore made between regional and community statutes voted by the Flemish parliament. The Flemish government is elected by the Flemish parliament. At least one of the (maximum) 11 members must reside in the Brussels-Capital Region and thus represent the Dutch-speaking population of that region. This member cannot, however, take part in the vote on Flemish regional matters, for the same reasons as indicated for the Flemish parliament.

The exercise of regional competencies by the German-speaking community

The Constitution offers the possibility for the Walloon region to defer some of its competencies to the German-speaking community.[33] The German-speaking community parliament and the Walloon regional parliament have to adopt identical statutes indicating the competencies that may be exercised by the institutions of the German-speaking community. Until now, this possibility has been used in a very limited manner in order to transfer the powers for the protection of monuments and landscapes.[34] Contrary to the merger between the Flemish region and community, this transfer of power does not entail any institutional change as such. Its sole objective is to avoid any intervention by the Walloon regional authorities in the German-speaking community's exercise of its powers.

The "dismantling" of the French community

According to Article 138 of the Constitution, all or part of the powers of the French-speaking community may be exercised by the Walloon region and by the French Community Commission of the Brussels-Capital Region. The latter is part of the complex institutional solution that was negotiated for Brussels. In order to protect the Flemish-speaking minority in Brussels, the members of the Brussels regional parliament, in the same manner as the members of the two Houses of the federal parliament, are divided into a Dutch and a French language group, called the Dutch and the French Community Commissions. The members of these two Community Commissions together compose the Joint Community Commission. This latter Commission exercises legislative powers in Brussels in the person-related community matters vis-à-vis institutions which cannot be identified as belonging to the Flemish or French communities as well as directly vis-à-vis persons.

The transfer of powers from the French community to the Walloon region and the French Community Commission in Brussels can only take place through identical decrees enacted with a two-thirds majority vote by the French community parliament, and with an absolute majority vote by the Walloon regional parliament and by the assembly of the French Community Commission in Brussels. These decrees have to indicate the powers and financial means that are transferred. In this way, an extensive portion of the French community's powers has been transferred towards the Walloon region on the one hand, and towards the French Community Commission in Brussels on the other hand.[35] The same possibility for transfer does not exist either for the Flemish or the German-speaking communities.

The "dismantling" of the French community is to a large extent inspired by financial issues.[36] Although the communities in principle have taxation powers, the Flemish and French communities cannot levy taxes, unlike the German-speaking community, because of the lack of a (constitutional) rule defining the territorial application of such taxes. This is – again – a consequence of these two communities encountering each other in the region of Brussels-Capital. This does not result in any problems on the Flemish side because of the "merger" between the Flemish region and the Flemish community. This merger makes it possible to use regional financial means also for community matters. As such a merger is lacking in the southern part of the country, the financial problems of the French community were at least partially resolved through the transfer of its powers to the Walloon region and to the French Community Commission in Brussels. The partial dismantling of the French community also reflects the predominant regionalist tendency on the francophone side. The French-speaking socialist party is a decisive political force in Wallonia. The dismantling of the French community is a way to diminish the political influence of the more liberal (conservative) French-speaking inhabitants of the Brussels region who have but little interest in the specific, mostly economic problems of the Walloon region.

Asymmetries within the institutions of the Brussels-Capital Region

The dismantling of the French community has led to another asymmetry, this time within the institutions of the Brussels-Capital Region. Through the dismantling of the French community, legislative powers of the French community have been transferred to the French Community Commission in Brussels. Henceforth, this Community Commission, which is composed of the members of the French language group of the Brussels regional parliament, acts as a legislator in its own right and can enact "decrees", i.e. community statutes, vis-à-vis the institutions established in the Brussels-Capital Region which belong exclusively to the French community. The Flemish Community Commission has no such legislative powers but, being an extension of the Flemish community in Brussels, acts only as an administrative body.

Directly and indirectly elected community and regional parliaments

When one takes into account the several asymmetries mentioned above, apart from the federal parliament there are currently seven legislative bodies operational in federal Belgium: the Flemish parliament, the Walloon regional parliament, the German-speaking community parliament, the Brussels regional parliament, the French community parliament, the Assembly of the Joint Community Commission and the Assembly of the French Community Commission.

As the elections are organised on a territorial basis, in particular within the limits of the respective language regions, only the first four of these parliaments are directly elected. The 75 members of the Brussels-Capital regional parliament and the 25 members of the German-speaking community parliament were already, prior to the 1993 state reform, directly elected. Until the 1993 state reform, the members of the Flemish parliament, the French community parliament and the Walloon regional parliament were only indirectly elected. They held seats in those parliaments on the basis of their respective membership in the Dutch and French language groups of the federal parliament. This so-called "double mandate" used to put a heavy burden on the democratic legitimacy of the members of the community and regional parliaments. The double mandate was therefore to a large extent abolished: 118 members of the Flemish parliament are directly elected in the Flemish region; the other six members are the six first-elected members of the Dutch language group of the Brussels-Capital regional parliament. As from the next elections, these Brussels members will be directly elected as well. The Walloon regional parliament has 75 members, all directly elected in the Walloon region.

After the 2004 elections, the total number of members of the Brussels regional parliament increased from 75 to 89 in order to reinforce the representation of the Flemish in parliament. Instead of the distribution of seats of each language group on the basis of the total number of votes obtained by the parties of the language group concerned, the seats were distributed between the French and the Dutch language group in accordance with a legally fixed ratio: 72 seats for the French language group and 17 for the Dutch language group. A minimum representation of the Dutch language group was therefore guaranteed. This new legislation was upheld by the Court of Arbitration.[37]

The other parliaments are derived from the first four. The French community parliament has 94 members in total, all being members of the Walloon regional parliament along with 19 members elected from and by the French language group of the Brussels regional parliament. The Assembly of the Joint Community Commission is composed of the members of the Dutch and French language groups of the Brussels regional parliament; the members of the Assembly of the French Community Commission are the members of the French language group of the same Brussels regional parliament.

"Big" and "small" communities and regions

Certain asymmetries also exist which distinguish the smaller sub-entities, i.e. the Brussels-Capital Region and the German-speaking community, from the other – larger – communities and regions.

The subordinate position of the legal norms enacted by the Brussels regional legislator

As mentioned already, the establishment of regional institutions in Brussels in the 1988 state reform could only be achieved on the basis of a complex political compromise. On the Flemish side, there was strong opposition to the creation of regional institutions in Brussels, which would be equivalent to the Flemish and Walloon regions. The Brussels-Capital Region would be controlled by a French-speaking majority and would, when combined with the Walloon region, outnumber the Flemish region.

A significant although in the end rather symbolic part of the political compromise was the position in the hierarchy of norms to be taken by the legal norms which would be enacted by the Brussels regional parliament. A distinct name even had to be invented to indicate the Brussels regional statutes. Unlike the "decrees", i.e. statutes enacted by the other communities and regions, the statutes enacted by the Brussels regional parliament are called "ordinances". Like the "decrees", "ordinances" may repeal, extend, amend or replace prevailing legislative provisions in the competence matters transferred to the Brussels-Capital Region. They are also subject to the same judicial review by the Belgian constitutional court (the "Court of Arbitration"). Unlike decrees, ordinances are also subject to a limited judicial review by the other courts. This judicial review differs in two ways from the general rules governing the judicial review of administrative action. First of all, the reference standards are limited to the provisions of the Constitution and the Special Majority Act on the Brussels Institutions, with the exception of those reviewed by the Court of Arbitration.[38] Furthermore, the Council of State, the highest administrative court, is not entitled to annul an ordinance but may, unlike "decrees", refuse to apply an ordinance in a case submitted to it.[39]

Contrary to the other communities and regions, the federal authorities have a limited administrative supervisory role in matters of zoning and town planning, public works and transport "in order to protect the international role of Brussels as the country's capital".

The "constitutive autonomy" of the three major sub-entities

Only the three major sub-entities, i.e. the Flemish community (also exercising the Flemish regional powers), the French community and the Walloon region dispose of the so-called "constitutive autonomy".[40] Neither the

Brussels-Capital Region, nor the German-speaking community, have such powers to themselves regulate matters relating to the election of their parliament and to the composition and functioning of their parliament and government. The Constituent Assembly did not discuss extensively the reasons why the Brussels-Capital Region and the German-speaking community had to be excluded. Brussels' status as the country's capital and the delicate institutional equilibrium within the Brussels-Capital Region might be called upon, although it could also have been possible to grant the constitutive autonomy in principle to the Brussels-Capital Region, leaving it to the Dutch and French language groups within the Brussels regional parliament to decide whether or not this power should be exercised. On the other hand, there is no justification at all to withhold the constitutive autonomy from the German-speaking community.

The exercise of the powers relating to the constitutive autonomy must be exercised through special majority decrees passed by a two-thirds-majority vote in the parliament concerned. This majority condition is, surprisingly, less demanding than the traditional double two-thirds majority required for amending the federal Constitution.

The constitutive autonomy is rather limited when compared with other federal states and certainly does not provide sufficient legal grounds for the communities and regions to adopt their own constitution.

The autonomy status of the German-speaking community

The German-speaking community exercises the same powers as the other two communities, with the exception of the use of languages. This is not a true exception, however, because the communities are generally not competent to regulate the use of languages in municipalities having a special linguistic regime and all the municipalities making up the German-speaking community have such special linguistic status.

Contrary to the autonomy status of the other communities and regions, which is entrenched in special majority legislation, the institutions, powers and financial means of the German-speaking community are regulated by ordinary majority statute. This results from the basically dualistic nature of the Belgian federal state structure. Contrary to the two larger communities, the German-speaking community is not represented at the federal level by its own language group in parliament, nor is there a guaranteed representation in the Council of Ministers. Moreover, its representation in the senate is more symbolic than effective.[41]

Conclusion

From the above, it may seem that the Belgian federal state structure has been established as the only possible institutional solution to the complex problems arising from the coexistence of the two large language communities. The devolution of far-reaching autonomy towards the communities and regions was accompanied by consociational arrangements at the federal level guaranteeing the effective participation of the French-speaking minority in federal policy.

Federal state building in Belgium is essentially a way out of the permanent deadlocks and compromises at the central level. With each stage of the state reform, more powers and financial means are withdrawn from the centre. It is not clear yet where these dynamics will end.

The institutional solutions that were put in place reflect to a large extent the fundamental relationship between the two large communities. On the one hand, the Flemish community constitute the (not so dominant) majority at the federal level confronting a very substantive French-speaking minority and, on the other hand, the French community constitute a dominant majority in Brussels-Capital confronting a Flemish minority. The parity-based decision-making and protective mechanisms in favour of the French-spreaking community at the federal level is only acceptable because similar protection was established for the Flemish minority in Brussels.

From the beginning, room was left for asymmetrical institutional solutions. This made it possible to take into account the specific situation of the communities and regions. This seems also to become an increasingly important condition for the coexistence of the communities in Belgium.

Appendix 1

Belgium, regions and communities

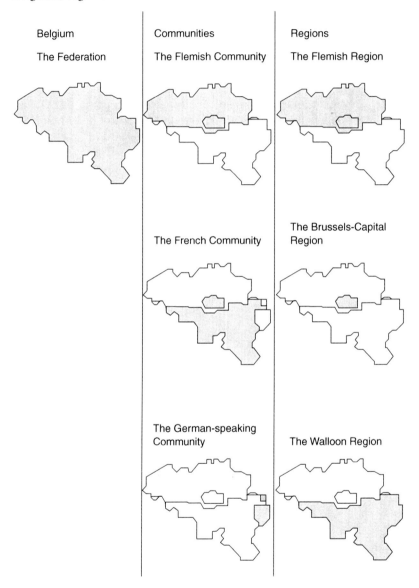

Belgium
The Federation

Communities
The Flemish Community

Regions
The Flemish Region

The French Community

The Brussels-Capital Region

The German-speaking Community

The Walloon Region

The grey areas correspond with the (sub-)entity indicated in the title. (source: © Federale Voorlichtingsdienst/Belgian Federal Information Service).

Notes

1 See for more details about the 2001 state reform: P. Peeters, "'Lambermont' or the Fifth Belgian State Reform – a General Overview", *2003 European Public Law*, 9 (1), 1–12.
2 Article 1 of the Constitution.
3 See Appendix 1: Map "Belgium, regions and communities" (Belgian Federal Information Service).
4 P. Peeters, "The Process of Change: From Unitary to Federal: the Belgian Case", in B. de Villiers and J. Sindane (eds), *Managing Constitutional Change* (Pretoria: HSRC Publishers, 1996), pp. 97–124.
5 K. Lenaerts, "Constitutionalism and the Many Faces of Federalism", *American Journal of Comparative Law*, XXXVIII, 1990, pp. (205), 206.
6 In 1846, there were 2.4 million Dutch-speaking and 1.8 million French-speaking inhabitants (E.H. Kossman, *De Lage Landen 1780–1940. Anderhalve eeuw Nederland en België* (Amsterdam: Brussel, 1979), p. 118.
7 L. Huyse, *De gewapende vrede. Politiek in België na 1945* (Leuven: Kritak, 1986), pp. 56–7.
8 A. Alen and R. Ergec, "Het territorialiteitsbeginsel in de Belgische en de Europese rechtspraak", *Rechtskundig Weekblad*, 1998–99, pp. 417–24.
9 Until then, a language census was periodically held, every ten years, by which the linguistic status of a municipality could change.
10 After the Second World War, national parliament preferred the name "German-speaking community" instead of "German community".
11 A. Alen, "Patterns of Multilingualism: The Case of Belgium", Workshop "Multilingualism – The Baltic Republics Today", University of Joensuu, 11–13 November 1995, with reference to L. Hooghe, *Executive Federalism in Canada* (Brussels: Study Centre for Federalism, 1991), p. 10.
12 The German-speaking community parliament has been elected directly as from 1973.
13 The federal authorities remain competent for other, for instance English-speaking schools, in the Brussels metropolitan region on the basis of their residuary powers.
14 Even if the exercise of such community powers may have an extraterritorial effect: Court of Arbitration, judgment no. 9, 30 January 1986; A. Alen and P. Peeters, "The Competences of the Communities in the Belgian Federal State: the Principle of Exclusivity Revisited", *European Public Law*, 1997, 3, pp. 165–73.
15 E.C.H.R., 23 July 1968, Belgian Linguistic Case, Series A, Vol. 6; E.C.H.R., 2 March 1987, Mathieu-Mohin and Clerfayt, Series A, Vol. 113.
16 B. O'Leary, "An Iron Law of Nationalism and Federation? A (neo-Diceyian) theory of the Necessity of a Federal *Staatsvolk*, and of Consociational Rescue", *Nations and Nationalism* 7 (3), 2001, pp. (273), 285, 291.
17 I.D. Duchachek, *Comparative Federalism* (Lanham–New York–London: University Press of America, 1987), p. 248.
18 C.J. Friedrich, *Tendances du Fédéralisme en théorie et en pratique* (Bruxelles: Institut belge de Science politique, 1971), p. 135.
19 A. Alen, *Belgium: Bipolar and Centrifugal Federalism* (Brussels: Ministry of Foreign Affairs, 1990); A. Alen (ed.), *Treatise on Belgian Constitutional Law* (Deventer-Boston, Kluwer Law and Taxation Publishers, 1992), p. 123; P. Peeters, "The Process of Change from Unitary to Federal: the Belgian Case", in B. de Villiers and J. Sindane (eds), *Managing Constitutional Change* (Pretoria: HSRC Publishers, 1996), pp. 97–124; Ronald Watts, *Comparing federal systems in the 1990s* (Kingston, Ontario: Queen's University, 1996), p. 105.

20 D.J. Elazar, *Exploring Federalism* (Tuscaloosa, AL: University of Alabama Press, 1987), p. 244.

21 I.D. Duchacek, *Comparative Federalism* (Lanham–New York–London: University Press of America, 1987), p. 248.

22 R. Watts, *Comparing Federal Systems in the 1990s* (Kingston, Ontario: Queen's University, 1996), p. 105.

23 Ibid.

24 See *inter alia* K. Deschouwer and Th. M. Jans, "L'avenir des institutions, vu de Flandre", in A. Leton (ed.), *La Belgique. Un Etat fédéral en évolution* (Bruxelles: Bruylant, 2001), pp. (209), 219–20.

25 A. Alen, J. Billiet, D. Heremans, K. Matthijs, P. Peeters and J. Velaers, *Vlaanderen op een kruispunt. Sociologische, economische en staatsrechtelijke perspectieven* (Leuven: Universitaire Pers Leuven, 1990), p. 244.

26 P. Peeters, "The Process of Change from Unitary to Federal: the Belgian Case", in B. de Villiers and J. Sindane (eds), *Managing Constitutional Change* (Pretoria: HSRC Publishers, 1996), p. 121.

27 W. Dewachter, *De dualistische identiteit van de Belgische maatschappij*, Koninklijke Nederlandse Academie van Wetenschappen (Amsterdam: Noord-Hollandsche, 1992), p. 17.

28 C.D. Tarlton, "Symmetry and Asymmetry as Elements of Federalism: a Theoretical Speculation", *Journal of Politics*, 27, 1965, pp. (861), 868.

29 Ibid. p. 869.

30 Article 137 of the Constitution.

31 Article 1, par. 1, of the Special Majority Law of 8 August 1980 on Institutional Reform.

32 F. Delpérée and M. Verdussen, "Le système fédéral. L'organisation", in F. Delpérée (ed.), *La Belgique fédérale* (Bruxelles: Bruylant, 1994), pp. 68–9.

33 Article 139 of the Constitution.

34 Decree of the Walloon regional parliament of 23 December 1993 and Decree of the German-speaking Community parliament of 17 January 1994.

35 See the decrees published in the *Belgian State Gazette* (*Belgisch Staatsblad-Moniteur belge*) of 10 September 1993. The transfer related to powers concerning physical education, sports, tourism, social promotion, professional recycling, student transportation and a portion of health policy and social aid to persons.

36 V. Bartholomée, "Le système fédéral. L'assymétrie", in F. Delpérée (ed.), *La Belgique fédérale* (Bruxelles: Bruylant, 1994), pp. 83–4; B. Blero and F. Delcor, "Les transferts de compétence de la Communauté à la Région", in *Les Réformes Institutionnelles de 1993. Vers un Fédéralisme Achevé?* (Bruxelles: Bruylant, 1994), pp. 71–116.

37 Court of Arbitration, nr. 35/2003, 25 March 2003.

38 The only reference standards for the judicial review of the Court of Arbitration used to be the rules governing the distribution of legislative powers between the federal state, the communities and the regions, the constitutional principles of equality and non-discrimination (Art. 10 and 11 Const.) and the freedom of and right to education (Art. 24 Const.). The judicial review of the court has recently been extended. Henceforth, the court has also jurisdiction to review the compliance of federal, community and regional legislation with all other fundamental rights and liberties set out in Title II of the Constitution and with the Articles 170 and 172 (equality in tax matters; principle of legality) and 191 of the Constitution (equality Belgians–foreigners).

39 A. Alen (ed.), *Treatise on Belgian Constitutional Law* (Deventer-Boston: Kluwer Law and Taxation Publishers, 1992), p. 154.

40 C. Berx, *De Ruime Grondwetgevende Bevoegdheid van Deelstaten: een Rechtsvergelijkende Studie* (Antwerpen-Apeldoorn: Maklu, 1994), p. 167; K. Rimanque, "De

Instellingen van Vlaanderen, de Franse Gemeenschap en het Waalse Gewest", in A. Alen en L.-P. Suetens (eds), *Het Federale België na de vierde Staatshervorming* (Brugge: die keure, 1993), pp. 180–9; F. Tulkens, "L'autonomie Constitutive": un Nouveau Concept de Droit Constitutionel Belge?" *Administration publique (trimestriel)*, 1994, pp. 159–64; M. Uyttendaele, "L'autonomie Constitutive en Droit Fédéral Belge. Réflexions sur L'unicité du pouvoir Constituant dans un Etat fédéral", *Administration publique (trimestriel)*, 1993, pp. 221–30; P. Vandernacht, "Les Nouvelles Règles de Fonctionnement et de Composition des Organes des Entités Fédérées à la Lumière des Dernières Réformes Institutionnelles", in M. Uyttendaele (ed.), *Les Réformes Institutionnelles de 1993. Vers un Fédéralisme Achevé?* (Bruxelles: Bruylant, 1994), pp. 341–75.

41 M. Uyttendaele, *Regards sur un Système Institutionnel Paradoxal. Précis de Droit Public Belge* (Bruxelles: Bruylant, 1997), pp. 847–52.

4 Federalism and competing nations in India

Harihar Bhattacharyya

Whether India is properly to be described as one nation or two or more really does not matter, for the modern idea of nationality has been almost divorced from statehood. The national state is too small a unit today and the small states can have no independent existence. . . . The national state is thus giving place to the multinational states or to the large federations.

Jawaharlal Nehru (1946)[1]

The problem

The basic question that I seek to raise in this chapter relates to India's unity, stability and survival as a polity in the midst of manifold and complex social and cultural diversity (many religions, languages, tribes and communities), and in conditions of mass poverty, illiteracy, extreme regional unevenness in development and widespread inequality. The question has assumed special significance in the aftermath of the disintegration of the multi-ethnic and national Soviet Union, and the split up of the Federal Republic of Yugoslavia. India's record of relative unity and integrity stands in sharp contrast to many post-colonial federations, which have failed, or broken down. In the age of what Eric Hobsbawm has called "nation-splitting",[2] India's relative unity and integrity, and survival as a state is remarkable indeed.

India is not a nation state in the classic sense of the term but a multinational federation. The nation state presupposes, as G.J. Bereciartu (1994) argues, the existence of a political community that tends to homogenize all of the communities existing within its territory, and hence is totalitarian in orientation expressed through linguistic unity, and uniformity of customs and culture.[3] In order to point out the inconsistency between the nation state and federation, W.H. Riker claimed: "Nation-states derive from, and justify, and separate out a single ethnic group, while federations may, and often do, bring together political units with ethnic bases."[4] India lacks the above socio-cultural preconditions ("linguistic unity", or a "single ethnic group" etc.), and also the fixed and undisputed "political community" to qualify herself as a nation state. Had India been a nation state in the above sense, this vast and diverse country would have disintegrated long ago, as often predicted in the ongoing writings on Indian politics since the country's independence (1947). Daniel Elazar rightly pointed out that although "the ideology of the nation-state – a single state embracing a single nation – remains very strong, the nation-state itself is rare".[5] Despite what Jawaharlal Nehru, a top nationalist leader, thinker and the first Prime Minister of India, said above, the ideological sway of the nation state has remained strong in India since its founding moment although it has increasingly remained far removed from a growing political reality of India marked by ethno-national pressures from below for a federal political recognition of identity.

The answer to the question of India's relative stability and unity as a multinational country must take one to Indian federalism which has provided the space for various nations competing often with each other, and with the pan-Indian political nation for recognition and power. Where does, then, Indian federalism stand in relation to nationhood in India? The nature of India's nationhood has remained since pre-independence (before 1947) days a debatable issue in the ongoing historical and political thinking of India; it is yet to be taken seriously in India's limited federal debate.[6] The passage quoted above from Jawaharlal Nehru, the architect of the post-colonial state in India, is one indication of how the issue of nationhood perturbed the pre-independence generation of nationalists. In Rabindranath Tagore, India's Nobel Laureate (1913) poet and novelist, and philosopher, India's nationhood was defined in terms of the everyday life processes of people who evolved for generations a way of living with their differences, a life which was based on the denial of centrality to the state.[7] Still earlier, in the writings of Bhudev Mukhopadhyay, a less known nineteenth century social thinker of Bengal, the state was considered to be central to the life of the state.[8] Little wonder, in a vast diverse country without a common language, or culture, the issue of nationhood has remained problematic. A.R. Desai writing just before independence located the problem in the challenge to Indian nationhood posed by the "growing political awakening among nationality groups such as the Andhras, the Malayalis, the Karnatakis, the Baluchs and others".[9] Desai further wrote: "The movements of those nationalities were inspired by the urge of self-determination, by their will to live and develop their life freely as distinct nationalities."[10] Irfan Habib,[11] a leading historian of India, finds India's nationhood more puzzling. Habib raised the question in the following: "Is then India a nation? We must without hesitation answer this question in the negative. India is a country certainly; but it is not a nation, because it does not meet the requirements of either a common language or a common culture."[12] In Chatterjee's estimate (1986 and 1993), the national question in India has remained unresolved. He argues also that the so-called "national unity" in India is actually not "national" but "confederal".[13]

In India's federal debate, as we have already indicated, the "national" character of the federation has escaped the attention of scholars. J. Das Gupta's work acknowledges "India's bold experiment of combining

democratic responsiveness to cultural differences with a federal reconciliation of regional community, identity and autonomy".[14] What Das Gupta
has called "cultural differences" are perhaps not the right words for various
ethnic nations in India comprising the multinational India. In my previous
work (2001) I have sought to establish India as a multicultural federation,
and showed how India's national identity was continuously being negotiated
vis-à-vis the growing autonomy needs of ethno-national groups, the relationship between Indian federalism and nationalism remains neglected in
the existing knowledge on the subject. In the "Introduction" to *Multiple
Identities in a Single State* (1995) edited by B. Arora and D. Verney, federalism is seen merely as a "constitutional distribution of powers between a
national government and a number of state or provincial governments".[15]
They have recognized the role of federalism in diverse countries including
India but only as having "contributed to the settlement of *regional* (i.e. *subnational*) [emphasis added] problems while preserving a strong union".[16] To
put rather bluntly, a theoretical understanding between Indian federalism
and national identity, which is essential to establish the "national" character
of the Indian federation, whether it is multinational, or mono-national, is
simply lacking in the ongoing literature on Indian federalism. And yet, the
resolution of the problem is a must before one seeks to explain India's relative successes in maintaining unity, integrity and political stability in
complex diversity and with no common language.

Theory

Brendan O'Leary has recently advanced perhaps the most provocative theoretical formulation on the relation between federalism and nationalism in
which the Indian case has been used as an example.[17] His thesis is as follows:

> a stable democratic majoritarian federation, federal or multinational,
> must have a staatsvolk, a national or ethnic people, who are demograph-
> ically and electorally dominant – though not necessarily an absolute
> majority of the population – and who will normally be the co-founders
> of the federation.[18]

The underlying idea of the theory is that the dominant ethnic group that
opts for a federation does not fear it because it is the "decisive majority of
the federal population".[19] Its sheer numbers make it to dominate the rest of
the federation. O'Leary further states: "A Staatsvolk, a people who own the
state, and who could control it on their own through simple democratic
numbers, is a prime candidate to lead a federation."[20]

In his estimate, India qualifies to have a *Staatsvolk*, if the primary division
is taken to be religion, which makes the Hindus comprising 80 per cent of
the population (1991). But "if the primary division is linguistic rather than
religious, then India appears to lack a *Staatsvolk*".[21]

As O'Leary has rightly indicated, the linguistic India does not have a *Staatsvolk* because Hindi, the national language, is not spoken by the major- ity of the population. Also, the (about) 40 per cent Hindi speakers, as shown in the Census Reports of India (1981), are a differentiated lot because there are some languages like Maithili and Bhojpuri that though are included in the Census definition of Hindi, actually are very different from Hindi. Con- sidering that, the actual speakers of Hindi would be around 30–35 per cent.

Do then India's Hindus, about 82 per cent of the population, make India's *Staatsvolk*? To begin with, the term "religion", so far as the Hindus are concerned, must be used with care. Unlike Christianity and Islam, Hin- duism is not an organized religion, but amorphous, region-specific, and very plural in beliefs and practices. The Hindus are divided in terms of lan- guages, regions and castes. This has served to explain the failures on the part of the right-wing Hindu nationalist political parties and groups in India, of late, to have constructed "Hindutva", the political Hindu identity, akin to what O'Leary has called *Staatsvolk*.[22]

Alternative facts of history

Historically, the Indian National Congress (INC), the main nationalist polit- ical platform of the Indians before independence, to be sure, rejected the British Cabinet Mission Plan (1946) of a federation of the Hindus and the Muslims, and the autocratic native states (more than 500 in number), but not a federation properly so-called, that is, the one based on democracy. By the early 1920s, the INC reorganized itself on the basis of linguistic groups under- going an internal federalization, so to say. Defying the colonial boundaries, it created, for instance, in the Bombay Province, three committees, namely, the Maharastra Provincial Committee (Marathi language), the Gujarata Provincial Committee (Gujarati language) and a Bombay Provincial Committee for the Bombay city. Again, in the Madras Province, three committees were created: the Tamil, the Telegu and the Malayalam Provincial Committees.[23] This ver- nacular tilt, though immediately geared around building mass bases in a mul- tilingual country, on the part of the INC already expressed a federal preference. Chatterjee detected a political truth in the attempt: "The language groups were the primary platforms for the union of nationality and democracy in their fight against colonialism."[24] The INC though composed predomi- nantly of the Hindus did not fear a federation. Had it been so, then even after the Partition of India, and birth of Pakistan in 1947, the Constituent Assem- bly (1946–49) of India dominated by the INC again would not have opted and devised a federal democratic constitution for India.

Alternative argument

The two basic points that I seek to raise here are as follows. First, there was evidently nothing "Hindu" behind India's design of a federal democratic polity. The so-called Hindu (federal) generosity towards major religious groups, most notably the Muslims, in post-independence India did not simply arise because the Muslims of India after Partition were (and still are) spread throughout India and lacked any sufficient regional concentration to claim statehood.[25] Jammu and Kashmir, India's only Muslim majority state, was an erstwhile princely state, and not the effect of India's federalization. When Jammu and Kashmir acceded to the Indian Union (October 1947), it did so as a constituent unit of the federation (with more autonomy than any other states in India under Article 370 of the Indian Constitution) without disturbing its territorial integrity. The post-independence federalization in India's north-east witnessed the birth of three Christian-dominated states (Nagaland, Mehgalaya and Mizoram), but then, the legitimacy basis of their creation was not religion, but tribal ethnicity.

Second, the so-called pan-Indian "national" identity, that one hears a lot of, is ethnically vague lacking any distinct cultural commonality such as language. In a foreign land, a Tamil (whether Hindu or Muslim) from India's Tamil Nadu would appear to be as foreign as a Tamil (Hindu or Muslim) from Sri Lanka to a Bengali (Hindus or Muslim) from West Bengal (a state in India). Their cultural world is so different! The pre- and post-independence political history of India is replete with example of alternative articulations of nationhood at ethnic levels that go against the so-called pan-Indian (Hindi, Hindu and elitist (higher caste)!) and hegemonic nation. E.V. Ramaswamy Naicker's concept of a Tamil nation, for instance, was defined in total opposition to the pan-Indian nation propagated most powerfully by the INC.[26] If there is any basis of unity between a Bengali from West Bengal and a Tamil from Tamil Nadu, it is political, as citizens of the Union of India expected to share certain common political values, and principles. The pan-Indian identity in post-independence India was to be necessarily political, or civic dissociated from any particular ethnic marker. In other words, it is political nationality, which, though hegemonic, has been the focal point of unity among many ethnic nationalities in India since independence.

Nationhood: thin and thick

In ongoing theoretical literature on nationalism, nationality and nationhood, one often comes across the distinctions between political, or civil and ethnic components of nationhood, or between the subjective and the objective elements, or factors of nationality.[27] Eric Hobsbawm[28] has made a distinction between pre-modern ethnic identities (he calls "proto-nationalism") and modern nationalism which is faulty because he neglects to consider that even the so-called pre-modern ethnic identities articulate their demands and express themselves in typically the idioms and languages of self-determination of nations.

The great German sociologist Max Weber considered the nation as essentially a political concept involving a political project although it has a social and cultural content. Weber defined the nation as follows:

> In so far as there is at all a common object lying behind the obviously ambiguous term "nation" it is apparently located in the field of politics. One might well define the concept of nation in the following way: a nation is a community of sentiments, which would adequately manifest itself in a state of its own; hence, a nation is a community, which normally tends to produce a state of its own.[29]

Weber did not equate the nation with the people of a polity because in a given polity, many groups often emphatically assert their independence in the face of other groups.[30] He also asserted that a common language was not absolutely necessary to a nation.

Cliford Geertz's (1993) observations of the nationality situation in the post-colonial states are more pertinent to the understanding of the multinational situation in India. According to him, there are two competing yet complementary components – ethnic and civic – in the nationalisms of the post-colonial states.[31] Ethnic nationalism, according to him, refers to a commitment to primordial loyalties, which endow individuals with a distinct identity while civic nationalism implies a desire for citizenship in a modern state. In the first case, the aim is to search for an identity and a demand that that identity be publicly acknowledged as having import etc. The aim in the civic case is practical: its a demand for progress, for a rising standard of living, more effective political order, greater social justice and so on.[32]

According to Geertz, the tensions between the two identities, or nations in the post-colonial countries are chronic and severe. The first reason as to why this is so is the clash between state, or civic, and ethnic boundaries. Second, the civic base of national unity in the new states is weak and fragile because it is maintained "not by calls to blood and land but by a vague, intermittent and routine allegiance to a civil state".[33] He wrote at length on the issue quoting even Jawaharlal Nehru as follows:

> In modernizing societies where the tradition of civic politics is weak and where the technical requirements for an effective welfare government are poorly understood, primordial attachments tend, as Nehru discovered, to be repeatedly, in some cases almost continuously, proposed and widely acclaimed as preferred bases for the demarcation of autonomous political units.[34]

In India, one thus witnesses two levels, or layers of nationhood: ethnic which is thick, and based deeply in culture, language, religion, tradition and social structure, and political, or civic which is thin but hegemonic in intent. While the former is non-negotiable, the latter is subject to negotiation.[35]

Nationhood may be thick among the Bengalis in West Bengal, the Tamils in Tamil Nadu, the Nagas in Nagaland, the Sikhs in Punjab and so on although their thick (ethnic) nationhood is not devoid of a political content. Often the "political" in the thick nations have raised, as in the case of the Sikhs in Punjab, problems of political accommodation in a "secular democracy". The thin nationhood in India is the domain of civic/political nationality: the relation between the Union (of India), on the one hand, and the thick nations, on the other. This is the basis of India's political unity, so to say. This is a matter of degree, and a variable layer in the sense it is affected by the deal the particular thick nation(s) gets from the Union regarding its autonomy. This thin layer of nationhood, on the other hand, is not devoid of any cultural content, but it lacks any distinct cultural basis. It has served since independence as the basis of India's "national" political identity. It is ethno-national identity and autonomy, which has been the main plank of negotiation vis-à-vis the "national" political identity. The extent to which an ethnic nationalist identity will be integrated with the "national" identity as Indians has often depended on the deal it has received regarding its autonomy and identity. While this is true in almost all cases in the peripheral regions, with perennial grounds of discontent and political extremism, the ethnic nationalism in the so-called mainland is not free from it. If the people of West Bengal feel genuinely that there has been a persistent neglect of the state by the Union government, then this will exacerbate Bengali ethnic nationality vis-à-vis a pan-Indian national identity. In the early 1950s southern India was the hotbed of aggressive ethnic nationalism, which led to the creation of Andhra Pradesh and Tamil Nandu. The height of aggressive and violent ethnic nationalism that one witnessed among the Sikhs in Punjab in the 1960s, and again in the 1980s, due to perceived neglect of the Union government and interference in autonomy, served to thin further their "civic" or political attachment to the Union. India's ethnic nations such as the Bengalis, Telegus, Tamils, the Nagas, Sikkimese and Assamese have been competing for the best protection of their autonomy and identity within the Union of India. From the Union side, the preconditions have included the acceptance of the Constitution of India along with all the political values embedded. Moreover, the Union has defined the following ground rules regarding nationality recognition in India: secessionism is to be given up; religion cannot be used as the basis of statehood; the demand for linguistic state must be supported by all the major groups in the state; and there must be demonstrable popular support for ethnic national recognition.[36] These internal ethno-national political processes have served to form the basis of the so-called "bargaining federalism" that one comes across in the writings on Indian federalism.

Unity in diversity: thin nationhood

The so-called "unity in diversity" has remained the kernel of India's thin nationhood, as a political community. Jawaharlal Nehru wrote in his famous book *The Discovery of India* (1946/1981) under the section "The Variety and Unity of India":

> The diversity of India is tremendous; it is obvious; it lies on the surface and anybody can see it. It concerns itself with physical appearances as well as with certain mental habits and traits. There is little in common, to outward seeing, between the Pathans in the Norwest and the Tamils in the far south. Their racial stocks are not the same, though there may be common strands running through them; ... yet with all these differences there is no mistaking the impress of India on the Pathans, as this is obvious on the Tamils.
>
> The Pathans and the Tamils are two extreme examples; the others lie somewhere in between. All of them have their distinctive features, all of them have still more the distinguishing mark of India.[37]

The above two passages testify more to the existence of various thick nations than the unity among them. The unity that Nehru claimed to have seen among them was more a myth than a reality, an elite imagination indicated by Benedict Anderson.[38] For Nehru, as much as many other nationalist thinkers before him, most notably Rabindra Nath Tagore and Bhudev Mukhopadhyay, the emerging nationhood of India was thus a "unity in diversity", a nation based not on any particular ethnic group or marker, but the one that partakes of the commonness of the country's diversity. Nehru pointed out again:

> Some kind of a dream of unity has occupied the mind of India since the dawn of civilization. That unity was not conceived as something imposed from outside ... it was something deeper and within its fold, the widest tolerance of belief and customs was practised and every variety acknowledged and even encouraged.[39]

It is seen that Nehru emphasized the ancientness of the Indian nation by basing it on a broad cultural unity, or commonality. Unlike Switzerland, the concept of "unity in diversity" in India was not political, to begin with. Until India's independence (1947), there was little real basis of using the term "unity in diversity" in any political sense except perhaps the decades-long anti-colonial movements against British colonialism for independence. That was why culture was considered to be the sovereign domain of the nation by almost all the leading nationalist thinkers.[40]

A brief history of Indian federalism

India as a democratic federation dates from 1950 when the Constitution of India was inaugurated. During the last couple of decades prior to independence in 1947, various unsuccessful experiments in decentralization and federalism were attempted by the colonial authorities, the last being the federation between the Hindus, the Muslims and the native autocracies numbering 561 envisaged in the so-called British Cabinet Mission Plan of 1946. With the Partition of India between India and Pakistan in 1947 on the basis of religion, the major threat of separation was removed. But, nonetheless, the Constituent Assembly (1946–49) opted for a federation to be called a "Union of States". The term "federation" was avoided for two reasons. First, the situation in the aftermath of the Partition of India, following the "great" communal killings of 1946–47 was grave indeed. The term "federation" at that time was suspect, considered as a recipe for disintegration. Second, as Dr B.R. Ambedkar, the Chairman of the Drafting Committee and the architect of the constitution, pointed out, Indian federation was not the result of a compact among independent, "sovereign" states.

And yet, a democratic (parliamentary) federation rather than a unitary state form was adopted though with a very strong centre. The basic reason why a federation was adopted was to accommodate the country's manifold diversity – linguistic regional, tribal and so on. The reorganization of the Indian territories on the basis of language after independence was a pledge of the Indian National Congress, the main party of India's independence. The INC itself was reorganized in the 1920s in such a way so as to accord with the provinces. The Provincial Committees of the INC were, in many cases, the linguistic units. Formally, the Indian federation is not designated as either "multinational", or "multiethnic", but the underlying objective seems to be the one to accommodate various ethno-national identities through the institutional provisions for statehood, and other non-territorial measures for the symbolic recognition of identity. The Preamble of the Constitution of India begins with the words "We, the People of India", which suggests that only an Indian nationhood is recognized, officially speaking.

Multinational India: demographic

India, demographically speaking, is the second largest country (its population is over a billion now) after China, and socially and culturally the most diverse in the world. Formed over many thousands of years as a country of immigrants who brought their own cultures and traditions, India's diversity is proverbial. Although predominantly inhabited by the "Hindus" (over 82 per cent) who are, however, regionally rooted and specific, plural in beliefs and practices, and divided by castes and languages, India contains large proportions of Muslims (about 12 per cent) spread over the country with more than a million in as many as 13 states (out of 28), Sikhs, Buddhists, Christian, Jains and so on (Table 4.1).

Three features stand out from Table 4.1 regarding regional concentration of religious groups in India. First, there is the only Muslim majority state in India, namely, Jammu and Kashmir in which the Muslims form a majority in Kashmir. This was due, not to any reorganization of territory, but to the fact that the Kashmiri Muslims have been living in Kashmir for centuries. Second, there are three Christian majority states in India, all in the northeast, namely, Nagaland, Mehgalaya and Mizoram. These states, again, were created since the 1960s, by carving out of Assam, not on the basis of religion, but of tribal ethnicity. Third, Sikhs are concentrated in Punjab where they form a majority. Punjab was created in 1966 as a result of reorganization of Indian territories on ethno-religious basis.

India's linguistic diversity is proverbial. By one estimate, there were some 1,632 languages spoken in India.[41] So far, 18 languages have been "officially recognized" and placed under the eighth Schedule of the Constitution (Table 4.2). Today, the speakers of these 18 languages constitute about 91 per cent of the population. Many of India's languages are very ancient with strong literary traditions. Some of the so-called regional languages, most notably Tamil (a south Indian language), are in fact older than Hindi, spoken by the largest (but not the majority) number of Indians. During the period of British colonial rule, language and region did not always coincide. Thus, the provinces created by the British in India were not linguistically homogeneous. Many of the provinces as well as the princely autocracies (numbering 561) were bilingual, or even trilingual. In the wake of India's national liberation movements, many of the region-based linguistic groups became self-conscious, and demanded self-determination.[42] The Linguistic Provinces Commission (popularly known as the Dar Commission) formed on 17 June 1948 to advise the Constituent Assembly (1946–49) correctly sensed the situation: "Indian nationalism is deeply wedded to its regional languages;

Table 4.1 Religious composition of Indian population (1991)

Religions	*Population (in '000s)*	*Percentage of total population*
Hindus	687,646	82.00
Muslims	101,596	12.12
Christians	19,640	2.34
Sikhs	16,259	1.94
Buddhists	6,387	0.76
Jains	3,352	0.40
Other religions	3,269	0.39
Religion not stated	415	0.05
Total	838,567	100

Source: Census Reports of India, 1991.

Table 4.2 Official languages in India (1991)

Languages	Speakers (in '000s)	Percentage of total population
Hindi	337,272	40.20
Bengali	69,595	8.30
Telegu	66,017	7.87
Marathi	62,481	7.45
Tamil	53,006	6.32
Urdu	43,406	5.18
Gujarati	40,673	4.85
Kannada	30,377	3.91
Malayalam	30,377	3.62
Oriya	28,061	3.35
Punjabi	23,378	2.79
Assamese	13,079	1.56
Sindhi	2,122	0.25
Nepali	2,076	0.25
Konkani	1,760	0.21
Manipuri	1,270	0.15
Kashmiri	56	0.01
Sanskrit	49	0.01
Other languages	31,142	3.71
Total	838,583	100.00

Source: Census Reports of India, 1991.

Indian patriotism is aggressively attached to its provincial frontiers."[43] In the post-independence period, it is language, not religion, which, when coupled with regional identity, has provided the most powerful instrument for political recognition as an ethnic identity.

According to Watts (1966),[44] the Indian Constitution exhibits the usual characteristics of a federation: as dual polity, a distribution of powers between the Union and the state governments, a relatively rigid constitution and a Supreme Court to protect the constitution. The very first Article of the Constitution of India describes the federation as: "India, that is, *Bharat*, shall be a Union of States". The "States" are recognized as the indispensable parts of the federation although the Indian federation itself was not the result of a compact, or agreement among sovereign units. The federation that was created by the Constituent Assembly (CA) composed of representatives elected by the people (on a limited franchise) was not meant, on the face of it, to be a multinational federation. Nowhere in the Constitution is it mentioned as such. There were representatives from, but not of, various "provinces" in the CA. However, there were also representatives of the Indian states (that is, the princely states) in the CA, but they were not predominant. The classic centralist-provincialist debates, as one found in the Philadelphia Convention, were conspicuous by their absence in the Indian

CA. According to the founding fathers of the constitution, sovereignty lay in the people. The Preamble of the Constitution begins with the words "We, the People of India." The units (the states) of the Indian federation did not create the federation. The states are, on the contrary, the result of the federation. The growing federalization of the once very centralized federation since independence, due to strong ethno-linguistic pressures from below and as a result of the political recognition of identity, has witnessed the growing number of states added to the federation.[45] The political map of India since her independence in 1947 underwent significant changes in order to undo, and to right size the various administrative units created during the period of colonial rule. The territorial legacies of the Raj were tremendous: apart from the 11 Governor's provinces such as Bengal, Bihar, and Madras, which were large, and ethnically heterogeneous, there were some 561 princely states (autocracies) of varying sizes and complexion, ethno-linguistically speaking. The creation of linguistically homogeneous states after independence was a nationalist pledge of the Indian National Congress from as early as the early 1920s. Thus, the basic principle of reorganizing Indian territories after independence involved the creation of political units that corresponded with ethno-linguistic identities of the people.[46]

State-creating institutional mechanisms: accommodating thick nations

The constitutional provisions for the creation of new states in India are rather flexible. The Indian federation, constitutionally speaking, is an indestructible union of destructible states. The Indian Constitution (Articles 3–4) empowers the Union Parliament (*Lok Sabha* (popularly elected Lower House, and *Rajya Sabha*, the Council of States) to reorganize the states for territorial adjustment. It is provided that Parliament may by law: (1) form a new state by separation of territory from any state, or by uniting two or more states, or parts of states, or by uniting any territory to a part of any state; (2) increase the area of any state; (3) diminish the area of any state; (4) alter the boundaries of any state and (5) alter the name of any state etc. The legislative requirement on the part of Parliament to do so is by a simple majority, and by the ordinary legislative process. However, the presidential recommendation for introducing such a bill is required, and the president is required, before he recommends, to refer the bill to the legislature of the state to be affected by the proposed changes within a specified period of time. The president is not bound to accept the view of the state legislature. So far more than 20 Acts have been passed by the parliament to give effect to states' reorganization. In the cases of the three new states the constitutional procedures have been followed, and the Legislative Assemblies of the three affected states have debated the proposed changes and the bill for years before agreeing to the proposed changes. Democratic method has informed the legislative process.

Post-independence accommodation of ethnic identity

Since the inception of the Indian Republic in 1950, statehood, i.e. the creation of new states, has remained a live issue predicated on India's manifold diversity (most notably language), and its appropriate use and utilization by the political elites. In the beginning (1950) there were 27 states of differential status and powers which were reduced by the first major territorial reorganization in 1956 to 14 with equal powers and functions. The first state created in recognition of linguistic principle in post-independence period was Andhra Pradesh (Telegu language, 1953), and that too, after its legendary leader, P. Sriramulu's fast unto death. This prompted the government of India to form the States Reorganization Commission in 1953, and on the basis of its recommendations, to pass the famous States Reorganization Act, 1956. The basis in the first major reorganization of states in 1956 was strongly linguistic: the federal units were created in order that they corresponded mostly with linguistic boundaries. Since 1956, the formation of new federal units in India has remained more or less a continuous process. The bases for state creation have been ethno-regional and linguistic. In the 1950s and the 1960s, the linguistic factor played the most determining role with the sole exception of the case of the creation of Punjab (1966) in which the linguistic factor combined with religion. In the 1970s, India's north-east (now comprising seven federal units) became the area of major states' reorganization which gave birth to three new states as a political recognition of tribal identity. In the 1980s, another three states were created (two in the north-east, and Goa in the south-west). The essence of the statehood demand has always been the congruence between federal political boundaries and the ethno-linguistic boundaries of the people. At the heart of such demands has remained the urge for decentralization and autonomy for the protection of identity and for development. The political processes which have accompanied the legal-constitutional ones are often protracted negotiations between the governments (Union and state), and the ethnic movements, and the resultant bipartite or tripartite "Ethnic Peace Accords" signed, and honoured by subsequent legislation for institutionalizing peace in the shape of democratically formed local governing bodies.

Relative autonomy of the states

Indian federation is based on the relative autonomy of the states. Dr B.R. Ambedkar, the architect of the Indian Constitution, stated in the CA that the "States under our constitution are no way dependent upon the Centre for their legislative or executive authority."[47] The Supreme Court, the country's federal court, in its various landmark judgments has emphasized upon the relative "sovereignty of the states" (the famous Bommai Case 1994). The Constitution provides for the distribution of powers between the Union and the state governments in terms of three Lists (Union List with 99 items,

State List with 66 items and Concurrent List with 52 items), and the states have exclusive powers of legislation over 66 items in the State Lists that deals with such matters as public order and police, local government, public health, land tenure, reforms and taxes, agriculture, state taxes and duties, fisheries, trade and commerce within the state, development and so on. The states are also entitled to legislate on items in the Concurrent List such as civil procedure, marriage, welfare and labour, economic and social planning, education and so on. The three Lists are quite exhaustive. The residual powers have been vested with the Union government, the reason being the mode of formation of this federation, as Watts (1966) pointed out, through devolution of a once centralized state. Following the Anglo-Saxon tradition, the Indian Constitution has assigned each order of government executive authority for which it has legislative authority.

The other area of the relative autonomy of the states is the political process within the states. As in the nation as a whole, the same Westminster parliamentary democratic system based on multiparty competition on first-past-the-post principle of election is followed in the forming governments in the states. Except the controversial Article 356 of the Constitution, which, when misused politically by the ruling parties at the Union opposed to the one(s) at the state(s), interferes with the state autonomy, the states in India have, by and large, enjoyed relative autonomy in their political process. The Indian states are thus ruled by state-based parties of ethnic groups, brands of leftist and communists, as well as the all-India level parties. No wonder, the states have remained a potent source of nurturing ethnic nationalism in India particularly so when the linguistic communities have been territorially rooted.

Non-territorial measures: the official recognition of languages

The non-territorial measures of accommodating linguistic identity in India consist of the following. First, the right to language forms part of the funda-mental "cultural and educational rights of minorities" (Article 30 of the Indian Constitution), which stipulates that the minorities shall have the right to establish and administer educational institutions of their choice. The state shall not impose upon them any culture other than their commun-ity's own culture.

Second, there is provision (under Articles 345 and 347) for "officially rec-ognizing" languages by placing a particular language(s) under the eighth Schedule of the Constitution. So far 18 languages have been "officially" recognized in India (Table 4.2). This method seeks to accommodate linguis-tic group(s) in three ways. First, it satisfies the need for identity (linguistic) for the aggrieved community. Second, it entitles the linguistic community to demand to read, among others, all official communication and documents in their language. Third, such languages as "officially" recognized and placed under the eighth Schedule of the Indian Constitution, become the third language in India's so-called "three-language formula" i.e. Hindi (national language), English (link language) and the eighth Schedule language, as mentioned above. In actual political process, the demand for the official recognition of languages has most often been intertwined with the movements for political recognition of identity.

Third, there is an individual dimension to it. Although "Hindi" in *Devnagari* script is the "official language of the Union" (Article 343), any petitioner (Article 350) in submitting any representation for the redress of any grievance to any officer of the Union or a state, is authorized to use any languages used in the Union, or in the state. That is, any officer cannot reject such representation on the grounds that it is not written in Hindi. It is further stipulated that every state and the local authorities within a state have to provide adequate facilities for instruction in the mother-tongue at the primary stage of education to children of the minority groups. No less than the president of India has been authorized by the Constitution (Article 350A) to issue such directive to the states to such effects.

Two remaining issues regarding the identity implications of languages must also be pointed out. In India, there are both stateless linguistic minorities (Table 4.2) who speak a language, which is not "officially" recognized, and who do not have a state. Second, there are states, most notably in India's north-east where the local language/dialects spoken by overwhelming numbers of the people are not yet "officially" recognized. This is, for instance, the case in Meghalaya, Mizoram and Nagaland where the state-level official languages are not those spoken by the majority of the people in the states.

Conclusion

Indian federalism backed by democracy has performed a double task. First, it has satiated the ethnic, i.e. thick nations, by providing institutional arrangements (both territorial and non-territorial) within which thick nations, based on language, or tribal ethnicity, or region, or a combination of language, religion and region, have been able to maintain and to celebrate their identity. Second, relatively satiated thick nations have facilitated the development of the thin nation, that is, the nation as a political community, by participating in the national political processes in accordance with the Indian Constitution. In India, statehood as well as the non-territorial measures for the protection of identity have served as a basis of unity at the political level, and facilitated the development of the political nation. In India, again, it must be pointed out, when nation as a political community was to be a post-colonial experience, federalism coupled with democracy, by providing for the institutional expression of thick nations, has been performing the task more or less successfully. The lingering doubts in the west about the prospects of India's democracy seem to have gone. Note the following editorial comment by the *New York Times* (8 October 1999) after the conclusion of India's general elections in late 1999:

> As 360 million Indians voted over the last month, the world largest and most fractious democracy once again set a stirring example for all nations. . . . India's rich diversity sometimes looks like an obstacle to unity. But the latest election has proved that a commitment to resolving differences peacefully and democratically can transform diversity into a source of strength.[48]

The political history of post-independence India is replete with examples when centralization and the weakening of the federal polity has encouraged and often hastened the process of "nationalist" separation in parts of India leading to political extremism and violence, and vice versa. Federalism in India rather than defeating national self-determination, has thus served to promote internal self-determination of many thick nations. In the US, the role of federalism in nation building is still a matter of some debate.[49] Indian federalism, only half a century old, has remained as the institutional terrain within which both the political/civic and the many thick nations have been taking shape.

Notes

1 Jawaharlal Nehru, *The Discovery of India* (Delhi: Oxford University Press, 1981/1946 orig.), p. 531.
2 Eric Hobsbawm, *Nations and Nationalism Since 1780* (Cambridge: Cambridge University Press, 1991), especially the last chapter entitled "Nationalism in the late 20th century".
3 G.J. Bereciartu, *Decline of the Nation-State* (Reno, NV: University of Nevada Press, 1994, orig. 1986), p. 166.
4 W.H. Riker, "European Federation: The Lessons of Past Experience", in J. Hesse and V. Wright (eds), *Federalizing Europe? The Costs, Benefits, and Preconditions of Federal Political Systems* (Oxford: Oxford University Press, 1996), p. 9.
5 D. Elazar, *Exploring Federalism* (Tuscaloosa, AL: University of Alabama Press, 1987), p. 9.
6 Harihar Bhattacharyya, *India as a Multicultural Federation: Asian Values, Democracy and Decentralization (In Comparison with Swiss Federalism)* (Fribourg: Institute of Federalism, 2001), "Introduction", especially pp. 15–37 for a critical sum up of the debate.
7 Partha Chatterjee, *The Nation and its Fragments* (Princeton, NJ: Princeton University Press, 1993), pp. 110–15. See also his *Nationalist Thought and the Colonial World: A Derivative Discourse* (Delhi: Oxford University Press, 1986) for the recent debate on the issue.
8 Chatterjee (1993), pp. 110–15.
9 A.R. Desai, *Social Background of Indian Nationalism* (Bombay: Popular Prokashan, 1946/1976), p. 381. While Baluchistan has gone over to Pakistan in the Partition scheme of India in 1947, most of the nationality groups mentioned by Desai have obtained statehood in Indian federation in various phases of federal reorganization since the early 1950s.

10 Ibid., pp. 387–8. Both pre- and post-independence histories of India are replete with examples of the growth of nationalism among various territorially rooted linguistic groups such as the Telegus, Tamils, Tripuris, Nagas, Mizos, Khasi and Garos, Oriyas, Konkanis, Gorkhas, and so on. Many of such ethnic nationalisms, most notably the Tamil, claimed ethnic superiority over the so-called Indian nationhood, which was accused of being elite, Brahmanical and male. For details, see M.S. Pandian "Nation from its Margins: Notes on E.V. Ramaswamy's Impossible Nation", in Rajeev Bhargava, Amiya Kumar Bagchi and R. Sudarshan (eds), *Multiculturalism, Liberalism and Democracy* (Delhi: Oxford University Press, 1999), pp. 286–308.

11 Irfan Habib, "Emergence of Nationalities", in K.M. Kurian and V.N. Varughese (eds), *Centre-State Relations in India* (Delhi: Macmillan, 1981).

12 Ibid., p. 31.

13 Chatterjee (1993) quoted in J. Hutchinson and Anthony D. Smith (eds), *Nationalism* (Oxford: Oxford University Press, 1993), p. 214.

14 Jyotirindra Das Gupta, "India's Federal Design and Multicultual National Construction", in Atul Kohli (ed.), *The Successes of India's Democracy* (Cambridge: Cambridge University Press, 2001), p. 49.

15 Balver Arora and Douglas Verney (eds), *Multiple Identities in a Single State* (New Delhi: Konark Publications Pvt. Ltd, 1995), p. 1.

16 Arora and Verney (1995), p. 1.

17 Brendan O'Leary, "An Iron Law of Nationalism and Federation? A (neo-Diceyian) Theory of the Necessity of a Federal Staatsvolk, and of Consociational Rescue", *Nations and Nationalism*, 7 (3), 2001, 273–96.

18 O'Leary (2001), pp. 284–5.

19 O'Leary (2001), p. 285.

20 O'Leary (2001), p. 285.

21 O'Leary (2001), p. 297.

22 What Paul R. Brass, a noted authority on India's ethnicity and nationality, had said about the ineffectiveness of India's ethnic conflicts to seriously affect her unity goes against O'Leary's thesis of *Staatsvolk*: "These conflicts . . . normally do not threaten the political unity of the country because of the absence of a dominant ethnic group identified with the Indian state as a target for nativist ideologies." Paul R. Brass. *Ethnicity and Nationalism: Theory and Comparison* (New Delhi: Sage Publications, 1991), p. 326.

23 Partha Chatterjee, *Itihasher Uttaradhikar* (in Bengali) (Kolkata: Ananda Publishers, 2000), p. 74.

24 Chatterjee (2000), p. 74.

25 It must, however, be pointed out that although the Indian Constitution recognizes the fundamental right to religion, the use of religion as a basis of statehood within the Union of India has been prohibited.

26 M.S.S. Pandian, "Nation from its Margins: E.V. Ramasway's Impossible Nation", in Rajeev Bhargava, Amiya Kumar Bagchi and R. Sudarshan (eds), *Multiculturalism, Liberalism and Democracy* (Delhi: Oxford University Press, 1999), esp. pp. 287–307.

27 J. Hutchinson and Anthony D. Smith (eds), *Nationalism* (Oxford: Oxford University Press, 1993), and M. Guibernau and John Hutchinson (eds), *Understanding Nationalism* (Cambridge: Polity Press, 2001) are the most recent excellent works on the subject.

28 Eric Hobsbawm, *Nations and Nationalism Since 1780* (Cambridge: Cambridge University Press, 1990).

29 H.H. Gerth and C.W. Mills (eds), *Max Weber: Essays in Sociology* (London: RKP, 1948), p. 177.

30 Cliford Geertz, "Primordial and Civic Ties" (pp. 29–34) in Hutchinson and Smith (1993), p. 30.

31 Quoted in Hutchinson and Smith (1993), p. 30.

32 Geertz (1993), p. 30.

33 Geertz (1993), p. 31.

34 Geertz (1993), p. 31.

35 Several bipartite or tripartite ethnic peace accords starting with the Naga-Hydari Peace Accords (1947) in India are concrete examples of this negotiation. For the texts of such accords, see P.S. Datta (ed.), *Ethnic Peace Accords* (New Delhi: Vikas Publishing House, 1995).

36 Brass, (1991), p. 315.

37 Nehru (1946/1981), pp. 61–2.

38 Benedict Anderson, *Imagined Communities: Reflections on the Origin and Spread of Nationalism* (London: New Left Books, 1983).

39 Jawaharlal Nehru (1946/1981), p. 62.

40 Partha Chatterjee, *The Nation and its Fragments* (Princeton, NJ: Princeton University Press, 1993).

41 Quoted in D.D. Basu, *Introduction to the Constitution of India* (New Delhi: Prentice Hall of India, 1997), p. 387.

42 For a case study, see Harihar Bhattacharyya, "The Emergence of Tripuri Nationalism 1948–50", *South Asia Research*, 9 (1–2), May 1989. The first systematic articulation of Indian nationalism in the writings of Bankim Chandra Chattapadhyay, the nineteenth century Bengali administrator-novelist expresses the tension between the Bengali and the Indian national identity. See for instance, Partha Chatterjee, *Nationalist and the Colonial World: A Derivative Discourse* (London: Zed Books, 1986), and also Chatterjee (1993).

43 Quoted in Bhattacharyya (2001), p. 100.

44 Ronald L. Watts, *New Federations: Experiments in the Commonwealth* (Oxford: Clarendon Press, 1966), p. 19.

45 The last three new states were created in 2000. For details, see Harihar Bhattacharyya, "India Creates Three New States", *Federations: What's New in the Practice of Federalism?*, 1 (3), 2001.

46 I have discussed the various phases of reorganization of Indian territories elsewhere, in greater detail. See, for instance, Bhattacharyya (2001).

47 Quoted in Basu (1997).

48 Quoted in Atul Kohli (ed.), *The Successes of India's Democracy* (Cambridge: Cambridge University Press, 2001), p. 1 ("Introduction").

49 S.H. Beer, *To Make a Nation: the Rediscovery of American Federalism* (Cambridge, MA: Harvard University Press, 1993), pp. 1–25.

5 Multinational federation
The case of Malaysia[1]

Ismail Bakar

Introduction

The Federation of Malaysia is a union of 13 states: 11 states in peninsular Malaysia (Johor, Kedah, Kelantan, Malacca, Negeri Sembilan, Pahang, Penang, Perak, Perlis, Selangor and Terengganu) and two states, that is, Sabah and Sarawak, in the northern part of Borneo. In terms of geography, Sabah and Sarawak are separated by about 400 miles from peninsular Malaysia by the South China Sea. The present Federation of Malaysia is the successor to the Federation of Malaya 1948, which then comprised only the 11 states of peninsular Malaya. These were the original members of the federation when it was first created in 1948 and subsequently gained independence from the British in 1957. In 1963, the Federation of Malaysia was formed when Sabah, Sarawak and Singapore joined the Federation of Malaya. However, in 1965 Singapore was expelled from the federation to become an independent state, leaving the 13 members of the federation as it exists today.

This chapter explores the aspects of ethnic diversity of the Malaysian federation, its characteristics – in particular language, religion and culture, and its effect on national unity and national integration within the federal framework. Given to these diversities, how can federation cope with these differences, that is, to unite diverse ethnic groups together in common shared values? What type of identity should Malaysians promote? Since the creation of the Federation of Malaya in 1948 there are endless ethnic conflicts with regards to communal rights which translate into serious political tensions. The problem was further complicated by the inclusion of Sabah and Sarawak into the Federation of Malaya in 1963. As we shall see, the ethnic cleavages in Sabah and Sarawak were more complex compared with those in peninsular Malaysia and make the task of uniting and integrating both states with the peninsular more taxing. In the case of Malaysia, ethnic conflicts can be examined from three dimensions: first conflicts between *Bumiputera* (this literally means 'sons of the soil', comprising Malay and other indigenous/natives),[2] especially Malays, with non-Malays notably in peninsular Malaysia. Most of the conflicts here are rooted in this question:

why are *Bumiputera* accorded special privileges in government policy? Second, is the conflict among Malay Muslims in peninsular Malaysia in particular due to differences in their political beliefs – one group is attached to Islam which aimed at creating an Islamic state and the other group is the moderate Malay Muslims. This conflict is more critical as it involves severe party competition which not only poses a threat to the federation but also to interracial relations. Third, is the conflict among *Bumiputera* in Sabah and Sarawak, that is, between Muslim *Bumiputera* (largely Malays) and non-Muslim *Bumiputera* (natives). This conflict is less severe but it remains significant to the federation for two reasons: first, these conflicts were perceived by non-Muslim *Bumiputera* of Sabah and Sarawak as an attempt of 'Malaynisation' and Islamisation of their culture and religious freedom which makes the national integration of Sabah and Sarawak with the rest of states in the peninsular states (comprises Malays/Muslim) more difficult due to the fear of Malay hegemony; and second, conflicts within *Bumiputera* itself over the issue of ethnic politics, that is, conflicts arising from the Melanau minority that dominate state politics in Sarawak; and conflicts between the Kadazan Dusun majority with other natives in Sabah.

Ethnic diversity and source of conflicts

Before we advance our discussion on multinational federation, it is imperative to look first at ethnicity in Malaysia. Ethnic cleavages are one of the most prevalent sources of internal divisiveness in the federation. As with other federations, the Federation of Malaysia reflects diversities – multilinguistic, multi-religious and multicultural. However, unlike other federations, the Federation of Malaysia was not formed along communal lines in that constituent units were not formed or divided according to linguistic, religious or according to a particular ethnic group. Thus, it could not be claimed that any one state was exclusive to one particular ethnic group unlike in India as in the case of Kashmir and Punjab.

The main ethnic identity of Malaysia is Malay and other indigenous/natives (collectively known as the *Bumiputera*) followed by Chinese and Indian (see Table 5.1). In peninsular Malaysia, *Bumiputera* represent the largest proportion followed by Chinese and Indian, while in Sabah and Sarawak, natives represent the majority followed by Chinese. Among the natives in Sabah, Kadazan Dusuns are the majority, while Ibans are dominant in Sarawak. Tables 5.2 and 5.3 show the distribution of ethnic identities according to state groupings: peninsular Malaysia, Sabah and Sarawak. Although at first glance the Chinese are a minority, demographically they have political significance in that the majority are urban dwellers, while *Bumiputera* are more dispersed in the rural areas.

The position of Malay and other indigenous people are safeguarded by the Constitution, a result of political bargaining reached in the first federal creation in 1948 until the attainment of independence in 1957.[3] This has

Table 5.1 Malaysian population

	Total (million)	% of total			
		Bumiputera*	Chinese	Indian	Others
1947	4.908	49.8	38.4	10.8	1.0
1957	6.279	49.8	37.2	11.3	1.7
1961	7.232	50.0	36.0	11.3	2.7
1970	8.819	50.0	37.0	11.0	2.0
1980	11.473	55.1	33.9	10.3	0.7
1991	18.380	60.6	28.1	7.9	1.4
2000	23.275	65.1	26.0	7.7	1.2

Source: Department of Statistics, Malaysia.

Note
* Comprises of Malays, after 1963 includes other origins of Sabah and Sarawak.

Table 5.2 Population of peninsular Malaysia, 2000

	Total	%
Bumiputera	11,183,388	64.0
Malays	(10,914,654)	(97.6)
Other *Bumiputera*	(268,734)	(2.4)
Chinese	4,892,563	28.0
Indian	1,680,132	8.0
Total	17,487,349	100

Source: Population and Housing Census of Malaysia, 2000, Department of Statistics, Malaysia.

Note
The numbers shown are Malaysian citizens.

become a form of social contract between the *Bumiputera* and non-*Bumiputera* and hence the position of *Bumiputera* cannot be questioned. To safeguard their position, Article 160 defined 'Malay' as 'a person who professes the religion of Islam, habitually speaks the Malay language, [and] conforms to Malay custom'. For Sabah and Sarawak, Article 161A (6) of the Federal Constitution defined the native of Sarawak as 'a person who is a citizen and either belongs to one of the races specified in Clause (7)[4] as indigenous to state or is of mixed blood deriving exclusively from those races', while for Sabah, 'a person who is a citizen, is the child or grandchild of a person of a race indigenous to Sabah and was born (whether on or after Malaysia Day or not) either in Sabah or to a father domiciled in Sabah at the time of the birth'.

To further safeguard the Malays and indigenous/natives privileges, Article 153 of the Federal Constitution states, 'It shall be the responsibility of the *Yang di-Pertuan Agong*[5] to safeguard the special position of the Malays

Table 5.3 Population of Sabah and Sarawak, 2000

Sabah	Total	%	Sarawak	Total	%
Bumiputera	1,601,356	80.5	*Bumiputera*	1,463,435	72.9
Kadazan Dusun	(479,944)	(30.0)	Iban	(603,735)	(41.3)
Bajau	(343,178)	(21.4)	Malays	(462,270)	(31.6)
Malays	(303,497)	(19.0)	Bidayuh	(166,756)	(11.4)
Murut	(84,679)	(5.2)	Melanau	(112,984)	(7.7)
Others	(390,058)	(24.4)	Others	(117,690)	(8.0)
Chinese	262,115	13.2	Chinese	537,230	26.7
Others	125,190	6.3	Others	8,103	0.4
Total	1,988,661	100.0	Total	2,008,768	100.0

Source: Population and Housing Census of Malaysia, 2000, Department of Statistics, Malaysia.

Note
The numbers shown are Malaysian citizens.

and natives of any of the Sabah and Sarawak and the legitimate interests of other communities in accordance with the provisions of this Article.'[6] In order to safeguard the special position of *Bumiputera*, 'the *Yang di-Pertuan Agong* shall exercise his functions under this constitution and federal law in such manner as may be necessary'.[7] However, today many Malaysians have become disenchanted with the spirit of this provision for uniting Malaysia because government policy has consistently failed to meet this requirement and is regarded by non-*Bumiputera* as a kind of discrimination, such as the New Economic Policy (NEP).

As well as being a multiracial society, Malaysia is very much multi-religious: mainly Islam, Hinduism, Buddhist, Confucian, Christian and native animism. But religion follows an ethnic line: Malay professes Islam; Chinese are Taoist, Confucian, Buddhist and a small number of Muslims; Indians are mostly Hindu with a few professing Islam; while indigenous peoples follow either animism or profess another religion. For Sabah and Sarawak, most of the natives (except Malays) are Christian or practise animism. Although religion could play an important role for uniting people in a diverse society like Malaysia, nonetheless, strong religious beliefs could also do much to undermine the society, especially with regards to the integration of Sabah and Sarawak into the Federation of Malaysia. The position of Islam in the federation is paramount, especially in respect to other religions. Article 3 of the Federal Constitution states that, 'Islam is the religion of the federation; but other religions may be practised in peace and harmony in any part of the federation.' Although there is freedom to practise one's own faith, Article 11 restricts the propagation of any religious teaching (other than Islam) to Muslim: 'every person has the right to profess and practise his religion and, subject to clause (4) to propagate'.[8] This is also contended by other ethnic groups professing religions other than Islam for fear that the imposition of Islamic values in government policy is an attempt at Islamisation.

Apart from religion, another dividing factor is the multilingual aspect of the federation. Article 152 (1) states that '[t]he national language shall be Malay language'. Although this does not mean that using other ethnic languages is prohibited,[9] it is nonetheless a cause of some anxiety because the promotion of the Malay language symbolises Malay dominance. As such, whenever the issue of language emerges, it is inevitably transformed into a racial issue because it tends to be viewed by other ethnic groups as a threat to their culture and more importantly as an attempt at 'Malaynisation'.

More than language, the cultural issues are equally contentious. Undoubtedly culture reflects identity, but for multicultural societies, which culture should be promoted for the sake of national unity and national identity? Respect for strong ethnic diversity implies a cultural paradox that makes efforts to unite people more difficult. The cultures of Chinese, Indians and natives are markedly different from Malays' culture since it is mainly characterised by and large by Islamic beliefs. Any form of cultural activities which do not conform to Islamic teaching is regarded by Muslims as non-Islamic (*haram*) and hence the promotion of non-Islamic cultural attributes is rejected by Muslims. This makes the creation of Malaysian identity based on the pluralism of cultures even more difficult if it is not in conformity with Islamic rites.[10]

Looking at the Constitution, clearly the position of Malays and indigenous peoples were safeguarded in the federation, compared with other immigrants (non-*Bumiputera*). These special privileges and protection for *Bumiputera* have become social contracts between *Bumiputera* and non-*Bumiputera*. But this contract was rooted in the early period of the Malayan Union in 1946 and during the formation of the federation in 1948, that is, during the colonial period.[11] During the period of British colonialism, a large number of immigrants from China and India were brought into Malaya to work in the tin mines and rubber plantations. This situation created a plural society in Malaya and in the long term caused socioeconomic and political fears among Malays.[12] Politically, this brought into prominence fears of non-Malay political domination, as the numbers of foreign labour far outstripped that of the Malay population. The Malays were concerned that the non-Malays were temporary immigrants whose first loyalty continued to be to their own countries.[13] In particular 'most Chinese and Indians who came to Malaya during the first three decades of the twentieth century ... were little more than "birds of passage", who left once they had made their money'.[14] The loyalty of Chinese and Indians towards Malaya was questionable, which prompted Malay resistance over the equal citizenship status proposed by the Malayan Union. This was the main reason for Malays' nationalist discontentment against the Malayan Union projects promoted by the British in 1946. Although 'the Malayan Union proposals ... were favourable and beneficial to many of the Chinese ... [they] were sceptical about choosing to become Malayan Union citizens, as they were still proud to maintain their status as Chinese nationals'.[15] Indeed at this juncture, Chinese and Indian nationalisms were not Malaya-centred but oriented 'exclusively to events transpiring in China and India, respectively'.[16] Their 'nationalism' towards Malaya was only prompted by the opposition of the Malays led by UMNO (the United Malays National Organisation) towards the Malayan Union and which later witnessed the birth of Chinese and Indian political parties, namely, Malayan Chinese Association (MCA) and Malayan Indian Congress (MIC), to protect and promote their rights in a future Malaya. With continued strong Malay opposition headed by UMNO towards Malayan Union, finally the Malayan Union was abolished, barely two years after its inauguration. The failure of the Malayan Union promoted by the British government was indeed a result of growing nationalism among Malays, especially the young generation which inspired a new political movement aimed at gaining independence from the colonial power following the Japanese occupation in Malaya, but more importantly stemmed from political self-awareness among Malays for fear of Chinese political prominence in Malaya. When the Federation of Malaya gained independence in 1957, the Federal Constitution that was drafted was based on political bargaining between three main ethnic groups, that is, Malays (represented by UMNO), Chinese (represented by MCA) and Indian (represented by MIC), which together formed the Working Party to study a constitutional proposal. The Alliance Working Party came to agreements that Malay special privileges (Malay language as the national language, the position of Islam in the federation and the status of Malay rulers) should be retained, safeguarded and entrenched in the Constitution in return for liberal citizenship for Chinese and Indians.[17] Thus the Constitution is a result of communal political bargaining. When the Federation of Malaysia was formed in which Sabah and Sarawak joined the Federation of Malaya in 1963, the position of natives from these states was also safeguarded and entrenched in the Constitution as a condition to enter the federation.[18]

The *Bumiputera*, especially Malays, regard this social contract as necessary to retain their hegemony in political power to safeguard their political and socio-economic interest. This is evident notably from the distribution of the economic wealth of the nation, which is more accommodating towards the *Bumiputera*, who were being left behind by non-*Bumiputera*, in particular the Chinese. In terms of economic well-being, the Chinese are dominant, while Malays are politically dominant. The Malays' argument for privileged economic treatment against the non-*Bumiputera* economic ascendancy boils down to a matter of Malays' rights by virtue of their being the 'sons of the soil'. However, it seems unlikely that these claims for greater economic equality between the communities will resolve matters because tensions between *Bumiputera* and non-*Bumiputera* go much deeper than mere economic inequalities. Indeed, even if economic inequalities were diminished, other racial barriers would remain because of major differences in culture, customs, language and religion. This is a source of ethnic conflict that poses a serious threat to the federation. Once one community's interest is threatened, the result is catastrophic, as evidenced in the 1969 riots between Malays and Chinese. When the Chinese demand more political power, and when Malays fear losing control over political dominance, coupled with economic inequality, the result is inevitable. Other related events, such as the Memali incident in Kedah in 1985,[19] the confrontation between Indians and Malay-Muslims in Penang in March 1998, and the 'Kampong Medan' incident between Malays and Indians in March 2001 were also the manifestation of cultural and religious conflicts. Thus, the spirit of the social contract of the Federal Constitution, which was the result of political bargaining between three major ethnic groups that accorded privileges to the *Bumiputera*,[20] must be understood and respected.

The question of national unity and national integration

The Federation of Malay(si)a has existed for more than four decades. Given the basic divisiveness of the community, how has Malaysia survived until today? The simple answer is due to strong central government which has successfully promoted government sponsored unity and integration programmes. Besides, the 'strong central government' theme of the federal creation helps to curtail any future potential ethnic conflicts at the margin. There are two issues regarding 'unity in diversity' in Malaysian federalism: first, inter- and intra-ethnic unity – *Bumiputera* (Malays and other natives), Chinese and Indian; and, second, unity and integration among member states in the federation. Both are equally significant for federalism and federation to flourish. As such 'given the communal situation, there would seem to be four main possibilities, analytically: assimilation of the various communities; accommodation of the communities on the basis of leaving things as they are; partition of the country; or chaos'.[21] Partitioning of the country or 'balkanization' according to ethnic grouping is definitely out of the question for Malaysia as it would weaken the country, bringing chaos and instability that would cause the federation to collapse. Hence, the primary task that lies ahead is to focus on assimilation and accommodation of diverse ethnicity. However, complete assimilation is also impracticable because, as noted above, the main ethnic group is Malay which is culturally different from other ethnic groups due to its attachment to Islam. Political accommodation through negotiation therefore seems the only practical way to unite diverse ethnicities. Musolf and Springer assert that

> the existence of deep communal divisions in a developing context can exacerbate attempts to negotiate interests and regulate political conflict. Thus, the fact that Malaysia is a deeply-divided society magnifies the problem of political development and adds weight to the argument for developing institutional arrangements which minimize conflict.[22]

The establishment of the Ministry of National Unity and the Department of National Unity contributed to this success, that is, in bringing together multi-ethnic communities into one common shared value. Besides, the role of the Ministry of Youth and Sport and the Ministry of Education are equally crucial in producing 'new Malaysians' loyal to the country.

In 1970, after the 13 May 1969 racial riot, the government proclaimed the new ideology/doctrine, *'Rukun Negara'* (Articles of Faith of the State), aimed at uniting all ethnics by inculcating one common set of beliefs:

> Our nation, Malaysia, being dedicated to achieving a greater unity of all her peoples; to maintaining a democratic way of life; to creating a just society in which the wealth of the nation shall be equitably shared; to ensuring a liberal approach to her rich and diverse cultural traditions; to building a progressive society which shall be oriented to modern science and technology.
>
> We, her people, pledge our united efforts to attain those ends guided by these principles:
>
> - Belief in God
> - Loyalty to King and Country
> - Sanctity of the Constitution
> - Rule of Law
> - Good Behaviour and Morality

Although this doctrine was neither embedded in the Constitution nor given legal status, it has become an implicit rule to be practised and upheld by all Malaysians loyal to the country. The doctrine was further strengthened by a combined economic, legal and political apparatus that emphasised the feeling of nationhood.

In terms of economy, the formulation of the New Economic Policy (NEP) in 1970 after the ethnic riots of 13 May 1969 seemed necessary to bring about a more equal wealth distribution among ethnic groups. Poverty, income inequality and economic crises are factors that could easily engender communal tension. However, strong government determination to provide a social safety net has minimised potential ethnic conflicts. The 13 May event was indeed 'a political manifestation of economic ill'.[23] The NEP aimed at promoting greater national unity by reduction and, subsequently, eradication of poverty as well as restructuring society to correct the economic imbalance between *Bumiputera* and non-*Bumiputera*, thus reducing and eventually eliminating the identification of race with economic well-being. Some observers have criticised the NEP as a form of social and economic discrimination against non-*Bumiputera*. However, the use of the term 'discrimination' to describe the NEP is entirely inappropriate; indeed I share the view of A.B. Shamsul to describe the NEP as a form of 'accommodation' of the economic needs of the country in the quest for unity in diversity.

To understand the real spirit of the NEP, it is necessary to understand the historical background of both *Bumiputera* and non-*Bumiputera*. Indeed in 1952 the High Commissioner of the Federation of Malaya, Sir General Templer, had realised that the

> ideal of a united Malayan nation does not involve the sacrifice by any community of its traditional culture and customs, but before it can be fully realized the Malays must be encouraged and assisted to play a full part in the economic life of the country, so that the present uneven economic balance may be redressed.[24]

With the NEP, the *Bumiputera* can now stand almost on an even footing with non-*Bumiputera*. Although the achievement of the NEP for meeting *Bumiputera* equity (at least 30 per cent of national economic wealth) is still below the target after three decades of NEP, at least it helps to close the gap between *Bumiputera* and non-*Bumiputera* (especially with Chinese). On a positive note, the NEP has succeeded in redressing the socio-economic imbalance among ethnic groups. Today the *Bumiputera* have had success in businesses and occupied a high percentage of professional posts.

With regard to the political system in Malaysia, it is possible to endorse the Dicey–O'Leary proposition in Chapter 10 about the significance of having a *Staatsvolk* in the federation. According to this model 'a stable democratic majoritarian federation, federal or multinational, must have a *Staatsvolk*, a national or ethnic people, who are demographically and electorally dominant' and '[a] Staatsvolk, a people who own the state, and who could control on their own through simple democratic numbers, is a prime candidate to lead a federation, whether the federation is a national federation or a multinational federation'. Based on this presupposition, clearly Malay is a *Staatsvolk* in Malaysia. However, being a *Staatsvolk*, Malay dominance cannot guarantee political stability without sharing power with other communally-based political parties due to the social contract that exists among major ethnic groups. Consequently consociational arrangements are inevitable, as O'Leary and McGarry argue above, 'where there is no *Staatsvolk* or where the *Staatsvolk's* position is precarious, a stable federation requires (at least some) consociational rather than majoritarian institutions if it is to survive'.[25]

For Malaysia, the grand party coalition is important for two reasons: first, to arbitrate, unite and reconcile communally-based party differences; and second, to strengthen federal–state relations as well as intrastate relations. The political system in Malaysia is characterised as: first, heavily based on communal cleavages; second, regionally based differences; and third, dominated by one party. Almost all political parties in Malaysia reflect a communal bias

> because of the communal nature of politics in Malaya [and Malaysia] all parties face the dilemma. If they do not try to appeal to a particular

community or communities, they will lose support to other parties. It would seem that non-communal parties cannot hope to survive, while communal parties might have some difficulty in winning a majority.[26]

For this reason, a coalition of communally-based political parties was formed in 1974, known as the *Barisan Nasional* (National Front) the successor of the Alliance Party formed in 1952. This coalition has managed a system of consociational arrangements for government in Malaysia since independence in 1957 so that power-sharing was based on inter-communal elite accommodation. Although there is a party formed on a non-communal basis, its support is less widespread compared to that of parties formed on the communal cleavages. This is because each communally-based party is fighting for its respective community's interest in the federation and therefore does not rally support from other communities. The three major components of the *Barisan Nasional* (the BN) are UMNO, MCA and MIC.[27] As the names indicate, all these parties represent their respective communal interests, that is, UMNO fights for Malays' interests, MCA fights for Chinese interests and MIC fights for Indian interests, but with the BN coalition communal interests are accommodated to minimise conflicts. In this regard, Michael Leifer (1973: 176) argued,

> In the case of Malaysia, communal allegiance has dominated the character of the political system albeit in a context where no one race commands an absolute majority and where viable and effective government is possible only through some form of inter-communal accommodation. In such circumstances any political grouping which seeks through such accommodation, to command the middle-ground of politics is vulnerable to challenge from parties which rest on an exclusively communal base.[28]

The records of the BN as a coalition of communally-based parties prove that the claim made by Michael Leifer is justified. Since independence, the BN and its predecessor (the Alliance Party) have dominated the party system up until today. 'One of the most significant characteristics of the BN (and its predecessor the Alliance Party) has been their ability under the leadership of UMNO to maintain a high degree of cohesion between their components parties.'[29] In Malaysia, the parties' coalition works hard in the cause of national unity, maintaining a parliamentary majority since 1957 and clearly contributes to political stability, shaping federal–state relations and the ability to maintain and preserve federalism and federation.[30]

The multiparty coalition, as demonstrated by the BN, has developed as an effective mechanism for the accommodation of Malaysia's communally diverse political elite, and since independence has never lost power, at least at the national level. As explained above, the favourable federal–state relations since independence are to some extent the outcome of political cohesion at federal and state levels, that is, the dominance of the BN led by UMNO. Being the largest component in the BN and most influential in the government, UMNO is of particular interest with regard to efforts to unite communally-based political parties as well as to ensure cordial centre-state relations in the quest for unity in diversity. However, despite the successful track record of the BN, there has always been conflict between the BN and state governments led by opposition parties due to differences in political belief and approach. This has caused political conflicts and disharmony, as evident in Kelantan (1959–78 and 1990 to present), in Terengganu (1999 to the present), which is ruled by an Islamic-based party PAS (Pan Malaysia Islamic Party/*Parti Islam Se Malaysia*) and also evident in Sabah during the PBS *(Parti Bersatu Sabah)* government (1985–94), which appealed to Kadazans/Christians as well as Chinese voters. Although there are instances where conflicts emerged within the same political grouping, that is, between the federal and state governments controlled by UMNO,[31] conflicts within the same party were less severe and less likely to threaten federal–state relations than conflicts arising out of different political parties.

The case of Singapore's expulsion from the Federation of Malaya barely two years after it joined in 1963 was a clear example of party competition due to differences in political approach. The escalating factor of Singapore's expulsion in 1965 was that the People's Action Party (PAP – the Singapore's ruling party) leader, Lee Kuan Yew, antagonised the Alliance (later the BN) – a coalition of UMNO, MCA and MIC) by attempting to oust MCA (a component member of the Alliance) in the 1964 general election. In its failure to oust the MCA, PAP subsequently sought a coalition with the Alliance. However, due to practical differences in political approach, the Alliance leader rejected PAP's intention to join the coalition. In its desperate attempt to be the champion of the Chinese in Malaysia, PAP began attacking the Alliance thus compromising the bargain agreed upon entering the federation and formed a coalition opposition party, Malaysia Consultative Solidarity, to challenge the Alliance. In particular, the PAP leader started to incite racial issues especially by denying Malays privileges in the federation and in return promoted the 'Malaysian Malaysia' concept. The PAP attitude of pouring boiling oil onto the Alliance at the time of the 1964 general election put the federation's very existence at risk. The practical political difficulties finally led to Singapore's expulsion from the federation on 9 August 1965, before it could bring disaster on the whole federation.

Although the party coalition has worked well to steer communally-based political parties towards national unity, it remains the case that if different political parties from the centre rule the states, tensions emerge that can result in divisive party competition to control state governments. This was evident in every general election, where the incumbent ruling party exerted its utmost effort to capture and recapture all states, by whatever means[32] to overcome their opponents. In order to win the competition, political opponents have to be derailed from the mainstream politics most notably through various forms of 'federal intervention' aimed at suppressing the spawning of state political-based parties which could undermine the multiracial/multi-ethnic society. This was notably evident from the fiscal federalism point of view, 'when a state was not viewed as being in line with the priorities of the federal leaders, clearly it risked becoming a target for financial sanction'.[33] There are three degrees of federal intervention[34] – 'mild intervention' (with the federal government typically co-opting local leaders), 'mid-intervention' (with the federal authorities using a mixture of administrative pressures and financial rewards to lure opposition politicians to the *Barisan Nasional*) and finally 'direct intervention', that is, by the declaration of a state of emergency and security apparatus. Apart from these interventions, the use of federal bureaucrats in states[35] also contributed to the ability of the federal government to control states' political behaviour. Indeed, the whole structure of government administration was tailored and geared towards the continued maintenance of a 'strong central government' which helped to curtail future potential ethnic conflicts at the margin. Hence despite the struggle to unite multi-ethnicities, the Malaysian federal system is under constant threat of the consequences of severe party competition between the governing federal political elites (BN/UMNO) on the one hand and political parties non-affiliated to the centre that control constituent state governments (PAS) on the other.

All forms of federal intervention coupled with the federal government's financial strength (due to exclusive control over revenue sources) were factors that gave the federal government political advantages, enabling the centre to bring its political rivals to heel in the name of national security, political stability, peace and harmony. Thus, since independence the Malaysian federation has experienced growing centripetal forces aimed at strengthening federal political elites in pursuit of building a nation-of-intent. If the federal political agenda is challenged or under threat, the upshot is strained federal–state relations in which all resources are directed at quelling state opposition. The notion of nation state (*negara bangsa*) promoted by the federal political elites is dedicated towards the formation of a unitary state in that Malaysia is gradually moving towards one unified state. This idea of a nation state rejected the constituent state government concept, primarily to undermine the growing states' rights campaign that followed escalating economic and political self-awareness. However, it was resisted by state political elites (from the opposition party) which have their own notion of nation-of-intent. The PAS government notion of nation-of-intent is clear, that is, the creation of an Islamic state. Typically the federal government response to the emergence of states' political awareness was made through 'federal intervention'. Although this decision did endanger federalism, it was the only way to ensure that the incumbent party retained a two-thirds majority in the parliament, apart from the 'delineation of election boundaries'[36] to favour the incumbent ruling party. This is why the central political leadership strongly opposes any attempt by non-affiliated political parties to win power in the constituent states for fear that its established position would be threatened.

Apart from the economic and political apparatus, it is also worth mentioning other means of uniting the multi-ethnic population, that is, through legal and security devices to prevent one ethnic group from provoking other ethnic groups that could turn into ethnic violence. To ensure this, the government has a battery of legal and security methods to prevent any untoward racial elements from destabilising the federation. The use of the Internal Security Act (ISA),[37] the Printing Presses and Publication Act (1984), the Sedition Act (1948) and the Police Act (1967) have proved highly successful in thwarting attempts to destabilise ethnic relations, although they have been criticised by human rights organisations as being misused by the government for political purposes. However, the use of this apparatus to maintain political stability and unite the populace would not last long especially if it involved the detention of communal political elites.[38]

Malaysian identity and the building of the nation state

National unity is a precondition for the creation of nation states and subsequently national identity. Building the nation state out of ethnic diversity undoubtedly involves the question of identity. The Prime Minister made a declaration on his Vision 2020 that,

> there can be no fully developed Malaysia until we have finally overcome the nine central strategic challenges that have confronted us from the moment of our birth as an independent nation. The first of these is the challenge of establishing a united Malaysian nation with a sense of common and shared destiny. This must be a nation at peace with itself, territorially and ethnically integrated, living in harmony and full and fair partnership.[39]

But given this ethnic diversity, which identity should Malaysia promote for the purpose of establishing a united Malaysian nation? Clearly, in the case of Malaysia, the government cannot promote national identity based on Malay identity being a *Staatsvolk*. This would simply be impracticable. Much ambiguity surrounds this issue in a country like Malaysia and national identity in Malaysia was promoted from 'authority-defined identity',[40] that is, *government promotion* of national identity based on Malay attributes – culture, language and religion. This notion of national identity was embedded in the National Culture Policy formulated in 1971. The reason for choosing Malay culture as a basis of national identity was rooted in the history of the country which was evolved from the *Kesultanan Melayu* (literally meaning the united kingdom of Malay *kerajaan*).[41] Although this does not reflect the real diversity of Malaysia, at least for the time being it has worked quite well in the process of building a nation state. The promotion of Malay-based identity in the process of nation state building is contentious, especially for the Chinese and Indians who are in favour of a pluralised national identity so that each ethnic culture would be accorded an equal position in the creation of an overarching national identity. The promotion of Malay-based identity in the building of a nation state also created much discontent among the *Bumiputera*, first, by Malay-Muslims who have their own concept of nation-of-intent based on Islamic principles which is currently being promoted by PAS – the PAS notion of nation-of-intent is based on Islamic jurisprudence[42] in that an Islamic state is to be established based on the *Shari'ah* laws – and second by non-Muslim *Bumiputera* (in particular in Sabah and Sarawak) due to fear of Malay hegemony which could erode their identity. Until an 'acceptable' notion of national identity and subsequently a nation of intent is found, Malaysia continues to exist as one state with many ethnicities and several nations.

Indeed, it was ethnic pluralism that very much characterised federalism in Malaysia and continues to make the federation complex and complicated. The problem with a multi-ethnic federation could become serious if either 'ethnic nationalism or sub-state nationalism' intensified due to the policies of any political party in power and what is most threatening is if the federal government was to ignore the diverse traditions, values and aspirations attached to each ethnic community. This would 'lead to the disintegration of the old nation and the creation of new national entities'.[43] Hence, building a united Malaysian nation out of ethnic diversity is the prime task for Malaysia.

Conclusion

Malaysia's population is extremely heterogeneous and hence uniting this diverse society is a prime task of the government. It is an extremely demanding task to bring diverse ethnic groups together in a system of common shared values that could be accepted by all ethnic groups because the sources of conflict are numerous: religious, linguistic, economic and cultural. Any discontent could easily turn into racial conflict and subsequently political chaos. As discussed above, the main conflicts in Malaysia are mainly between the following: *Bumiputera* and non-*Bumiputera* over socio-economic and political issues; among Malays due to differences in political beliefs; conflicts between states in peninsular Malaysia and Sabah and Sarawak due to fear of Malay hegemony; as well as conflicts among *Bumiputera* in both Sabah and Sarawak over the issue of ethnic politics. These conflicts necessitate the urgency of national unity as well as national integration within the federal framework. To ensure unity in diversity can be maintained, a combined economic, political and legal apparatus is indispensable. However the use of this apparatus to unite multi-ethnic groups with complete cultural and religious differences would not last long if there was no self-awareness of the need to live together in peace and harmony. Despite efforts to unite and integrate multi-ethnicity, the future of federalism in Malaysia still remains unsettled as the sources of conflicts are numerous and the list is growing. Until the spirit of nationhood can be effectively cultivated and strengthened, unity in diversity will have to depend mainly upon the security apparatus.

Notes

1 The opinions expressed in this chapter are those of the author alone and not of the Malaysian government.
2 The *Bumiputera* (the Malays and other indigenous groups) are descended from ancestors who settled in the area about 4,000 years ago. Non-*Bumiputera* (Chinese and Indian), on the other hand arrived later during the British rule as immigrant workers to work in tin mines and rubber plantation.
3 For a full account on the political bargaining of the Constitution, see Fernando (2002), *The Making of the Malayan Constitution* (MBRAS) Monograph, No. 31, The Malaysian Branch of the Royal Asiatic Society, Kuala Lumpur.
4 Article 161A, Clause 7 of the Federal Constitution defined the natives of Sarawak to include: Bukitans, Bisayahs, Dusuns, Sea Dayaks, Land Dayaks, Kedayans, Kalabits, Kayans, Kenyahs (including Sabups and Sipengs), Kajangs (including Sekapans, Kejamans, Lahanans, Punans, Tanjongs and Kanowits), Lugats, Lisumas, Malays, Melanos, Muruts, Penans, Sians, Tagals, Tabuns and Ukits.
5 The *Yang di-Pertuan Agong* (King) is the supreme head of the federation (Article 32).
6 Article 153 (1) of the Federal Constitution.
7 Article 89 of the Federal Constitution. See also Article 153 (2) of the Federal Constitution.
8 Clause (4) of Article 11 says 'state law and in respect of the Federal Territories of Kuala Lumpur and Labuan, federal law may control and restrict the propagation of any religious doctrine or belief among person professing the religion of Islam'.
9 'No person shall be prohibited or prevented from using (other than official purposes) or from teaching or learning, any other language' Article 152(1), Federal Constitution.
10 See M.I. Said, 'Malay Nationalism and National Identity', in M.I. Said and Z. Emby (eds), *Malaysia: Critical Perspectives – Essays in Honour of Syed Hussin Ali* (Kuala Lumpur: Malaysia Social Science Association, 1996), pp. 34–73.
11 For the discussion on the Malays' opposition to Malayan Union, see M.N. Sopiee, *From Malayan Union to Singapore Separation: Political Unification in the Malaysia Region, 1945–1965* (Kuala Lumpur: University of Malaya Press, 1976). See also A.B. Shamsul, 'Debating about Identity in Malaysia: A Discourse Analysis', *Southeast Asian Studies*, 34 (3), December 1996, pp. 476–99 and H. Singh, 'Ethnic Conflict in Malaysia Revisited', *Journal of Commonwealth and Comparative Politics*, 39 (1), March 2001, pp. 42–65. For the reports on the constitutional proposals for the Federation of Malaya in 1948, see *Constitutional Proposals for Malaya: Report of the Working Committee appointed by a conference of His Excellency the Governor of the Malayan Union, Their Highnesses the Rulers of the Malaya States and the Representatives of the United Malays National Organisation* (Kuala Lumpur: Malayan Union Government Press (Government Printer), 1946) and *Constitu-*

tional Proposals for Malaya: Report of the Consultative Committee together with Proceedings of Six Public Meetings, a Summary of Representations Made, Letters and Memoranda Considered by the Committee (Kuala Lumpur: Malayan Union Government Press (Government Printer), 1947).

12 In 1947 the total population of Malaya was 4.908 million, of which Malay consisted of 49.8 per cent, Chinese 38.4 per cent, Indian 10.8 per cent and others (mainly European) 1.8 per cent. Clearly non-Malays outnumbered Malays. See Table 5.1.

13 See M. Macdonald, 'Political Developments in Malaya', Address by the Rt. Hon. Malcolm Macdonald at a meeting of the Empire Parliamentary Association (EPA) held in the rooms of the Association, Westminster Hall, London on 27 April 1948. Address published by EPA, London, 1948.

14 See K.J. Ratnam, *Communalism in Malaysia* (Kuala Lumpur: Pustaka Ilmu, 1967).

15 For further discussion on Chinese reaction towards Malayan Union can be found in H.C. Oong, *Chinese Politics in Malaysia, 1924–1955: The Dynamics of British Policy* (Kuala Lumpur: UKM Publisher, 2000), especially Chapter 4.

16 See R.S. Milne and D.K. Mauzy, *Malaysia: Tradition, Modernity and Islam* (Boulder, CO and London: Westview Press, 1986).

17 See Fernando (2000).

18 See *Constitutional Proposals for the Federation of Malaya* (Cmnd. 210, London: HMSO, 1957); *Constitutional Proposals* (Kuala Lumpur: Government Printer, 1957); *Report of the Federation of Malaya Constitutional Commission 1957* (London: Colonial Office, No. 330, HMSO, 1957); *Report of the Commission of Enquiry, North Borneo and Sarawak, 1962* (Kuala Lumpur: Government Printers, 21 June 1962); *Agreement Concluded Between the United Kingdom of Great Britain and Northern Ireland, the Federation of Malaya, North Borneo, Sarawak and Singapore* (Cmnd. 22 of 1963), (Singapore: Government Printer, 1963).

19 Memali incident in November 1985 did not arise directly as a result of communal conflicts but rather political conflict among Malays, i.e. between UMNO and PAS elements that threatened 'peace and order'. As a result 18 people were killed.

20 See Article 155 of the Federal Constitution.

21 See R.S. Milne and D.K. Mauzy, *Politics and Government in Malaysia* (revised edition), (Singapore: Times Books International, 1980), pp. 364–5.

22 L.D. Musolf and F.J. Springer, *Malaysia's Parliamentary System: Representative Politics and Policymaking in a Divided Society* (London: A Westview/Dawson Replica Issue, 1979), p. 4.

23 Milne and Mauzy (1980: 324).

24 Robinson, J.B.P (1955: 182–3), cited from Milne and Mauzy (1980: 324).

25 See B. O'Leary, 'An Iron Law of Nationalism and Federation? A (Neo- Diceyan) Theory of the Necessity of a Federal *Staatsvolk* and of Consociational Rescue', *Nations and Nationalism*, 7 (3), 2001, pp. 273–96. See also A. Lijphart, *Democracy in Plural Societies: A Comparative Exploration* (New Haven and London: Yale University Press, 1977).

26 See R.S. Milne, *Government and Politics in Malaysia* (Boston, MA: Houghton Mifflin Company, 1967), p. 87.

27 UMNO was formed in 1946 by Onn Jaafar in Johor Bahru, primarily to organise Malay opposition towards Malayan Union. The Malay political consciousness arose during Japanese occupation in Malaya (1942–43).

> Although the Japanese Occupation was destructive and brought about hardship and misery to the people, it did awaken the political consciousness among the people which stimulated some desire for national independence.

> It acted as a catalyst for the emergence and development of nationalism in Malaya, especially Malays whose nationalism later became the basis of nationalism.

C. Sabaruddin, 'National Ideology and Bureaucracy', *Occasional Papers*, No. 5, June 1978 (Kuala Lumpur: The Malaysian Centre for Development Studies, 1978), p. 18. For further discussion on UMNO, see A. Fawzi, 'The United Malays National Organisation (UMNO): A Study of the Mechanics of a Changing Political Culture', Ph.D. thesis, University of Hull, 1992. The Japanese occupation also witnessed the rising of Chinese and Indian politics, leading to the formation of the Malaysian Chinese Association (MCA) and the Malaysian Indian Association (MIC). In 1955, the Alliance swept the first general election, winning 51 of the 52 elected seats in the still colonial, partially appointed legislature. The Alliance ministers then proceeded to negotiate the terms by which peaceful independence was secured from the British on 31 August 1957. As at 31 January 2003, BN had 15 members.

28 M. Leifer, 'Priorities and Political Order in Malaysia and Singapore – A Review Article', in *Journal of Commonwealth Political Studies*, XI (2), July 1973, pp. 176–9.

29 See S. Barraclough, *A Dictionary of Malaysia Politics* (Singapore: Heinemann Asia, 1988), p. 33.

30 See B.H. Shafruddin, *The Federal Factor in the Government and Politics of Peninsular Malaysia* (Singapore: Oxford University Press, 1987).

31 For example conflicts involving the UMNO-dominated Pahang government and UMNO-dominated federal government over the issue of the Endau-Rompin National Park, which finally witnessed the expulsion of the Pahang *Menteri Besar*. For further discussion on this issue, see Shafruddin (1987) especially Chapter 9.

32 Unscrupulous instruments include money politics, media control, use of government machinery and lack of freedom to speak. For further discussion on the supremacy of the executive power, see H. Crouch, *Government and Society in Malaysia* (New York: Cornell University Press, 1996); K.S. Jomo and C.H. Wee, 'The Political Economy of Malaysian Federalism: Economic Development Public Policy and Conflict Containment', *World Institute for Development Economic Research (WIDER)*, Discussion Paper No. 2002/113 (Helsinki, Finland: United Nations University, 1996); E.T. Gomez and K.S. Jomo, *Malaysia's Political Economy: Politics, Patronage and Profits* (Cambridge: Cambridge University Press, 1997); E.T. Gomez, *Politics in Business: UMNO's Corporate Investments* (Kuala Lumpur: Forum Press, 1990); Y. Rais, *Freedom under the Executive Power in Malaysia: A Study of Executive Supremacy*, Ph.D. thesis, King's College, University of London, 1994.

33 See M.A. Yusoff, *Federalism in Malaysia: A Study of the Politics of Centre-State Relations*, Ph.D. thesis, University of Manchester, 1998, p. 233.

34 See J. Chin, 'Politics of Federal Intervention in Malaysia, with reference to Sarawak, Sabah and Kelantan', *Journal of Commonwealth and Comparative Politics*, 35 (2), July 1997, pp. 96–120; J. Chin, 'Unequal Contest: Federal–State Relations Under Mahathir', in K.L. Ho and J. Chin (eds), *Mahathir's Administration: Performance and Crisis in Governance* (Singapore: Times Books International, 2001), pp. 28–61.

35 See Shafruddin (1987) and A. Zakaria, 'The Police and Political Development in Malaysia', in A. Zakaria (ed.), *Government and Politics in Malaysia* (Singapore: Oxford University Press, 1987), pp. 111–27.

36 See S.S. Rachagan, 'The Apportionment of Seats in the House of Representatives', in A. Zakaria (1987), pp. 56–70.

37 Enacted in 1960 replacing Emergency Regulation (Ordinance 10/1948) and in 1972 was revised to become Law of Malaysia (Act 82). It has wide discretionary powers of arrest and detention without trial. Initially it was used by the British to curb communist elements in Malaya after the Second World War but later the power extended to anything that could bring threat to security and law and order.

38 See Rais Yatim (1994) especially Chapter 6 'Detention without trial under the Internal Security Act 1960: An executive legacy to perpetrate freedom and a weapon to rule.'

39 M. Mahathir, 'The Vision 2020', Prime Minister's Office, Malaysia (originally a speech entitled 'Malaysia: The Way Forward' delivered by the Prime Minister, Dr Mohamad Mahathir at the Malaysian Business Council, Kuala Lumpur, 1991).

40 See Shamsul (1996).

41 Ibid.

42 See S.S. Muhammad, 'Establishing an Islamic State: Ideals and Realities in the State of Kelantan, Malaysia', *Southeast Asian Studies*, 37 (2), September 1999, pp. 235–56.

43 See J.C. MacPherson, 'The Future of Federalism', in S. Randall and R. Gibbins (eds), *Federalism and the New World Order* (Calgary: University of Calgary Press, 1994), pp. 9–13.

6 Federalization in multinational Spain

Luis Moreno

Introduction

The Kingdom of Spain is a compound national state that incorporates various degrees of internal ethno-territorial plurality, including minority nations and regions. After a long hyper-centralist dictatorship (1939–75), a peaceful transition to democracy (1975–79) and an active European involvement following its accession to the EEC/EU (1986), Spain has undergone deep transformations as a multinational state in contemporary times.

The text of the democratic 1978 Constitution reflected many of the tensions and political stumbling blocks that existed at the time of the inter-party discussion on the territorial organization of the state. This issue was regarded as one of the most contentious to agree upon in the general consensual climate for democratization. As a result, a constitutional 'open model' for political decentralization gained support from all major political parties and the citizenship at large.[1] The subsequent process of home-rule-all-round has aimed at providing internal territorial accommodation by combining both federal principles of self-rule and, to a lesser degree, shared rule (Elazar, 1987).

The Spanish 1978 Constitution does not include the word 'federal' in any of its provisions, or in any subsequent legislation. However, since the beginning of the 1980s the dynamics of the *Estado de las Autonomías* (State of Autonomies) are characterized by a latent federalization (Moreno, 2001a). Furthermore, the main features of the Spanish covenantal process concord with the federative criterion that legitimacy of each autonomous layer of government is constitutionally guaranteed (Burgess, 1993).

Spain is composed of 17 *Comunidades Autónomas* (Autonomous Communities), three of which are recognized by the 1978 Constitution as 'historical nationalities' (the Basque Country, Catalonia and Galicia). In these nationalities, Basque, Catalan and Galician are regional languages with full legal status alongside Castilian (or Spanish as it is usually referred to elsewhere), which is the official language of the whole Kingdom of Spain. Approximately a quarter of the Spanish population of 40 million is bilingual.[2]

Nearly 25 years after the approval of the first regional constitutional laws or Statues of Autonomy (Basque Country and Catalonia in 1979), the process of decentralization of powers has achieved a high degree of popular support largely transcending past patterns of internal confrontation.[3] In policy terms the process of decentralization has allowed for considerable regional autonomy and home rule.

Transferring of powers and services from the central state to the regional state, together with fiscal federalism arrangements, has allowed the public budgets of the *Comunidades Autónomas* to grow very considerably. Figures concerning the territorial distribution of public expenditure in Spain are illustrative: the regional level increased their share from 3 per cent of the total Spanish spending in 1981 to as much as 35.5 per cent in 2002 (see Table 6.1). If public spending is to be identified as a good indicator of the level of regional autonomy (Watts, 2001), then it should be concluded that the Spanish *Comunidades Autónomas* enjoy a much higher degree of self-government as compared to federated units in other formally established federations in the world (e.g. Latin America).

Rather than as a result of a well-defined constitutional separation of competencies and powers, federalization in Spain has developed in an inductive manner, step by step. Actions by Jacobin centralists encroached in sections of the public administration and in some influential Spanish parliamentary parties, together with those of their 'adversaries' in the minority nationalisms and regional governments (principally, Basque and Catalan), have favoured bilateral and *ad hoc* centre-periphery relationships. For quite different reasons both influential political and administrative elites at both central and regional spheres have shown reluctance to encourage horizontal and multilateral processes of decision making. As a result, the *Estado de las Autonomías* has not unfolded explicitly into a formal federation or federal-like system of government because of a less-developed shared rule in the general governance of the country. Likewise, the persistence of political terrorism in the Basque Country has highly conditioned inter-party negotiations for an eventual constitutional reform and formal federalization.

Table 6.1 Territorial distribution of public expenditure in Spain (%)

	1981	1984	1987	1990	1993	1996	1999	2002
Central	87.3	75.7	72.6	66.2	58.3	58.9	56.2	48.7
Regional	3.0	12.2	14.6	20.5	25.8	26.9	28.2	35.5
Local	9.7	12.1	12.8	13.3	15.9	14.2	15.6	15.8

Source: MAP (1997) for years 1981–90, and MAP (2002) for years 1993–2002.

Notes
a During 1999–2002, strong regional increases corresponded to the decentralization of education and health powers to all 17 *Comunidades Autónomas*.
b Spending on social insurance pensions has not been taken into account as it would have introduced a bias were it to be included as a central government matter.

Spain can be regarded as a remarkable example of how an exclusivist ethnic order (Franco's dictatorship), modelled after the ideal-type of a Castilian hegemonic *Volstaat* or core-nation (Brubaker, 1996), has evolved into a liberal and plural democracy. Likewise, the consensual agreement made explicit in the 1978 Constitution can be interpreted as an unwritten pledge to extend the procedures of political dialogue and consociationalism as guiding principles for future developments of internal accommodation.

In this chapter a review of historical events is meant to provide background information on ethno-territorial cleavages and politics of territorial accommodation in Spain. It is followed by a section devoted to substantiate the claim that the Spanish *Estado de las Autonomías* is a federation in disguise. After identifying features of the model of multiple ethno-territorial concurrence and dual identities in Spain, a discussion is carried out on the relationship between federalism, nationalism and consociational arrangements.

Spain: a historical nation of nations

Despite its secular internal ethno-territorial conflicts, Spain is an entity clearly identifiable as a country of countries, or a nation of nations. This unity goes beyond the simple aggregation of territories and peoples with no other affinity than their coexistence under the rule of one common monarch or political power. However, the social and cultural cohesion that makes up Spain's unity does not obliterate its internal rivalries. As has happened in the past, concurrence among Spanish nationalities and regions has brought about an extra cultural incentive for creativity and civilization, but it has also been used as an excuse for open confrontation as has happened in armed conflicts in modern times (Revolt of the Reapers, 1640–52; War of Spanish Succession, 1701–14; Carlist Wars, 1833–40, 1846–48 and 1872–75; or the Spanish Civil War, 1936–39).

History provides a good deal of arguments for the claiming of regional home rule and the decentralization of political power in contemporary Spain. Most minority nationalisms and regional movements find, in the fertile and complex Spanish history, reasons in the legitimization of their quests for autonomy, self-government or independence as early as pre-Roman times.[4]

Spanish majority nationalism has also found in history reasons for programmes of centralizing nation building, particularly during the nineteenth century. For Spanish liberals the task was to articulate an 'aggregate monarchy' into an institutionalized nation. For the reactionary authoritarians, the Spanish 'indissoluble' nation was also to prevail upon regional diversities.

Both types of minority and majority nationalisms can be regarded as sharing a common legacy and origins (de Riquer and Ucelay-Da Cal, 1994). An examination of Spain's history focusing on its internal relations of power, and on the peculiarities of what became the first modern state in Europe at the end of the fifteenth century, is essential for testing claims regarding the debate on federalization and territorial accommodation.

To begin with, two main structuring factors are to be taken into account when analysing the territorial history of Spain. First, the dichotomy between particularism and universalism, which was gradually forged in Spain's Middle Ages during the eight-century period of *Reconquista*, or Christian recovery of the lands of the ancient Roman *Hispania* from Muslim control (718–1492). Such a relationship highly conditioned the medieval aggregation of the various territories of the Iberian Peninsula. Since then, the particular and the general have determined most aspirations, expectations and frustrations in the process of internal accommodation of Spain.

Second, the case of Spain is to be categorized as a union state,[5] rather than a nation state (Rokkan and Urwin, 1983). Early state formation developed in a peculiar manner allowing varying degrees of autonomy of their constituent parts, which were incorporated by means of treaty and pact. While crown legitimacy prevailed state wide, the union structure entailed internal variations regarding pre-union arrangements and rights. Such configurations conditioned subsequent programmes of nation building in modern and contemporary times.

Medieval kingdoms, dynastic union and Bourbon homogenization

After the annihilation of the last Iberian stronghold in Spain (Numancia, 133 BC) the Roman presence in *Hispania* lasted five and a half centuries. During this period political unity was moulded by the action of this 'external' force. Later on, the barbarian invasions opened up a new process of political unification, strengthened by the occupying Visigoths from AD 540 onwards. These occupiers converted into fervent Christians. For the second time in Hispanic history, and owing to the political action of a foreign lineage, a political bonding of the Iberian peoples was forged, enabling them to live under the same god, king and common laws.[6]

For most of the eight centuries of the *Reconquista*, certain parts of the Peninsula acquired distinct forms of social organization. Some had diffuse political origins and, at the same time, became themselves the origins of the entities that evolved into a good number of today's regions and nationalities. They shared a common mission, as Christians, to defeat the Moors, to which end they established and dissolved numerous alliances. However, it was not only a struggle between Muslims and Christians. There were numerous treaties, interchanges, intrigues and even cases of 'good neighbourliness'.[7] In this manner, in a country which was then a fertile mix of civilizations for Christians, Muslims and Jews, the future significance of pacts as structural precursors of modern Spain[8] was established.

In the period between the seventh and twelfth centuries, geography was a decisive factor in the political fragmentation[9] of the *Reconquista*. In Christian Spain, a number of kingdoms claimed to be the political heirs of Visigoth

Spain, but their actions resulted in the constitution of peninsular 'sub-kingdoms', or autonomous dominions, such as those of Asturias (739), Leon (866), Navarre (905), Catalonia (987), Aragon (1035), Castile (1037) and Galicia (1065), or that of Portugal in 1139, year of the ascension of Alphonse I to the throne of Portugal, a would-be kingdom that refused to remained as a mere earldom pertaining to the Crown of Castile. For its part, after the dissolution of Cordoba's Caliphate, Moorish Spain broke down into *taifa* kingdoms, resulting in an intensification of both alliances and confrontations between Christians and Muslims.[10]

The lands belonging to the Crown of Aragon, led and guided by Catalonia and its capital, Barcelona, had full self-governing institutions and experienced an enormous economic growth during the thirteenth and fourteenth centuries. The area of influence of the Aragonese–Catalan–Valencia Confederation stretched to the French Languedoc and Provence, Naples, southern Italy and Sicily, Athens, Neopatria and numerous Mediterranean enclaves.

At the same time, the ambition of the Castilian princes, through conquests and royal marriages, brought about the unification of Leon and Castile (1230), as well as the incorporation of the Basque provinces of Gipuzkoa (1200), Araba (1332) and Biscay (1379),[11] and the Canary Islands.[12] In the *Compromiso de Caspe* (1412) representatives of the Aragonese, Catalan and Valencian parliaments agreed to elect Ferdinand I of Antequera (r. 1412–16) as heir to the Crown of Aragon. This event was to become the origin of the marriage between Ferdinand of Aragon, grandson of Ferdinand I, and Isabella of Castile, the future Catholic kings.

Modern political unification in Spain took place by means of the dynastic union under the Catholic Kings in 1469, year of the marriage of the future heirs to the Kingdom of Castile and the Crown of Aragon. In 1474 and 1479, the Catholic Kings took effective possession of the thrones of Castile and Aragon, respectively. As it was not the result of a unitary process of territorial amalgamation, the Spanish constituent territories (crowns, kingdoms, principalities, dominions) maintained much of their former institutional existence. The incorporation of such territories to the Hispanic monarchy was achieved at an early stage of the European Modern Age.

The Kingdom of Spain became an imperial power in the sixteenth century. It was feared for its expansionism and extended its influence throughout the five continents, while consolidating its own empire in Europe through a peculiar form of obedience to the King of Spain. The monarchs of the House of Habsburg favoured the formula of both political unity and territorial autonomy, and in general they maintained this attitude throughout their entire dynasty (1517–1700). The precedents for these were the political pacts of the Aragonese–Catalan–Valencian Confederation, adopted also by the Austrian branch of the same dynasty. 'The universalistic imperial aspirations that Spain and the House of Habsburg represented . . . rested entirely on local autonomy and inclined towards federative combinations' (Hintze, 1975: 99).

Imperial development in the sixteenth and seventeenth centuries focused on affairs beyond the frontiers of the Iberian Peninsula. The Habsburg Kings did not seek to unite Spain by homogenizing the cultures, laws and customs of its lands. Attempts by courtiers and royal favourites in Madrid to assimilate the peoples of Spain, provoked the Catalan Reapers' Revolt and the independence of Portugal (1640).[13]

When the Bourbon dynasty took the Spanish throne, a long period of mirrored responses to the processes of national homogenization carried out in neighbouring France began. Philip V, grandson of French King Louis XIV, abolished the Catalan *fueros* in 1714 after the Spanish War of Succession (1701–14). During the eighteenth century, and aiming to reflect the French absolutist model of state monarchy, the leading figures of the Spanish Despotic Enlightenment advocated the building of a Spanish nation above and beyond the internal boundaries of kingdoms, principalities and lordly estates (Domínguez Ortiz, 1976). The process was attempted to different degrees of success in other old European states, such as France's 'gallicization' and Britain's 'anglicization' of most of its territory. In any case, the 'Spanish mosaic' persisted formally throughout the Old Regime (seventeenth and eighteenth centuries). The writer José Cadalso described such diversity in his celebrated *Cartas Marruecas* (Moroccan Letters):

> an Andalusian has nothing in common with a Biscayan, a Catalan is totally different from a Galician; much the same happens between the inhabitants of Valencia and Cantabria. This Peninsula, divided during so many centuries into various kingdoms, has always displayed a variety of costumes, laws, languages and currencies.
>
> (Cadalso, 1978: 85)

Nation-building, weak liberalism and political modernization

Napoleonic Spain aimed to amalgamate despotism, enlightened or not, with the centralizing ideals of the French Revolution. The popular rising of 1808 against the Napoleonic occupation was a general affair all over Spain. With the War of Independence – or Peninsular War – Spain reaffirmed its cohesion as a national state in an emergency situation. Paradoxically, the popular uprisings to expel the foreign troops were led in many cases by the very advocates of the French enlightened programmes seeking cultural standardization.

The War of Independence was an historical landmark whose resolution, broadly speaking, would determine the peculiar processes of nation building and modernization in Spain, not only in the nineteenth century, but also in most of the twentieth century. During the conflict with the French (1808–14), the diverse territories of the Spanish Peninsula fought separately but united in a common aim to free themselves from those who illegitimately occupied their land.

The coordination between the various regional executives constituted a de facto federal-like government.[14] Politically, this was the most significant fact to contribute to the defeat of the Napoleonic troops. However, the liberal Constitution of Cadiz (1812) designed a centralizing unitary state much unlike other liberal models of territorial organization, as was that of the North American federative experience.

The *liberales* wanted to build the Spanish nation by applying a unifying programme in a country halfway towards bourgeois modernization. They imitated the hyper-centralist practices and strategies of their French counterparts, but were incapable of consolidating both their political reforms and their 'national revolution'. Such incapacity was due not only to the conflict with the forces of pre-modernity, but also to their own political contradictions. Most notable among these was the individualism and party factionalism they practised, which quite clearly contradicted the general conception of Spain they claimed to embrace.

Many territories of Spain, particularly those with a strong historical identity and a tradition of self-government, perceived liberal centralism as unnatural and stifling. Especially in Navarre, the Basque provinces and Catalonia there were protests at centralist reform and claims were renewed for the restitution of their ancient *fueros* or local rights. The circumstances of the time ensured that the *Carlists*[15] and those reactionaries who supported the *ancien régime* were able to benefit from the peripheral hostility towards liberal elites in Madrid.

All things considered, the liberal national building and political modernization in Spain during the nineteenth century achieved some of the intended goals. Formal education extended throughout the country. The use of the Spanish language (Castilian) generalized. The internal market also consolidated, together with a centralized bureaucracy, a homogenization of the juridical life and the accomplishment of a national network of communication and transport. However, the problems for the internal territorial accommodation would remain for years to come. As a matter of fact, the struggle against centralism can be considered as the single most constant factor in Spain during the nineteenth century.

An episode towards the end of the period heralded by the Glorious Revolution (1868) is especially relevant to single out: the experience of the First (Federal) Republic of 1873 and the phenomenon of *cantonalism*. In general terms, the republicans were federalists. After the 1873 elections, the Constituent Assemblies ratified solemnly the Federal Republic as the form of state. In a chaotic political climate, caused by the weakness of Parliament and the central institutions, the feverish activity of those supporting a canton-made federation emerged from the periphery. This untimely attempt to form a 'bottom-up' Spanish federation was carried out in a moment of considerable tension internally and abroad.

The *cantonalista* experience caused alarm because of its centrifugal character and its potential for creating uncertainty. Again, force was used: the military coup of Generals Pavía and Martínez Campos 'simplified' the political situation. With the restoration of the Bourbon monarchy (1876–1923), and the dictatorship of Primo de Rivera (1923–30) which ensued, a new centrally-led attempt to impose uniformity on the country manifested itself. This process ended once again in failure.

The establishment of universal male suffrage in 1890 had the notable effect of placing incipient Catalan nationalism, or *Catalanisme*, squarely in the Spanish political scene. The disparity between Catalonia's social structure and that of an impoverished rural Spain was an important factor in the rise of Catalan nationalism (Giner, 1980). Differences in socio-economic composition between Spain's two major cities, Madrid and Barcelona, also became increasingly evident.[16] These elements fuelled a sense of hopelessness amongst members of the Catalan elites, who put their electoral support behind home-rule parties. The most important was the *Lliga Catalana* (later known as the *Lliga Regionalista*) which was founded in 1901 and subsequently came to enjoy significant influence under the leadership of Francesc Cambó.

The Basque Nationalist Party, founded by Sabino de Arana Goiri in 1895, was less successful than the Catalanist *Lliga* in obtaining support across class lines, partly because of its religious emphasis and ethnocentric claims. Early Basque nationalism stressed traditional community values in opposition to bourgeois industrial society, the effects of which included a considerable influx of migrants from the rest of Spain into the Basque Country. A racially-based Basque essentialism was the ideological foundation of early Basque nationalism, which combined with a powerful populism and religious exclusivism to produce a discourse quite distinct from that of Catalan nationalism. The latter ideology was more intellectual and less based on 'folklore' from the outset, and has always been less secessionist in character.

Catalan nationalism seems to have provoked greater resistance by the Spanish central elites than Basque nationalism precisely because it offered an alternative view of Spain, something which Basque nationalism more frequently turned its back on. Both nationalisms, however, could be seen as political manifestations of a vigorous and prosperous periphery, which contrasted sharply with the often inept and parasitical centralism of the Spanish state to which it was subordinated.

Regionalism came in different forms in other Spanish territories, reflecting the ethno-territorial diversity of a plural Spain and, in many cases, inspired by the action of the Catalan and Basque movements. Partly as a consequence of the federal experience of the First Republic (1873), there were clamours for recognition in Galicia, Valencia, Andalusia and Asturias. Chronologically, the appearance of explicit claims for regional autonomy in contemporary Spanish politics occurred in the years just before and after the beginning of the twentieth century.

A widespread distrust and hostility against the central government fuelled regional sentiments. Not only peasants, day labourers and unskilled workers, but also members of the middle classes and significant sections of the intellectual elites had a perception of state institutions as alien, remote and brutal. Perceptions and sentiments toward the Spanish state were also favourable depending on social class and place of residence within Spain. For instance, inhabitants of large areas of Castile and Andalusia, and even of a 'historical nationality' such as Galicia, regarded state institutions as the main source of life opportunities and eventually adopted a strong Spanish identity. This would translate into a centralist and homogenizing understanding of Spain's social reality. As a consequence, administrative, juridical, military and political officers became increasingly reluctant of the idea of Spanish plurality, something which would have far-reaching effects in subsequent civil and political conflicts, as in the Civil War (1936–39).

The Second Republic, the Franco dictatorship and the 1978 Constitution

In spite of its short existence, the Second Republic (1931–39) contributed greatly to the resolution of ethno-territorial conflict in Spain. The most notable improvement was the constitutional design of the state as a regional model, situated somewhere between a unitary and a federal state. This led to statutes of autonomy for Catalonia,[17] the Basque Country[18] and Galicia.[19] However, the regional autonomy question also played a fundamental part in the political polarization leading up to the Civil War (1936–39). Even within the republican forces the issue of regional autonomy created no little turmoil.

Although the autonomist movement was still young, it was spreading throughout Spain by the time the Civil War broke out (18 July 1936). With the victory of General Franco's forces (1 April 1939), a long period of political decentralization ensued, aiming once again to build a uniform national Spain.

Two of the great obsessions of the Franco dictatorship (1939–75) were anti-communism and anti-separatism. The 'sacred unity of the homeland' was regarded as an indispensable unifying element and as the very *raison d'être* of General Franco's despotic regime. To a large extent, Francoism justified itself through its ability to suppress and extirpate all forms of home rule,[20] regionalism and sub-state nationalism. In the end, the Franco dictatorship provoked the opposite effect to such centralist state moulding: 'Even under the most extreme totalitarian circumstances such a task (e.g. Spanish "national" homogenisation and cultural assimilation) cannot be easily accomplished. One consequence of attempts to erode communal identities and national traits can be their intensification' (Giner, 1984: 87).

From the 1960s onward, demands for regional autonomy became significantly more intense. During the final years of Franco's regime, the opposition forces developed a programme claiming both democratic rights and political decentralization. In the 'historical nationalities' (Basque Country, Catalonia and Galicia), the opposition forces were able to articulate a political discourse denouncing the absence of democracy and the continuous official attacks on their identities. In these communities, democratic and ethno-territorial claims became inseparable. In this way the ideology of self-government and political decentralization made its way into Spanish contemporary democratic consciousness.

After Franco's death in 1975, the transitional process to democracy began in earnest. There was general agreement among the democratic parties that decentralization was essential. However, the specific model to be adopted was unclear. In the end, the broad political consensus which made the drafting of the 1978 Constitution possible also brought with it an element of ambiguity in the territorial organization of Spain. In fact, two different conceptions, which had traditionally confronted each other, were given expression in the Spanish 1978 Constitution: on the one hand, the idea of an indivisible Spanish nation state, and on the other, the notion that plural Spain was an ensemble of diverse peoples, historic nationalities and regions.

Estado de las Autonomías: federation in disguise?

The expression *Estado de las Autonomías* has became popular in Spain in the daily use not only of politicians, lawyers and media, but also of the citizenship at large. Experts on studies of nationalism and decentralization of power have also coined such an expression outside Spain. Indeed, the contribution of the *formula autonómica* to the theoretical debate on the territorial organization of contemporary democracies has been significant. Its close conceptual link with federalism is, notwithstanding, undeniable.

The federalizing nature implicit in the internal logic of the *Estado de las Autonomías* corresponds with the federal texture of Spanish society. However, there is no general agreement on whether Spain should be considered properly as a federal system or a federation. As pointed out earlier, the word 'federal' is neither included in any of the provisions of the 1978 Constitution nor in the subsequent constitutional legislation passed by the Spanish Parliament. From this terminological perspective there should be no further discussion. However, beyond the constraints of the formal terminology the political articulation of ideas, interests and institutions in Spain need to be reassessed.

Together with *de jure* considerations there exist important de facto arrangements that lend support to the arguable inclusion of Spain in the category of federations. In order to substantiate such claims some basic federalizing criteria is to be contrasted as follows:

a   Spain's 'autonomical' system combines both 'self-rule' and 'shared rule'.
b   Spain is a democracy where two tiers of government – central and regional – enjoy constitutionally separate powers and representative parliamentary institutions.

c   The Spanish Constitution is the legitimate source for the right of self-government by the *Comunidades Autónomas*. The authority of the regional layer is not a surrogate of the central government.
d   Spain is composed of 17 *Comunidades Autónomas*, each and everyone having democratic constitutional statutes of autonomy for their internal organization.
e   Spain's Constitutional Court is the ultimate arbitrator for the demarcation of concurrent powers and governmental competencies.[21]
f   Spanish Parliament is bicameral with a Senate envisaged as a 'territorial upper chamber'.

No ideal-type of federation has been put into effect which could serve as a reference model to measure the federative qualities of the federal-like systems existing in the world today. Spain could well be considered as a multinational federation in disguise where the development of the joint action between the two main governmental tiers (central and regional) needs further consolidation. At the beginning of the process of decentralization, powers were allocated with no little intergovernmental friction. Later on, challenges to laws, decree laws and legislative decrees, either by the Spanish or the regional parliaments, have been judged by the Constitutional Court in a manner that confirms the federalizing trend towards the 'sharing of rule' between central and regional levels (Agranoff and Ramos Gallarín, 1997).

However, Spain would not fully qualify as a federation if we take into account the functional shortcomings in the actual institutionalization of the 'shared rule' principle. Despite its constitutional definition as 'territorial chamber', the Spanish Upper House mainly performs duplicating functions with regard to the fully-fledged Chamber of Deputies, or Lower House. Since 1978 the Senate has merely doubled the legislative functions of the Congress of Deputies. Its value has been basically instrumental, offering the parties of government and opposition a second chance to agree on legislative projects or to introduce amendments where legislative readings in the Lower House were hurried or superficial. This has contributed to its poor political reputation and to its low estimation among the citizenship with respect to its place and function.

If the institutional involvement of the Autonomous Communities in state-wide decision making via the Senate has been very limited, intergovernmental relations by means of the so-called 'sectoral conferences' (*conferencias sectoriales*) have contributed to horizontal consultation despite that they are not institutions for joint decision making. Exchange of information is an important element facilitated at the sectoral conferences, which have become mechanisms of 'institutional courtesy' (Grau i Creus, 2000), and which reflect to a certain degree a trend towards practices of cooperative federalism (Börzel, 2000).

Intergovernmental relations are still very dependent on the colouring of the political party in charge of the different levels of governments. Consequently, most of the conflicts are political-contingent rather than policy-oriented. That is why 'bilateralism' is still the preferred manner to reach political agreements rather than the multilateral institutionalization of 'shared rule' in a genuine federal Senate. Power-sharing at the federal level is a crucial feature of federations, which is not institutionalized in the case of Spain. With the proviso of the dysfunctional existence of the Upper House as chamber of territorial representation of the citizens of the *Comunidades Autónomas*, Spain's *Estado de las Autonomías* satisfies nevertheless the other crucial federative criteria above reviewed.

Multiple ethno-territorial concurrence and dual identities

The gradual establishment of the *Estado de las Autonomías* in Spain has generated a complex of relations which can be explained as *multiple ethno-territorial concurrence* (Moreno, 1995). 'Concurrence' should be understood in this context as the simultaneous occurrence of political transactions at state and sub-state levels, within the framework of a multinational state. The term should not simply be made equal to ethno-territorial 'competition'. In a situation of ethno-territorial concurrence there are competitive actions between majority and minority nationalisms and regionalisms, or between the latter. However, there is no compulsion per se to eliminate concurrent actors.

The Spanish mode of multiple ethno-territorial concurrence involves, in the first place, two 'axioms', which refer to general features that are common to most of the contemporary world's decentralized and federal systems; (a) conflicting intergovernmental relations and (b) the politicization of ethno-territorial institutions. Second, two 'premises' relate to the stage prior to the unfolding of Spain's process of decentralization; (c) the differential fact, or political 'distinctiveness' claimed by the minority nations within Spain; and (d) the centralist inertia, or path dependent assumption by the central administration of being hierarchically 'superior'. Third, three 'principles' are the fundamental pillars upon which the territorial rationale of the 1978 Constitution rests upon, explicitly or implicitly; (e) the democratic decentralization, by which liberal democracy and territorial autonomy are intimately related, (f) the comparative grievance, in order to vindicate powers and competencies among the *Comunidades Autónomas* and (g) the inter-territorial solidarity, so that basic levels of wealth are similar throughout Spain. Last, three 'rules' are the most compelling elements in the social and political structuring of the future development of federalization in Spain; (h) the centrifugal pressure, put on the centre by regional parties or elites, (i) the ethno-territorial mimesis, or the practices of policy equalization among the *Comunidades Autónomas* as none wants to be 'left behind' and (j) the inductive allocation of powers, a consequence of a gradual top-down process of decentralization. These elements are responsible for the asymmetry, heterogeneity and plurality which embody the *Estado de las Autonomías* (Moreno, 2001b).

The case of Spain shows the lack of one single and all-embracing national state identity extended throughout the country. Spain's multiple ethno-territorial identities expressed in the 17 *Comunidades Autónomas* illustrates how nationalism and federalism can 'work' together. The concept of dual identity or compound nationality concerns the way in which citizens identify themselves in sub-state nations or regions. It incorporates in variable proportions the regional (ethno-territorial) identity and the national (state) identity. As a result of this, citizens share their institutional loyalties at both levels of political legitimacy without any apparent fracture between them.[22]

Both multiple ethno-territorial loyalties and degrees of self-government are in accordance with the variable manifestation of such citizens' dual identification: the more the primordial regional (ethno-territorial) identity prevails upon modern state identity, the higher the demands for political autonomy. Conversely, the more developed the national (state) identity is, the less likely it would be for ethno-territorial conflicts to arise. Complete absence of one of the two elements of dual identity would lead to a deep socio-political division. If this was the case, demands for self-government would probably take the form of a claim for outright sovereignty and independence. In other words, when citizens in a sub-state community identify themselves in an exclusive manner, the institutional outcome of such antagonism will also tend to be exclusive.

Not surprisingly, in the Basque Country single exclusive regional identity is higher than 20 per cent and highest among all *Comunidades Autónomas* (26.8 per cent in the period 1990–95). Note, however, that in a survey immediately carried out before the 2001 Basque elections, those who declared to feel 'only Basque' were 23 per cent of the total as compared to 41 per cent who identified themselves 'as much Basque as Spanish'.[23] These figures may help to put into perspective the statement made by the *Lehendakari* (President) of the Basque government before the Basque Parliament on 27 September 2002. He then proposed a new Pact for Cohabitation (*Pacto para la Convivencia*) to be based on the free association and co-sovereignty between the Basque Country and Spain, according to a confederation-like proposal which falls short of independence or secession.[24]

Multiple ethno-territorial concurrence and dual identity are distinctive features of Spain's latent federalization, but can also be found in other democratic federations. Both elements provide the legitimizing bases for making unity and diversity workable. Polyarchies do not necessarily have as compelling alternatives those of secessionism and assimilationism. Rather than a stepping stone towards territorial dissolution, federalism and ethno-territorial accommodation can consolidate liberal democracy in multinational states (Linz, 1997).

Castilian Staatsvolk *and consociational accommodation*

In plural Spain both nationalism and federalism can be regarded as two conceptual sides of the same political coin for the achievement of territorial accommodation. No federal-like arrangements would have been working out in the process of transition to democracy had it not been for the political need to accommodate both Spanish national and minority nationalisms alongside other regional claims for territorial home rule. Spain validates, in this respect, the claim that federal systems can make compatible internal national oppositions and dual identities.

On exploring the relationship between federalism and nationalism, particularly in the case of multinational federations, it has been advanced that 'a stable democratic majoritarian federation, federal or multi-national, must have a *Staatsvolk*, a national or ethnic people, who are demographically and electorally dominant – though not necessarily an absolute majority of the population – and who will be the co-founders of the federation' (O'Leary, 2001: 244–5). This claim is meant to be consistent with liberal nationalism (Tamir, 1993), national federalism (Forsyth, 1989) and national cultural homogeneity (Gellner, 1997).

Spain provides a good example of how *Staatsvolk* dynamics are to be cautiously analysed on processes of federation building. As pointed out earlier, dictatorial Francoism attempted an identification of an 'eternal Spain' as the ideological expression of an old and unpolluted 'Castilian spirit' with a universal language and ideals beyond the limits of time and space. Epitomes like 'God's Empire' (*El Imperio hacia Dios*) or 'Spain, a unit of destiny in the universal (*España, una unidad de destino en lo universal*), and a simulated 'timeless' Castilian culture pertaining to the whole of Spain were used in an attempt to assimilate the Spanish mosaic of cultures and peoples.

According to the views of such majority (ethnic) nationalism, Spain was a single nation rather than a plural nation of nations. Francoism attempted to enforce a programme of 'national' homogenization patterned along the lines of a Castilian *Staatsvolk*, which was bound to fail with the return of democracy. By having made the Spanish nation equal to an ideal-type of uniform Castile, democrats all around Spain came to face an insuperable dilemma between civil liberties and decentralization, or between cultural homogeneity and representative government.

The subsequent development of the *Estado de las Autonomías* has clearly shown the fallacy of regarding Castile as a national unit. As a matter of fact only from the ethnolingual point of view such a nationality could be taken into account (64 per cent of the total population reside in Castilian-speaking territories such as Andalusia, Aragon, Canary Islands, Cantabria, Asturias, Extremadura, La Rioja, Madrid or Murcia, together with the traditional 'old' and 'new' Castilles).

However important language is for social mobilization and nation building, it would be unlikely for an ethnic community to be politicized solely around it. At this point, identity could well be the necessary extra element providing national cohesion on collective perceptions, interpretations and aspirations. But as we have previously examined, the wide existence of dual identities in the Castilian-speaking *Comunidades Autónomas* makes implausible an identity attachment to an ideal *Castilla* which does not exist as such neither ethnically nor politically.

Could it be hypothesized, nevertheless, that all mono-lingual Castilian-speaking regions in Spain would be willing to constitute one political community congruent with their ethnolingual commonality in the foreseeable future? 'No' ought to be the answer to this question if we bear in mind the effects produced by the federalizing developments accomplished in the last decades. Processes of socialization in the consolidation of the *Estado de las Autonomías* have reinforced regional boundary building and ethno-territorial diversities. Citizens in, say, Aragon or Andalusia regard themselves ethnically much less as Castilian speakers than as active members of their own regional communities. The role of the meso-governments of the 17 *Comunidades Autónomas* in the production and reproduction of regional identities in Spain has been very important (Martínez-Herrera, 2002).

From the viewpoint of the Basque, Catalan and Galician minority nationalisms, Spain ought to be constitutionally composed according to linguistic lines. This approach lends support indirectly to the idea of recreating the Castilian *Staatsvolk*. Not surprisingly, such sub-state nationalisms are generally more favourable of establishing confederal options for territorial accommodation in Spain than of working out federal arrangements *tout court*. They are suspicious of versions of one-nation federalism as in the cases of Australia, Germany or the USA. Along these lines, Jordi Pujol declared himself a federalist prior to his election as President of the Catalan Generalitat in 1980:

> In the specific case of Spain I could conceivably be a federalist, if the federation was based on genuine and authentic nationalities of the state, viz. Euskadi [Basque Country], Galicia, the whole of Castile, and the Catalan Countries (or just Catalonia, if Valencia and the Islands ... rejected being associated with the Principate [Catalonia]).
>
> (Pujol, 1980: 26)

After 25 years of widespread decentralization and latent federalization, Spain has preserved their territorial stability according to a broad consensus among parties and elites of a consociational nature. Spain has not followed literally the four features theorized by Arend Lijphart (1977). As regards autonomy in culture, this competency falls under the exclusive constitutional powers of all *Comunidades Autónomas*. Power sharing is de facto exercised in the daily practice of intergovernmental life by the great number of concurrent policies needing joint action. And parliamentary support of the nationalist parties to the central government has been so important as to reach in some cases the category of 'informal vetoes' against possible decisions invading areas of their regional jurisdiction. Quota representation of minority groups in state institutions and public sector has not been necessary. Other than the absence of discrimination against citizens from the 'historical nationalities', or any other regions,[25] minority nationalisms have set as a priority the achievement of influence and power in their own territories by means of controlling institutions of self-government and making eventual allegiances with central elites and government.

In the general pattern of consociational practices and agreements which has facilitated federalization in Spain, Basque terrorism has highly conditioned not only the achievement of peace and stability in *Euskalherria*,[26] but has also interfered in the general climate of inter-party agreement inside and outside the Basque Country. Let us remind ourselves that consociational practices between nationalists and non-nationalist parties to accommodate the various Spanish idiosyncrasies and identities were also the pattern for political agreement for most of the period of Basque home-rule since 1978. It remains to be seen whether those practices can return to the Basque Country despite the fact that electoral polarization seems to reflect an increasing civil fracture (Moreno, 2004).

Developments in the Basque Country have had an undeniable effect on the dynamics of agreements between state-wide political parties themselves, most of which also have federal or decentralized organic structures. The limited degree of enthusiasm raised by the constitutional reform in order to 'federalize' the Senate is based upon the reluctance to re-edit the same consensual climate which made possible the drafting of the 1978 Constitution, and which now appears rather difficult.

Conclusion

The ethnolingual variety of Spain, a country which for most of its contemporary history has been governed by central actors, institutions and political forces that have traditionally been both weak through inefficacy and strong through violence, has too often resulted in damage to its unity. With the ongoing federalization old patterns of confrontation seem to have been overcome. Actions by both majority and minority nationalism however put into test the resilience of the general consensual pact inaugurated with the 1978 Constitution, and the consociational practices for territorial accommodation since then.

The case of Spain's *Comunidades Autónomas* illustrates the potentialities for accommodating different identities and aspirations for self-government within the framework of a plural polity. As in other formal multinational federations or union states, Spain can provide some useful contrasts on how to build macro communities of trust beyond single national sentiments and attachments. Such insights are most relevant concerning supra-national unions like the European Union (EU) (Moreno, 2002).

Much like future developments in the EU, Spain faces a variety of challenges on how to integrate – rather than to assimilate – existing collective identities forged at the various levels of political legitimacy. If achieved by means of shared rule and self-rule it would avoid being seen as an exogenous process, which is superimposed 'from above' by a central authority upon the internal interaction of communities with long-standing cultures and histories.[27]

Notes

1   Conservatives, centrists, nationalists, socialists and communists were involved in broking a constitutional-wide inter-party consensus. In the popular referendum held on 6 December 1978, the Spanish *Carta Magna* received 87.9 per cent 'yes' votes, 7.8 per cent 'no' votes, and 4.3 per cent null or blank votes. Abstention reached 32.9 per cent of the registered electorate.

2   Catalan and its dialects are spoken by 4.2 million in Catalonia, 2.1 million in Valencia, 0.2 million in the Balearic Islands and 0.05 million in Aragon; Basque is the vernacular language of 0.7 million in the Basque Country and 0.05 million in Navarre; and Galician is that of 2.3 million *gallegos*. Other official languages, as declared in their regional Statues of Autonomy, are Bable (spoken by 0.4 million in Asturias) and Aranese (0.004 in Catalonia). There are also a number of Spanish dialects widely spoken in other regions (Andalusia, Canary Islands, Extremadura, Murcia) (Sanmartí Roset, 1997: 67).

3   In 2002, public assessment of the setting-up of the *Comunidades Autónomas* was considered 'positive' by 67 per cent as compared to 51 per cent in 1994. Those who had a 'negative' opinion decreased from 19 to 13 per cent, while the same 11 per cent of the surveyed expressed neither 'positive' nor 'negative' views (CIS, 1998, 2002).

4   The influential Catalan nationalist Enric Prat de la Riba described how in the sixth century BC, Phoenician explorers found the Iberian *etnos* covering from Murcia (in the south-east of the Iberian Peninsula) to the river Rhone in France. This was 'the first link [. . .] in the chain of generations that have forged the Catalan soul' (Prat de la Riba, 1917: 99–102).

5   The United Kingdom could also be included in such a category. Let us remind ourselves that after the Union of the Crows (1603) and the Act of Union (1707), Scotland's civil society continued to enjoy a degree of autonomy in crucial areas such as education, law, local government and religion (Paterson, 1994).

6   King Chindasvinto (r. 642–9) and his son Recesvinto (r. 649–72) were able to collate the Visigothic laws in the *Liber iudiciorum* or *Lex Wisigothorum*, which became applicable to the whole of the Peninsular territory.

7   Throughout the medieval period, and parallel to the tendency towards warring and expansionism, the habit of making pacts with and respecting the rights of the defeated, whose cultural and technical knowledge was generally superior to that of the victors, was consolidated. Thus, with the growth of the Christian kingdoms, the 'reconquered' communities (Mozarab, Mudejar and Jewish) obtained legal statutes, or *fueros*, that protected the integrity of their customs and ways of life (Moreno, 2001a).

8   According to historian Américo Castro, 'In the year 1000 . . . Christian Spain was essentially what it would be in 1600, and could be clearly distinguished from France and Italy' (Castro, 1984: 13).

9   While the north-east of Spain structured around the values of Christianity and the figure of St James, and the Castilians rebelled against the old kingdom of Leon-Asturias, Catalonia remained part of the Carolingian Empire since 987 as the 'Hispanic Landmark' (*Marca Hispánica*). Catalan nationalists, including Jordi Pujol himself, have identified the Caroligian Frankish origins of the *Comtats* founded by Charlemagne as the origins of Catalonia, and as such different from

the rest of the Spanish lands. According to Américo Castro, 'Catalonia neither belonged completely to Spain, nor ceased to be part of it' (ibid.: 81).

10 For historians such as Claudio Sánchez-Albornoz and Angus MacKay, during the long medieval period, and in contrast to the rest of Europe, the concepts of border and reconquest became essential symbolic and actual referents in the historical development of the country. Later they would be replaced by the enterprise of the Spanish Empire and the expansion overseas (Sánchez-Albornoz, 1956; MacKay, 1977).

11 For Salvador de Madariaga (1979) the three Basque provinces were not constituent of the Basque Country – which was a modern political creation. In any case, all three provinces took good care of their *fueros* or local rights, before and after they joined the Castilian Crown: 'They would not recognize Lord or King without the prior and solemn pledge for honouring their *fueros*' (Pi i Margall, 1911: 251).

12 In 1436, and after a lengthy dispute with the Kingdom of Portugal, Castile obtained the recognition of its sovereignty over the Canary Islands from Pope Eugene IV.

13 In a confidential memorandum of 25 December 1620, the Duke of Olivares, who governed Spain for 22 years, advised Philip IV to become King of Spain, and not to remain content with being King of Portugal, Aragon, Valencia and Count of Barcelona: 'You should see to it that these kingdoms of which Spain is composed are ruled by the laws and in the manner of Castile. In doing so, your Majesty would become the world's most powerful sovereign' (reproduced in Linz, 1973: 43). The attempt resulted in the eventual banishment of the Duke in 1643, and Catalonia's loss of Roussillon, Conflent and Cerdanya. The Catalan national anthem, *Els Segadors* ('The Reapers') evokes the events of 1640.

14 The territories elected two representatives to the *Junta Central*, supreme unit of governance in occupied Spain. Besides those functions of general action (coordination of war activities, colonial and foreign relations, and general services), the rest of the administrative affairs were run at the regional level.

15 Carlists were traditionalist Catholic supporters of the pretender Charles who claimed the Spanish throne after the death of his brother, King Ferdinand VII. The Carlist movement proclaimed a virulent anti-liberalism, fuelled by a frantic fear of secularization, rationalism and modernity. In the nineteenth century, three Carlist civil wars ripped Spain apart: 1833–40, 1846–48 and 1872–75. The current Basque separatist movement (ETA, HB, KAS, EH) is characterized by an emotional and messianic style which is not so far removed from the Carlist traditionalism which preceded it, and which it has now to a large extent replaced (Giner and Moreno, 1990).

16 Between 1877 and 1920, the proportion of Madrid workers in the industrial sector grew considerably from 18.4 to 42.5 per cent of the workforce, but remained behind Barcelona in this respect, with 37.1 per cent in 1877 to 54 per cent in 1920. Perhaps it was more significant that the proportion of 'unproductive' middle classes in Madrid, consisting of civil servants, members of the armed forces and domestic staff (23.6 per cent in 1877 and 15.3 per cent in 1920), was greater than that of Barcelona (5.9 per cent in 1877 and 5 per cent in 1920) (data taken from Linz, 1967: 209).

17 On 14 April 1931 the Spanish Second Republic was proclaimed. On the same day the Catalan nationalist leader, Francesc Macià, declared the creation of the Republic of Catalonia within the framework of a Spanish Confederation. After negotiations with representatives of the central government, the *Generalitat*, Catalonia's government of medieval origin, was re-established.

18 Three days after the proclamation of the Second Republic, an assembly of Basque mayors gathered by José Antonio Aguirre, leader of the Basque

Nationalist Party, claimed their right to autonomy within a Spanish federal republic. At the end of 1933, the statutory project did not include Navarre and was supported in a referendum by 47 per cent in Araba (Alava), and almost 90 per cent of Biscayans and Gipuzkoans. The proposal was put forward in the Spanish Parliament in December of 1933. Finally on 1 October 1936, the Basque statute of autonomy was passed, with similar rights and powers to that of Catalonia.

19 In Galicia, the *Organización Regional Gallega Autónoma* (ORGA, Autonomous Regional Organization of Galicia), led by Santiago Casares Quiroga, had instigated the drafting of a proposal for autonomy. On 28 June 1936, a referendum was held and around 70 per cent of the Galician electorate voted. The final result was 991,476 votes for and 6,805 against.

20 With the partial exception of Araba (Alava) and Navarre. These two *foral* territories were able to keep their fiscal privileges as a 'reward' for the participation of many *Carlist* from those provinces who joined Franco's forces during the Civil War (Giner and Moreno, 1990).

21 The need for a pact between government and opposition in the Spanish Parliament for the election of the members of the *Tribunal Constitucional* has so far proved to be a barrier against open political sectarianism in the appointment of its members. Furthermore, the important sentence of the Constitutional Court (5 August 1983) on the LOAPA Act ('Organic Law on the Harmonization of the Autonomy Process') passed by the Spanish Parliament, reinforced the open and federalizing interpretation of the 1978 Constitution very much against the views of centralist leaders within centre-right UCD and centre-left PSOE main parties.

22 The question put to them in successive surveys has been as follows: 'In general, would you say that you feel ... 1. Only Basque, Catalan, Galicia, etc.; 2. More Basque, Catalan, Galician, etc., than Spanish; 3. As much Basque, Catalan, Galician, etc. as Spanish; 4. More Spanish than Basque, Catalan, Galician, etc.; 5. Only Spanish; 6. Don't know; 7. No answer'. In the period October 1990–June 1995 a degree of duality was expressed by around 70 per cent of the total Spanish population (i.e. categories 2, 3 and 4). Approximately 30 per cent of all Spaniards expressed a single identity ('Only Spanish', or 'Only Andalusian, Basque, Catalan, etc.'). According to 2002 data, percentages were 78 and 22 per cent, respectively (CIS, 2002). For an analysis of the Catalan case, see Moreno *et al.* (1998). In Scotland/United Kingdom surveys using this identity scale were first carried out in the mid-1980s (Moreno, 1986).

23 The aggregate percentages of those with a degree of dual identity were 61 per cent as compared to 28 per cent of those declaring a single or exclusive self-identification (i.e. 'Only Basque' or 'Only Spanish'). Note that among supporters of the most voted nationalist party in the Basque Country (PNV), a third declared to be 'Only Basque', the same amount of those who identify themselves 'As much Basque as Spanish' (*El País*, 7 May 2001).

24 According to the *Lehendakari*, the citizens of the Basque Country are entitled to self-determination and to decide in a popular referendum the future of its political status and the sharing of its sovereignty within a multinational Spain. Note that full independence is supported by a quarter of the Basque surveyed population.

25 The recruitment of state-wide civil servants in Spain has traditionally followed the French model of non-discriminatory competitions. Conversely to the *verzuiling* system, or 'pillarization' of Dutch society and politics, consociationalism in Catholic Spain has not developed according to the expectations and goals of the various cultural and religious 'denominations'.

26 For radical Basque nationalism, *Euskalherria* is a nation made up of the Spanish

'historical territories' (provinces) of Araba, Gipuzkoa, Biscay as well as Navarre (all of these located in Spain) and the French districts of Labourd (Lapurdi), Soule (Zuberoa) and Lower Navarre (Behenafarroa) in the French *département* of the Atlantic Pyrenees.

27 I thank the Spanish Secretary of State for Education and Universities (PR2002–0200) for financial support during the writing of this piece of research. I am also grateful to Enric Martínez-Herrera for comments and suggestions made on an earlier version of this text.

References

Agranoff, R. and Ramos Gallarín, J.A. (1997), 'Toward Federal Democracy in Spain: An Examination of Intergovernmental Relations', *Publius. The Journal of Federalism* 27 (4): pp. 1–38.

Börzel, T. (2000), 'From Competitive Regionalism to Cooperative Federalism. The Europeanization of the Spanish State of the Autonomies', *Publius. The Journal of Federalism* 30 (2): 17–42.

Brubaker, R. (1996), *Nationalism Reframed: Nationhood and the National Question in the New Europe*. Cambridge: Cambridge University Press.

Burgess, M. (1993), 'Federalism and Federation: A Reappraisal', in Burgess, M. and Gagnon, A.-G. (eds), *Comparative Federalism and Federation: Competing Traditions and Future Directions*. London: Harvester Wheatsheaf.

Cadalso, J. (1978), *Cartas marruecas. Noches lúgubres* (2nd edn). Madrid: Cátedra.

Castro, A. (1984), *España en su historia. Cristianos, moros y judíos* (3rd edn). Barcelona: Crítica.

CIS (1998), *Estudio 2.286*. Madrid: Centro de Investigaciones Sociológicas.

—— (2002), *Estudio 2.455*. Madrid: Centro de Investigaciones Sociológicas.

de Madariaga, S. de (1979), *España: Ensayo de Historia Contemporánea* (14th edn). Madrid: Espasa-Calpe.

de Riquer, B. and Ucelay-Da Cal, E. (1994), 'An Analysis of Nationalisms in Spain: A Proposal for an Integrated Historical Model', in Beramendi, J.G., Máiz, R. and Núñez, X.M. (eds), *Nationalism in Europe. Past and Present* (Vol. II). Santiago: Universidade de Santiago de Compostela, pp. 275–301.

Domínguez Ortiz, A. (1976), *Sociedad y Estado en el siglo XVIII español*. Barcelona: Ariel.

Elazar, D. (1987), *Exploring Federalism*. Tuscaloosa, AL: University of Alabama Press.

Forsyth, M. (ed.) (1989), *Federalism and Nationalism*. Leicester: Leicester University Press.

Gellner, E. (1997), *Nationalism*. London: Weidenfeld and Nicolson.

Giner, S. (1980), *The Social Structure of Catalonia*. The Anglo-Catalan Society Occasional Publications: University of Sheffield.

—— (1984), 'Ethnic Nationalism, Centre and Periphery in Spain', in Abel, C. and Torrents, N. (eds), *Spain: Conditional Democracy*. London: Croom Helm, pp. 78–99.

Giner, S. and Moreno, L. (1990), 'Centro y periferia: La dimensión étnica de la sociedad española', in Giner, S. (ed.), *España. Sociedad y Política*. Madrid: Espasa-Calpe, pp. 169–97.

Grau i Creus, M. (2000), 'Spain: The Incomplete Federalism', in Wachendorfer-Schmidt, U. (ed.), *Federalism and Political Performance*. London: Routledge, pp. 58–77.

Hintze, O. (1975), *Historical Essays* (compiled by F. Gilbert). New York: Oxford University Press.

Lijphart, A. (1977), *Democracy in Plural Societies. A Comparative Exploration*. New Haven, CT: Yale University Press.

Linz, J.J. (1967), 'The Party System of Spain: Past and Future', in Lipset, S.M. and Rokkan, S. (eds), *Party Systems and Voter Alignments: Cross-National Perspectives*. New York: The Free Press, pp. 197–282.

—— (1973), 'Early State-building and the Late Peripheral Nationalisms against the State: the Case of Spain', in Eisenstadt, S. and Rokkan, S. (eds), *Building States and Nations. Models, Analyses and Data across Three Worlds*, 2 vols. Beverly Hills, CA: Sage, pp. 32–116.

—— (1997), 'Democracy, Multi-nationalism and Federalism'. Working Paper 1997/103. Madrid: CEACS-Institute Juan March.

MacKay, A. (1977), *Spain in the Middle Ages. From Frontier to Empire, 1000–1500*. New York: St Martin's Press.

MAP (1997), *Estudio sobre reparto del gasto público en 1997 entre los distintos niveles de administración*. Madrid: Ministerio de Administraciones Públicas.

—— (2002), *Estimación del reparto del gasto público entre los subsectores de administraciones públicas (1982–2002)*. Madrid: Ministerio de Administraciones Públicas.

Martínez-Herrera, E. (2002), 'From Nation-building to Building Identification with Political Communities: Consequences of Political Decentralization in Spain, the Basque Country, Catalonia and Galicia, 1978–2001', *European Journal of Political Research* 41: 421–53.

Moreno, L. (1986), *Decentralisation in Britain and Spain: The Cases of Scotland and Catalonia* (PhD thesis). Edinburgh: National Library of Scotland.

—— (1995), 'Multiple Ethnoterritorial Concurrence in Spain', *Nationalism and Ethnic Politics* 1 (1): 11–32.

—— (2001a), *The Federalization of Spain*. London: Frank Cass.

—— (2001b), 'Ethnoterritorial Concurrence in Plural Societies: The Spanish *Comunidades Autónomas*', in Gagnon, A.-G. and Tully, J. (eds), *Justice and Stability in Multi-national Societies*. Cambridge: Cambridge University Press.

—— (2002), 'Multiple Identities and Global Meso-communities', Madrid: UPC Working Papers (02-25). Available online: www.iesam.csic.es/doctrab.htm.

—— (2004), 'Divided societies, electoral polarization and the Basque country', in Guelke, A. (ed.), *Democracy and Ethnic Conflict*. Basingstoke: Palgrave.

Moreno, L., Arriba, A. and Serrano, A. (1998), 'Multiple Identities in Decentralised Spain: The Case of Catalonia', *Regional and Federal Studies* 8 (3): 65–88.

O'Leary, B. (2001), 'An Iron Law of Nationalism and Federation? A (Neo-Diceyian) Theory of the Necessity of a Federal *Staatsvolk*, and of Consociational Rescue', *Nations and Nationalism* 7 (3): pp. 273–96.

Paterson, L. (1994), *The Autonomy of Modern Scotland*. Edinburgh: Edinburgh University Press.

Pi i Margall, F. (1911), *Las Nacionalidades* (4th edn) (1st edn: 1876). Madrid: Librería de los Sucesores de Hernando.

Prat de la Riba, E. (1917), *La Nacionalidad Catalana*. Valladolid: Imprenta Castellana. (Original edition in Catalan: Barcelona, L'Anuari de la Exportació, 1906.)

Pujol, J. (1980), *Construir Catalunya*. Barcelona: Pòrtic.

Rokkan, S. and Urwin, D. (1983), *Economy, Territory, Identity. Politics of West European Peripheries*. London: Sage.

Sánchez-Albornoz, C. (1956), *España: un enigma histórico*. Buenos Aires: Editorial Sudamericana.

Sanmartí Roset, J.M. (1997), *Las políticas lingüísticas y las lenguas minoritarias en el proceso de construcción de Europa*. Vitoria-Gasteiz: Instituto Vasco de Administración Pública.

Tamir, Y. (1993), *Liberal Nationalism*. Princeton, NJ: Princeton University Press.

Watts, R. (2001), 'Models of Federal Power-sharing', *International Social Science Journal* 167: 23–32.

7 Russia's multinational federation

From constitutional to contract federalism and the 'war of laws and sovereignties'

Cameron Ross

Introduction

In December 1993 Russia ratified its first post-communist Constitution which in Article 1 boldly proclaimed that it was 'a democratic federative rule of law state with a republican form of government'. However, there are now major concerns over the current regime's commitment to the principles of federalism and democracy. Since the inauguration of Vladimir Putin as Russian President in May 2000 federalism has come under attack and we have witnessed a concerted effort to rein in the power of the regional governors and presidents.

The problems of federalisation in Russia are rooted in the country's centuries long history of authoritarian rule and the absence of a federal and democratic tradition. The 1993 Constitution provided Russia with all of the major institutional prerequisites necessary for a federation.[1] However, as Elazar stresses, 'True federal systems manifest their federalism in culture as well as constitutional and structural ways' and 'the viability of federal systems is directly related to the degree to which federalism has been internalised culturally within a particular civil society'.[2] Moreover, as Watts stresses, federalism requires a legal democratic culture with a 'recognition of the supremacy of the constitution over all orders of government'.[3]

However, the Russian state which emerged out of the ashes of the USSR in January 1992 inherited a highly authoritarian political culture and a weak and inchoate civil society. Nor was there any genuine tradition of federalism which the leadership could call upon to support it in its new state building strategy. For although the USSR was formally a federation, and the Russian Soviet Federative Socialist Republic (RSFSR) was a 'federation within a federation', in reality Soviet federalism was a sham. As Heinemann-Gruder writes,

> Instead of a sense of partnership in intergovernmental relations, constitutionalism and a voluntary and internalised agreement on shared federal norms and values, political practices featured the centralism of

the Communist party and executive command chains, the hierarchical structure of the central planning apparatus, and the dominance of Russian elites and their culture over non-Russians.[4]

As Mikhail Gorbachev (General Secretary of the Communist Party), admitted in 1989, 'Up to now our state has existed as a centralised and unitary state and none of us has yet the experience of living in a federation.'[5]

Federalism also requires the support of political elites. However, the collapse of communism in 1991 did not lead to a democratic 'circulation of elites' in Russia. On the contrary, 'nomenklatura' continuity was the norm, particularly in the ethnic regions where former communist elites were able to utilise the ethnic card to win and hold on to power. Post-communist elites have used federalism primarily as a smokescreen for the promotion of their own narrow political and economic interests.

Moreover, Russia's weak and fragmented party system has also hindered the development of federalism. A minority of the parties in the lower house of the Russian Parliament (the *Duma*) have nationwide organisations which could help to glue the federation together (much as the communist party did during the Soviet era), and a majority of the parties are hostile to Russia's ethno-territorial form of federalism. It is only since Putin came to power that we have witnessed the development of a parliamentary coalition ('United Russia') strong enough to command a majority of the votes in the *Duma*, and Putin has used this coalition to undermine, rather than defend federalism.

As we demonstrate below, the major challenge to the Russian state today is not confederalism or the threat of ethnic disintegration, but rather defederalisation and the creation of a centralised and authoritarian state under Putin. Behind the formal veneer of democracy and constitutionalism, federal relations in Russia are dominated by informal, clientelistic and extra-constitutional practices.

Below I discuss four major factors which have thwarted the consolidation of federalism in Russia: (1) the extremely high levels of socio-economic, constitutional and political asymmetry; (2) the 'war of constitutions' and the development of 'contract federalism'; (3) the problematic legacy of ethno-territorial federalism bequeathed to Russia from the USSR, and the challenge of ethnic secessionism; (4) Putin's radical assault on the principles of federalism and democracy.

Socio-economic, constitutional and political asymmetry

With a population of 145 million citizens incorporating 172 nationalities and an area covering 170 million square kilometres, Russia is one of the largest and most ethnically diverse multinational federations in the world. Furthermore, Russia has the largest number of constituent units of any federation. Founded on the dual principles of ethnicity and territory, the federation comprises 89 federal subjects, 57 of which are territorially defined subjects, and 32 which are ethnically defined subjects (including 21 republics and 11 national autonomies); see Table 7.1.

Asymmetry in Russia

Given the sheer size and ethnic diversity of the country it is not surprising that the Russian Federation should be asymmetrical. Indeed, as Stepan observes, with the possible exception of Switzerland, all mono-national democratic federations (Austria, Germany, Australia, the US, Argentina and Brazil) are constitutionally symmetrical and all multinational democratic federations (India, Belgium, Canada and Spain) are constitutionally asymmetrical.[6] Nor as Hahn reminds us is Russia unique in developing constitutional asymmetry through bilateral treaties. India and Spain provide special constitutional privileges to over ten of their federal subjects.[7]

It is not asymmetry per se that is the problem in Russia, rather it is the potent mixture of socio-economic, constitutional and political asymmetry. Moreover, as Hahn notes, Russia also has very high levels of 'non-institutionalised' or 'unofficial asymmetry', by which he means, 'violations of the federal constitution and of regional constitutions and laws' which have not been 'institutionalised' by formal agreements.[8]

Socio-economic asymmetry

The 89 different components of the Russian Federation vary widely in the size of their territories and populations. Thus, for example, the territory of the Republic of Sakha is 388 times greater in size than that of the Republic of North Osetiya-Alaniya. The population of Moscow (8.5 million) is 443 times greater than that of the sparsely populated Yevenk Autonomous *Oblast*.[9] There are also vast differences in the socio-economic status of the federal subjects. For example, income per capita in the oil rich Yamala-Nenetsk Autonomous *Oblast* is 178 times greater than in the Republic of Ingushetiya. Investment per capita across the federation varies by a factor of 20 and regional differences in per capita gross regional product vary by a factor of 30.[10] There are also considerable differences in the levels of unemployment, which in 2001 was just 2.1 per cent in Moscow but 34.9 per cent in Ingushetiya.[11] By comparison 'there is no more than a four-fold difference

Table 7.1 The federal structure of the Russian federation

Territorially defined federal subjects (57)	*Ethnically defined federal subjects (32)*
6 *Krais*	21 Republics
49 *Oblasts*	10 Autonomous *Okrugs*
2 federal cities (Moscow and St Petersburg)	1 Autonomous *Oblast*

in GDP between the European Union's poorest new recruits (Bulgaria and Romania) and the EU average',[12] and income per capita varies by a factor of just 1.5 in the German *Lander*.[13] In addition, one federal subject, the city of Moscow, overwhelmingly dominates Russia's federal economic and political landscape, with tax payments from the city regularly comprising one-third of the federation's total tax revenues.

Such high levels of inequality between regions are particularly worrying in multinational federations where the unequal distribution of resources can quickly take on an ethnic dimension exacerbating tensions and conflict between ethnic groups giving succour to separatist movements.

Constitutional asymmetry

One of the most destructive legacies which Russia inherited from the Soviet Union was its ethno-territorial form of federalism. The 'dual nature' of Russian federalism, which grants different constitutional rights and powers to different subjects of the federation, has created major tensions and divisions between federal subjects. Even although the Russian Constitution declares that all subjects are constitutionally equal (Article 5), in fact the 21 ethnic republics have been granted far greater powers than the other subjects of the federation. Constitutional asymmetry has also increased with the development of 'contract federalism'. During Yeltsin's presidency 46 bilateral treaties were signed between federal subjects and the federal government (see below).

Political asymmetry

Socio-economic and constitutional asymmetry in turn generate political asymmetry. Thus, for example, rich 'donor subjects' (regions which pay more taxes to the federal budget than they receive back) have been more successful in carving out higher levels of political autonomy than the impoverished 'recipient regions' who depend on federal transfers from the centre for their economic survival. And constitutional asymmetry has led to the creation of highly diverse political regimes in the regions ranging from 'partial democracies' at one end of the political spectrum to 'electoral dictatorships' at the other end.[14]

The 'war of constitutions' and the development of contract federalism

Over the period October 1991–October 1993 there was a fierce struggle for power between the Russian presidency and Parliament. Taking advantage of this period of political turmoil a number of republics were able to ratify radical 'confederalist' constitutions which granted themselves considerable powers of political and economic autonomy. As Umnova notes, at least four types of central–local relations were in operation during this period:

1) international relations (between Chechnya and Russia); 2) confederative relations (between Russia and the republics of Tatarstan and
Bashkortostan; 3) federative relations with elements of confederative and
unitary systems (in almost all of the ethnic republics and the richer
donor territorially based subjects); and 4) federative relations with elements of a unitary system (in the poor territorially based regions).[15]

In order to bring a halt to the 'parade of sovereignties' the Yeltsin regime
was forced to sign a Federation Treaty in March 1992 in which it conceded
major powers to the ethnic republics. In fact, there were three separate
treaties, with separate agreements for the ethnic republics, the ethnic
autonomies and the regions. Each of these three types of federal subject were
awarded with a different set of legal powers and status: national-state status
(for the sovereign republics), administrative-territorial status (for the *krais*
and *oblasts*, and the cities of Moscow and St Petersburg) and national-
territorial status (for the autonomous *oblasts* and autonomous *okrugs*).[16]

In the treaty the republics were recognised as sovereign states with rights
of secession and they were also granted independent powers over taxation
and ownership of their land and natural resources. In addition, the republics
were to have their own 'constitutions, legislation, elected legislative bodies
(parliaments), supreme courts, and presidents.'[17] In contrast the territorially-
based regions were given none of the above rights and their chief executives
(governors) were to be directly appointed by the President. The Federal
Treaty was ratified by the Russian Parliament in April 1992 and its text was
directly incorporated into the Russian Constitution which at that time was
the 1978 RSFSR Constitution which had been amended more than 300
times.

Incensed by the constitutional inequalities of the Federal Treaty a
number of regions refused to pay taxes to the Federal Budget, whilst a
number of others unilaterally elevated their status to that of republics. Thus,
for example, regions in European Russia created the Central Russian Republic, the Leningrad Republic and the Pomor Republic and a number of other
such 'bogus republics' were created in Siberia and the Urals.[18]

Tatarstan and Chechnya both refused to sign the Federal Treaty and in
November 1992 Tatarstan adopted its own rival constitution which declared
that, 'it was a sovereign state, and a subject of international law, *associated*
with the Russian federation on the basis of a treaty and the mutual delega-
tion of powers'. Chechnya which had declared its independence as early as
November 1991 proclaimed that it was an independent sovereign state and
a full and equal member of the world community of states.

The December 1993 Constitution

The Federation Treaty had been signed at a time when Yeltsin was weak and
he appeared to be losing his struggle for power with the Russian Parliament.

Yeltsin's victory over the Parliament in October 1993 turned the tables and Yeltsin now sought to take back in December 1993 what he had been forced to give up in March 1992. Thus, much to the chagrin of the ethnic republics the text of the Federal Treaty was left out of the new constitution, and Article 5 declared that all subjects of the federation were equal.

The Constitution also stripped the republics of their rights of sovereignty and secession. Thus, Article 4(1) states that, 'The sovereignty of the Russian Federation extends to the whole of its territory', and Article 4(3) declares that, 'The Russian Federation ensures the integrity and inviolability of its territory.' Further articles guarantee the supremacy of the Federal Constitution. Thus, Article 4(2) states that, 'the constitution of the Russian Federation and federal laws are paramount throughout the territory of the federation' and Article 15(1) declares that, 'the Constitution has supreme legal force, is direct acting and applies throughout the territory of the Federation. Laws and other legal enactments adopted in the Federation must not contradict the Constitution.'

The distribution of powers in the Constitution is set out in Articles 71–3. Article 71 defines those powers exclusively allotted to the federal government, whilst Article 72 lists those which come under the joint jurisdiction of the federal authorities and federal subjects. Whilst there are no specific powers set down for the federal subjects, Article 73 concedes that any powers not covered by Articles 71 and 72, are to rest with the federal subjects.

An important article in the Constitution is Article 78 which allows the centre to transfer 'the implementation of some of its powers' to the federal subjects and vice versa.[19] This article was used by the Yeltsin regime to promote the development of bilateralism and 'contract federalism'.

The Constitution also contains a number of ambiguous or even contradictory articles. For example, Article 11 states that central-periphery relations are determined 'by the Federal Treaty and other treaties', which suggests that the Federal Treaty and the Constitution are both still valid. Furthermore, whilst Article 5(4) declares that 'all components of the Russian Federation are equal with each other in their interrelationships with federal bodies of state power', some subjects are clearly more equal than others. Once again, as in the Federal Treaty, the republics were granted greater powers than the other subjects of the federation. Thus, for example, only the republics were granted their own constitutions, official languages and citizenship rights. Furthermore, in contradiction to Articles 4(1) and 4(3) discussed above, Article 5(2) defines the republics as 'states' implying that they have independent rights of sovereignty and secession.

The status of the autonomous *okrugs* is also ambiguous to say the least. According to the Constitution the *okrugs* have equal status with all other federal subjects even though nine of them are situated inside the territories of other subjects (*oblasts* and *krais*).[20] This would seem to suggest that the *okrugs* are simultaneously subordinate and equal to the regions in which they situated. The Constitution also ratified the creation of two other important federal bodies, a Constitutional Court and a new upper chamber of the Parliament, the Federation Council. The members of the Constitutional Court are appointed by the President subject to the approval of the Federation Council. Up until Putin's radical reform of the upper chamber in 2002 the Federation Council consisted of two ex-officio members from each of Russia's 89 subjects, namely the chair of each subject's legislative assembly and the head of each subject's executive body (named governors in the regions and presidents in the republics). The Federation Council is therefore according to Stepan's classification a 'demos-constraining' chamber as it gives equal representation to each of Russia's 89 subjects even although there are considerable variations in the size of their electorates.[21]

The upper chamber for most of its short history has been dominated by the presidency. Thus, although the Federation Council has the right to veto the legislation of the lower house both Yeltsin and Putin have been able to capture control over the use of such veto rights by packing the upper house with their own supporters.[22] (Putin's reform of the upper chamber is discussed in the fourth section of this chapter.) Furthermore, the President can also veto the legislation of both houses of Parliament and his veto can only be overturned by a vote of two-thirds of the members of each house.

The weak legitimacy of the Russian Constitution

A crucial aspect of any federal state is that it should be founded on a voluntary union or covenant. In Russia, Yeltsin's 'presidential constitution' was imposed on the country from above and although the Constitution was supported by 58.4 per cent of the voters nationwide (according to official statistics) it failed to be ratified in 42 of the 89 subjects. The election to ratify the Constitution was boycotted altogether in Chechnya.

It was not long before a number of those republics whose citizens had rejected the Federal Constitution declared that it was not valid in their territories and a 'war of sovereignties was waged between the republics and the federal centre'. By 1996 the Yeltsin administration reported that 19 of the 21 republican constitutions were in breach of the Federal Constitution. As Smith notes, such violations included, 'declaring the republic a subject of international law, establishing illegal taxes and dues, and proclaiming the right to decide questions of war and peace and the right to grant citizenship'.[23] Those constitutions (Chuvashiya, Sakha, Chechnya, Tatarstan and Tuva), ratified between the signing of the Federal Treaty in March 1992 and the ratification of the Russian Constitution on 12 December 1993, were the most confederal, including as they did declarations of sovereignty, rights of secession and citizenship. As we noted above, Tatarstan declared that it was an associate member of the Russian Federation. Only Chechnya went so far as to declare its complete secession and in 1994 and again in 1999 Russian troops had to be sent into the republic to restore federal control.

Bilateral treaties and the formation of a treaty-based federation

Over the period 1994–98 46 bilateral treaties were signed between the federal government and subjects of the federation which gave the local signatories a whole host of political and economic privileges. The vast majority of these treaties (42 of the 46) also contained provisions which violated the Russian Constitution. Thus, for example, Tatarstan's treaty which was signed in February 1994 legitimised Tatarstan's radical confederalist constitution and reaffirmed the republic's sovereignty over its economic and political affairs, including foreign trade and foreign policy.

Although Yeltsin adopted a presidential decree in 1996 which stated that all treaties had to conform with Articles 71 and 72 of the Constitution this was to no avail.[24] As Umnova demonstrates, the bilateral treaties significantly widened the number of areas coming under the joint jurisdiction of the federal authorities and the federal subjects as stipulated in Article 72 of the Constitution. For example, 'In Tatarstan there were 17 new spheres, in Bashkortostan and Sakha 11, in Kabardino-Balkariya 8, North Osetiya 14, Buryatiya 3, Sverdlovsk Oblast 8, Kaliningrad Oblast 11, and Udmurtiya 11.'[25] In other cases the treaties called for powers which were exclusively reserved for the Russian Federation government to be transferred to the sole jurisdiction of the federal subjects. In June 1999 the Russian Parliament also adopted a law to regulate the treaties which reiterated the fact that all new treaties had to conform to the Federal Constitution.[26] However, the law came too late to make any impact as no new treaties were forthcoming after the last bilateral treaty was signed with Moscow *Oblast* in June 1998.

Supporters of bilateral treaties argue that the agreements have made it possible to ease tensions between the centre and the federal subjects thereby allowing federal agencies 'the ability to take into consideration the specific features of each region'.[27] Moreover the bilateral treaties it is argued 'make the legal system more flexible and responsive to regional diversity and help promote consensus and compromise'.[28] The treaties also played a positive role in preventing the disintegration of the federation. Thus, as Heinemann-Gruder writes, 'the inclusion of regional elites into federal decision making and the bilateralisation of federal–regional relations contributed barriers to regionalist and secessionist strategies'.[29]

Opponents of the treaties stress that they, 'contradict the constitutional principles of federalism, destroy the unity of the legal system, weaken the supremacy of the federal Constitution and federal laws and violate the principle of the equality of subjects of the Russian Federation'.[30] The treaties have also been criticised for their lack of transparency and the absence of a democratic mandate. None of the treaties were ratified by regional or federal parliaments. Moreover, not one of the treaties was brought before the Constitutional Court for scrutiny.[31] As Hahn stresses:

> Conflict and bargaining among officials and bureaucrats, not the rise of civil society and culture, led the process. . . . Russia's asymmetrical

federalism was superimposed on weak semi- or quasi-democratic institutions and not embedded in strongly democratic institutions, as was the case, for example, in the democratic transition in Spain.[32]

By June 1998 when the last bilateral accord was signed, Russia was governed (or ungoverned) by five competing and contradictory sources of law: (1) the Federal Constitution, (2) the Federal Treaty, (3) federal laws, (4) bilateral treaties and (5) the constitutions and charters of the republics and regions.[33]

By the mid-1990s major economic and political powers had passed from the centre to the regions and regional politics were firmly under the control of regional elites. As the Ministry of Justice reported of the 44,000 regional acts adopted over the period 1995–97 almost half were in violation of the Russian Constitution and federal legislation.[34] For Sakwa, Russia's 'war of laws' created a process of 'segmented regionalism', which fragmented the sovereignty of the polity and transformed Russia from a multinational state into a 'multi-state state'.[35]

In 2000, Putin came to power with a mandate to reassert central control from Moscow, to rein in the powers of the ethnic republics and to bring an end to the 'war of laws' (see the fourth section of this chapter).

The fears of ethnic secessionism

During the period of the 'parade of sovereignties' (1991–93) there were real worries that the Russian Federation would follow the fate of the USSR and fall apart. Chechnya's unilateral declaration of independence and its refusal to sign the Federation Treaty only served to confirm deep seated fears that it would not be long before the other ethnic republics would follow suit. The creation of federal state, based on the dual principles of ethnicity and territory, was therefore seen by many members of the political elite as the only way to prevent the disintegration of the state.

Scholars of federalism have stressed both its positive and negative features. For those who stress its positive side, federalism is a source of empowerment for regional groups as it protects minorities from the tyranny of the majority. Furthermore, as Kempton notes, 'By providing a democratic alternative to nation-statehood federalism provides a viable alternative to regional secession and the potential disintegration of multinational states.' Stepan also alerts us to the positive 'association between federalism, multinationalism, and democracy' and the striking fact that 'every single long-standing democracy in a multilingual and multinational polity is a federal state'.[36] Other scholars of federalism have pointed to the success of federalism in such diverse countries as 'Canada, Belgium, India, Malaysia, Nigeria, Spain and South Africa'.[37]

For those who stress its negative features, federalism is the problem rather than the solution. By offering nationalists greater opportunities to mobilise their resources, federalism, it is argued, allows 'ethno-linguistic issues that might otherwise be secondary' to rise to the forefront of the political agenda.[38]

However, it is important to stress that fears of Russia's ethnic disintegration have been exaggerated. There are a number of demographic, economic and geopolitical factors which make it highly unlikely that the federation will fall apart. First, Russians make up 83 per cent of the population and the second largest ethnic group, the Tatars, comprises just 3.8 per cent.[39] Second, Russia's 21 republics make up just 15.7 per cent of the total population of the federation and in only seven of these republics does the indigenous population comprise a majority (Chechnya, Chuvashiya, Dagestan,[40] Ingushetiya, Kalmykiya, North Osetiya-Alaniya and Tuva). Third, of the 11 autonomous areas (the ten autonomous *okrugs* and the autonomous *oblast*) the eponymous population comprises a majority in only two; see Table 7.2.

If we assume that viable demands for secession can only come from those subjects whose territories border foreign states and where a majority of their population is indigenous, then this leaves us with just six republics which meet these criteria:[41] Chechnya, Dagestan, Ingushetiya, Kalmykiya, North Osetiya-Alaniya and Tuva.[42] Another factor which must be taken into consideration is the economic status of these republics. All six are totally dependent on the federal budget for their economic survival. Thus, it is not surprising that only Chechnya has gone so far as to declare its outright secession. Indeed, Chechnya's experience of two bloody wars and occupation by Russian troops is another important factor which has undoubtedly dampened down separatist demands from other republics.

Treisman also makes the important point that we should not view all separatist threats in Russia 'as expressions of primordial cultural aspirations'.[43] In many regions such threats have been used as a ploy to secure more funds from the centre. As Smith notes, 'It is the geopolitical leverage and rhetoric of nationalist politics – the threat or perceived threat of secession or withdrawal from the system of fiscal federalism – that result in the greater likelihood of a region's securing economic benefits.'[44] There is now considerable evidence to back up the claim that it is those republics which have been willing to go furthest in their claims of national sovereignty that have received the most economic privileges from the federal government.[45]

Putin's radical assault on the principles of federalism and democracy

President Putin came to power with a mandate to win back power from the federal subjects and to create a unified legal and security space across the federation. In order to restore the 'power vertical' Putin called for the instigation of a 'dictatorship of law'. No longer would the republics and regions be able to adopt legislation which violated the Federal Constitution and

Table 7.2 Ethnic composition of the republics and autonomies (1989 Census)

	Percentage of eponymous population(s)	*Percentage of Russian population*
Republic		
Adygeya	22.1	68.0
Altai	31.2	60.4
Bashkortostan	21.9	39.3
Buryatiya	24.0	70.0
Chechnya-Ingushetiya (divided into two separate republics in 1992)	70.7	23.1
Chuvashiya	68.7	26.7
Dagestan	90.8	9.2
Kabardino-Balkariya	57.6	32.0
Kalmykiya	53.0	37.7
Karachai-Cherkessiya	40.9	42.4
Kareliya	10.0	73.6
Khakassiya	11.1	79.5
Komi	23.3	57.7
Marii-El	43.3	47.5
Mordoviya	32.5	60.8
North Osetiya-Alaniya	53.0	29.9
Sakha (Yakutiya)	33.4	50.3
Tatarstan	48.5	43.3
Tuva	64.3	32.0
Udmurtiya	30.9	58.9
Autonomous areas		
Autonomous Oblast (1)		
Jewish	4.2	83.2
Autonomous Okrugs (10)		
Aga-Buryatiya	54.9	40.8
Chukotka	7.3	66.1
Yevenkiya	14.0	67.5
Komi-Permyakiya	60.2	36.1
Koryakiya	16.5	62.0
Khanty-Mansi	0.9	66.3
Nenents	11.9	65.8
Taimyr	13.7	67.1
Ust-Ordin Buryatiya	36.3	56.5
Yamal-Nenets	4.2	59.2

Sources: G.W. Lapidus and E.W. Walker, 'Nationalism, Regionalism, and Federalism: Centre-Periphery Relations in Post-Communist Russia', in G.W. Lapidus (ed.), *The New Russia: Troubled Transition* (Boulder, CO: Westview Press, 1995), pp. 88–9; E. Payin and A. Susarov, 'Line Five in the Mirror of Demography', *Rossiiskie Vesti*, 30 October 1997, p. 2. Translated in *CDPSP*, Vol. XLIX, No. 44 (1997), p. 11.

federal laws. Putin's 'dictatorship of law' would also guarantee that every Russian citizen, from Novgorod to Tatarstan, had the same set of universal rights and freedoms as guaranteed in the Federal Constitution.[46]

In the first of his federal reforms in May 2000, Putin divided the country into seven super-regions (federal districts) each of which contained about a dozen or so federal subjects, and he appointed a personal envoy to head each of them. Six of the envoys were former high ranking officials in the army and KGB.[47] The new districts included territorially defined regions and ethnically defined regions thus giving rise to fears that this was but a first step towards the abolition of the ethnic republics and the 'gubernisation' of Russia.

Putin's creation of the seven federal districts and the appointment of the presidential envoys does not actually violate the Constitution, which in Article 83 states that the President, 'appoints and removes plenipotentiary representatives of the President of the Russian Federation'. Thus, Putin can argue that such reforms are changes to his presidential administration, and not constitutional changes to the federation itself. However, as discussed below, Putin's federal reforms do represent an assault on the federal idea, and they certainly violate the 'spirit of the Constitution', if not the actual Constitution itself.

In a second major initiative in July and August 2000, which met fierce resistance from the upper chamber, Putin carried out a radical reform of the Federation Council.[48] In the place of the two ex-officio members from each of the federal subjects, the Federal Council, was henceforth (from January 2002) to be made up of two 'delegates' from each federal subject, one chosen by the head of the regional executive and the other by the chair of the regional assembly.[49] Thus, the governors and heads of regional legislative bodies no longer had direct representation in the upper chamber thereby losing their parliamentary immunity. Under the new system many of the federal subjects chose as their delegates Moscow insiders or powerful business leaders from outside their regions, thereby undermining one of the key prerequisites of a federation namely, 'the legislative entrenchment' of federal subjects in central decision making.[50] The independence of the upper chamber has also been weakened by the formation of a pro-Putin group ('Federatsiya') in the upper chamber and the election of Putin's choice of speaker (Sergei Mironov).

To placate the regional governors and legislative chairs for their loss of membership in the Federation Council, Putin co-opted them into a new presidential advisory body – the State Council which is chaired by the President. In a third major federal reform adopted in July 2000, Putin was given new powers to fire regional governors and to dismiss regional assemblies if they contravened the Constitution or federal laws.[51] However, the procedures for carrying out this law have proved very difficult to put into practice and not a single governor or regional assembly has been dismissed.[52] Moreover, the situation has become more difficult for the President since the adoption of a Constitutional Court resolution in April 2002 which has made the procedures for implementing the law even more complex and protracted. Whereas the original law 'required only one court to rule that federal laws had been violated more than once; now courts of three different jurisdictions, including the Constitutional Court, must render the decision'. Furthermore, 'the law now applies only to heads of regions elected after 16 October 1999'.[53]

Finally, Putin launched a major campaign to bring regional legislation into line with the Federal Constitution and he created a special commission headed by Dmitrii Kozak, the deputy head of his presidential commission, to oversee this work. By 2000 the number of normative legal acts adopted by the regions and republics exceeded 300,000 and, of these, approximately one-quarter violated federal laws.[54]

Putin also struck out at the powers of the ethnic republics. On 27 June 2000, the Constitutional Court declared that the declarations of sovereignty in the republics' constitutions were unconstitutional. The Federal Procurator instructed the envoys that all legislation was to be brought into line with federal norms by 1 January 2001. Reporting back on this date, Kozak confirmed that 80 per cent of the regional laws had been brought into line with federal law.[55] Putin also called for the bilateral treaties to be rescinded, and in his annual address to Parliament in April 2002 he reported that 28 of the 46 treaties had indeed been annulled.[56]

However, despite these achievements it would appear that the number of laws violating federal norms may actually be rising. Thus, for example, in Bashkortostan there are almost as many violations of federal law in its new constitution (51 of the 164 articles contain violations) which was adopted in November 2001, as there were in its old constitution. Likewise, Tatarstan's new constitution which was adopted in April 2002 still contains as many as 50 points of contention. Moreover, both Bashkortostan and Tatarstan continue to uphold their bilateral treaties with Moscow. The Tatarstan leadership has also steadfastly refused to renounce the republic's sovereignty and the new constitution also reiterates the republic's citizenship rights.[57]

In reply to criticism from Moscow for failing to bring his republics' legislation into line, President Shaimiev of Tatarstan gave this defiant reply to federal authorities, 'We realise that some will not like the mention of sovereignty in the Constitution of Tatarstan. However, the Russian Constitution recognises republics as states. Consequently, it is impossible to reject the notion of sovereignty either hypothetically or in practice.'[58] Putin's latest deadline for bringing all legislation into line by 14 July 2003, would also appear to have fallen on deaf ears.[59]

Why have Putin's envoys failed in bringing regional legislation into line? It may be that they simply lack the staff and resources to monitor the hundreds of thousands of laws in their federal districts. Or it may be that their organisations have been captured by regional elites, and the envoys have gone 'native'. Many of the senior members of the new federal districts are actually former members of regional executive bodies. Moreover the federal ministries have been wary of giving up power to the new federal districts. Putin may have ended up simply creating another layer of bureaucracy between himself and the federal subjects.

In a further major setback to Putin's reforms the Constitutional Court on 17 July 2003 adopted a resolution declaring that only it has the powers to determine whether regional constitutions violate federal norms.[60] The speaker of the Bashkortostan Parliament, Konstantin Tolkachev declared the Court's ruling 'revolutionary'. Up until this date courts of general jurisdiction had been granted the right to act as the spearhead of Putin's campaign in the regions and it was these courts which had been given the prime task of rescinding the hundreds of violations in the constitutions of the republics. As one constitutional expert in this area notes, 'since it will take the Court years to rule on specific cases, regional authorities will be able to adopt and implement any laws they want with little fear of federal action'.[61]

Whilst Putin has undoubtedly suffered a number of serious setbacks in the implementation of the above reforms, there is one important area, that of fiscal federalism, where he has been more successful. By instigating new tax and budget laws the President has radically changed the balance of tax revenues between the centre and the regions. 'In 2000, the split was 50:50 between the federal government and regional shares. In 2001, it widened to 56:44 and in 2002 the numbers were expected to be 62:38.'[62] Putin's success in weakening the economic autonomy of the regions will no doubt sooner or later also weaken their political autonomy.

One of the main reasons why Putin has been able to instigate such radical reforms is his ability to command a majority of seats in the *Duma* through his parliamentary coalition 'United Russia'. Unlike Yeltsin who struggled throughout his term in office with a hostile parliament, Putin has been able to turn his policies into laws. And now that the upper chamber has also been weakened with the removal of the regional governors and legislative chairs the stage would appear to be set for a new round of even more radical federal reforms from the President.

Thus, for example, Putin has indicated that he favours reducing the number of federal subjects from their current 89 to somewhere around 40. To achieve this end a new law was adopted in December 2001 which outlined the procedures necessary for the merging of federal subjects. However, the procedures for carrying out such mergers are very complex. All changes must be voluntary and requests must come from both the regions in question. Before the process can even begin the citizens of both regions must approve the merger in a referendum. Legislation is then drawn up which requires the approval of two-thirds of the members of the *Duma* and three-quarters of the members of the Federation Council. The first candidates for merger are likely to be Perm Oblast and Komi-Permyak Autonomous Okrug. The leaders of both these regions have already met with the President to discuss their unification.[63]

Conclusion

The federalisation of Russia has been thwarted by the weakness of Russia's civic culture and the lack of a federal and democratic tradition. Throughout its short history federal relations in Russia have been dominated by political and economic relations rather than constitutionalism and the rule of law. When the central leadership has been strong the constitutional powers of the regions have been curtailed, when the leadership is weak, as it was during the period of the 'parade of sovereignties' extra constitutional powers were ceded to the regions. When Yeltsin required bilateral treaties to buy votes and ensure that taxes would flow to the federal budget he was prepared to violate his own Federal Constitution and grant greater powers to a select group of federal subjects. Thus, by 1998 when the last bilateral treaty was signed, the Russian state had been transformed from a 'constitutional' to a 'contractual' federation. Moreover, levels of 'unofficial asymmetry' were running dangerously high. Thus, by the end of the Yeltsin era there were a number of competing and contradictory sources of constitutional authority: the Federal Constitution, the Federal Treaty, bilateral treaties, the constitutions of the republics and charters of the regions and, finally, federal and regional laws. Political criteria not constitutional criteria would decide which of these competing sources of law were to prevail and which federal subjects were to benefit and which were to lose out. As Vladimir Lysenko (deputy chair of the State *Duma* Committee on Federation Issues and Regional Policy) observed:

> the development of federalism in Russia, took place in an extremely inconsistent, spontaneous and chaotic manner. The formulation of the basic principles of the Russian version of federalism very often depended on the momentary interests of individual politicians ... rather than the strategic interests of the country.[64]

Vladimir Putin came to power in 2000 with a democratic mandate to restore the power of the centre and to bring an end to the 'war of laws and sovereignties'. However, whilst Putin's initiatives to bring regional legislation into line with the Constitution are to be welcomed, particularly in those ethnic republics whose citizens have been derived of universal democratic rights, there are now serious concerns about the future of federalism in Russia. Elazar's observation is relevant here: 'federalism implies a posture and attitude toward social as well as political relationships, which lead to human interactions that emphasise coordinative rather than superior-subordinate relationships, negotiated cooperation, and sharing among parties'.[65] Moreover, in federations, in contrast to unitary states, regional autonomy is not only devolved but constitutionally guaranteed. But in Russia, Putin's reforms have been driving the state towards the reinstitution of Soviet-style principles of hierarchy and centralised administrative control from Moscow. As Gadzhiev *et al.* note, 'For federalism, as for chess, what is important are the rules of the game, not the board or the pieces. Unfortunately in Russia everything is just the opposite. We have federative pieces on a federative board but play is according to unitary rules.'[66]

The President's reorganisation of the Federation Council, his usurpation of unilateral powers to dismiss regional assemblies and chief executives and his creation of seven unelected super-governors have all been major setbacks for Russian federalism. Moreover, federalism and democracy are intertwined and without the development of a civic and legal culture there can be no consolidation of federalism in Russia. In 1990, Boris Yeltsin on a tour of Russia told the ethnic republics, 'take as much sovereignty as you can swallow'. In Putin's Russia the catchphrase would appear to be, 'Give us back as much sovereignty as we would like to take.'[67]

Notes

1 Scholars of federalism have posited the following five prerequisites: (1) the existence of at least two tiers of government, both tiers of which have a formal constitutional distribution of legislative, executive and judicial powers and fiscal autonomy; (2) some form of voluntary covenant or contract among the components – normally a written constitution (requiring for amendment the consent of a significant proportion of the constituent units); (3) mechanisms to channel the participation of the federated units in decision-making processes at the federal level. This usually involves the creation of a bicameral legislature in which one chamber represents the people at large and the other the component units of the federation; (4) some kind of institutional arbiter, or umpire, usually a Supreme Court or a Constitutional Court to settle disputes between the different levels of government; (5) mechanisms to facilitate intergovernmental collaboration in those areas where governmental powers are shared or inevitably overlap. See, R. Watts, *Comparing Federal Systems* (Montreal and Kingston: McGill-Queen's University Press, 1999), p. 7; D.J. Elazar, *Exploring Federalism* (Tuscaloosa, AL and London: The University of Alabama Press, 1987), pp. 22–3.
2 D.J. Elazar (1987), p. 78.
3 Watts (1999), p. 99.
4 A. Heinemann-Gruder, 'Why Did Russia Not Break Apart?', in A. Heinemann-Gruder (ed.), *Federalism Doomed: European Federalism between Integration and Separation* (New York and Oxford: Berghahn Books, 2002), p. 148.
5 M. Gorbachev, 'Draft Nationalities Policy of the Party Under Present Conditions', adopted by the CPSU Central Committee Plenum, 20 September 1989, quoted in Stephan Kux, 'Soviet Federalism', *Problems of Communism*, March–April 1990, pp. 1–20, especially p. 2.
6 A. Stepan, 'Federalism and Democracy: beyond the U.S. model', *Journal of Democracy*, 10 (4), October, 1999, p. 31.
7 G.M. Hahn, 'Putin's Federal Reforms', *Demokratizatsiya*, 9 (4), Autumn 2001, p. 499.
8 Ibid.
9 A.N. Lebedev, *Status Sub'ekta Rossiiskoi Federatsii* (Moscow: Institute of State and Law, 1999), p. 24.
10 N. Ratiani, *Izvestiya* (4 June 2003) translated in *Johnston's Russia List*, No. 7209, 4 June 2003.

11 These figures refer to officially registered numbers – hidden unemployment is much higher.

12 Ratiani (2003).

13 G. Marchenko, 'Nuzhno li perekraivat' Rossiyu?', in Olga Sidorovoch (ed.), *Rossiiskii Konstitutsionalism: Politicheskii Rezhim v Regional'nom Kontekste: Shornik Dokladov* (Moscow: MONF, 2000), pp. 72–3.

14 See, Cameron Ross, *Federalism and Democratisation in Russia* (Manchester: Manchester University Press, 2002).

15 I. Umnova (2002), 'The Contemporary Russian Model of Russian Federalism: In Search of the Way to Peace, Democracy and Stabilisation', Internet article available at: www.federalism.ch/FTPMirror/ircc/InHouseSeminar/Umnova_Russian_Federalism_And_Peace.pdf, p. 7.

16 M. Stoliarov, *Federalism and the Dictatorship of Power* (London and New York: Routledge, 2001), pp. 86–7.

17 Ibid., p. 87.

18 V. Shlapentokh, R. Levita and M. Loiberg, *From Submission to Rebellion: The Provinces Versus the Centre in Russia*, (Boulder, CO: Westview Press, 1998), p. 109.

19 For a more extensive discussion of these points, see, Ross (2002).

20 The Agin-Buryat Autonomous *Okrug* (AO) within Chita *Oblast*; Chukotka AO (within Magadan *Oblast*); Yevenk and Taimyr AOs (Krasnoyarsk *Krai*); Khanty-Mansi and Yamala-Nenets AOs (Tyumen *Oblast*); Komi-Permyak AO (Perm *Oblast*); Koryakiya AO (Kamchatka *oblast*); Nenets AO (Arkhangelskaya *Oblast*); Ust-Orda Buryat AO (Irkutsk *Oblast*).

21 Stepan (1999), pp. 24–5.

22 The lower house can overturn the veto of the upper house if it can muster a vote of two-thirds of the members of the *Duma*. However, in Russia's highly fragmented lower chamber where parties are weak and undisciplined it is extremely difficult to achieve such a majority.

23 G. Smith, *The Post-Soviet States: Mapping the Politics of Transition* (London, Sydney and Auckland: Arnold, 1999), p. 139.

24 Presidential Decree Number 370, 12 March 1996 (with changes on 25 November 1996); 'Ob Utverzhdenii Polozheniia O Poriadke Raboty Po Razgranicheniyu Predmetov Vedeniya i Polnomochii Mezhdu Federal'nymi Organami Gosudarstvennoi Vlasti i Organami Gosudarsvennoi Vlasti Sub'ektov Rossiiskoi Federatsii', i O Vzaimnoi Peredache Osushchestvleniya Chasti Svoikh Polnomochii Federal'nymi Organami Ispolnitel'noi Vlasti i Organami Ispolnitel'noi Vlasti Sub'ektov Rossiiskoi Federatsii', *Sobranie Zakonodatel'stva Rossiiskoi Federatsii*, 12 (1996), p. 1058.

25 I.A. Umnova, *Konstitutsionnye Osnovy Sovremennovo Rossiiskovo Federalizma* (Moscow: DELO, 1998), p. 112.

26 'O Printsipakh i Poryadke Razgranicheniya Predmetov Vedeniya i Polnomochii Mezhdu Organami Gosudarstvennoi Vlasti Rossiiskoi Federatsii i Organami Gosudarstvennoi Vlasti Sub'ektov Rossiiskoi Federatsii', adopted by the State *Duma*, 4 June 1999 and ratified by the President on 24 June 1999. *Rossiiskaya Gazeta* (30 June 1999), p. 3.

27 Umnova, 'The Contemporary Russian Model', p. 10.

28 Ibid.

29 Heinemann-Gruder (2002), p. 156.

30 Umnova, 'The Contemporary Russian Model', p. 10.

31 The Constitutional Court does not have the power to initiate hearings but rather must have cases brought before it.

32 Hahn (2001), p. 502.

33 Umnova (1998), p. 50.

34 *Izvestiya*, 4 March 1997, p. 4.
35 R. Sakwa, 'Federalism, Sovereignty and Democracy', in C. Ross (ed.), *Regional Politics in Russia* (Manchester: Manchester University Press, 2002), p. 2.
36 N. Bermeo, 'The Import of Institutions', *Journal of Democracy*, 13 (2), April 2002, p. 98.
37 D. Kempton, 'Russian Federalism: Continuing Myth or Political Salvation', *Demokratizatsiya*, 9 (2), Spring 2001, p. 229.
38 D. Kempton, 'Three Challenges to Assessing Russian Federalism', in D. Kempton and T.D. Clarke (eds), *Unity or Separation: Centre-Periphery Relations in the Former Soviet Union* (Westport, CT, London: Praeger, 2002), p. 17.
39 E. Payin and A. Susarov, 'Line five in the mirror of demography', *Rossiiskie Vesti*, 30 October 1997, p. 2. *CDPSP*, XLIX (44), 1997, p. 10.
40 In Dagestan there are 33 national groups, none of which comprises a majority. Russians account for only 9.2 per cent of the total population of Dagestan.
41 Chuvashiya is landlocked with no borders on foreign states.
42 One other non-ethnically-based region which may eventually secede from the federation is Kaliningrad which is geographically cut off from the rest of the country nesting between the Baltic sea, bordering on Lithuania and Poland.
43 D. Triesman, 'The Politics of Intergovernmental Transfers in Post-Soviet Russia', *British Journal of Political Science*, 26, 1996, p. 329. See also Treisman, 'Russia's Ethnic Revival: The Separatist Activism of Regional Leaders in a Post-communist Order', *World Politics*, 49, January 1997, pp. 212–49.
44 Smith (1999), p. 197.
45 See A.M. Lavrov, 'Russian Budget Federalism: First Steps, First Results', *Sevodnya*, 7 June 1995, p. 5. Translated in *CDPSP*, XLVII (23), 5 July 1995, p. 3.
46 See, C. Ross, 'Putin's Federal Reforms and the Consolidation of Federalism in Russia: One Step Forward, Two Steps Back!', *Communist and Post-Communist Studies*, 36, 2003, pp. 29–47.
47 See, Presidential Decree Number 849, 13 May 2000, 'O Polnomochnom Predstavitele Prezidenta Rossiiskoi Federatsii v Federal'nom Okruge', and the accompanying Resolution, 'O Polnomochnom Prestavitele Prezidenta Rossiiskoi Federatsii v Federal'nom Okruge.' Published in *Rossiskaya gazeta*, 13 May 2001.
48 See, the Federal Law, Number 113-F3, 5 August 2000, 'O Poryadke Formorovaniya Soveta Federatsiya Federal'novo Sobraniya Rossiiskoi Federatsii.' Adopted by the state *Duma* 19 July 2000 and ratified by the Federation Council 26 July 2000, *Rossiskaya gazeta*, 5 August 2000.
49 The regional assemblies can veto the choice of the governor if they can muster the votes of two-thirds of their members. The regional assemblies appoint and dismiss their representatives by secret ballot.
50 P. King, 'Federation and Representation', in M. Burgess and A.-G. Gagnon (eds), *Comparative Federalism and Federation* (New York, London: Harvester-Wheatsheaf, 1993), p. 93.
51 The law on the removal of the governors and disbanding of legislatures which was adopted in July 2000 takes the form of amendments to the Federal Law 'Ob Obshchikh Printsipakh Organizatsii Zakonodatel'nykh (Predstavitel'nykh) i Ispolnitel'nykh Organov Gosudarstvennoi Vlasti Sub'ektov Rossiiskoi Federatstii', which was ratified by the President on 6 October 1999 and published in *Rossiskaya gazeta*, 19 October 1999.
52 Putin did secure the removal of governors in Primorskii Krai, Sakha and Ingushetiya, but only by offering them important jobs in Moscow and, apparently, threats of criminal investigations.
53 Radio Free Europe/Radio Liberty (RFE/RL), *Russian Federation Report*, 4 (13), 10 April 2002.

54 M.I. Vil'chek, 'O Kliuchevikh Problemakh Stanovleniya Instituta Polnomo-
    chnykh Predstavitelei Prezidenta RF', in *Polpredy Prezidenta: Problemy
    Stanovleniya Novovo Instituta* (Nauchnye Doklady, MGU, No. 3, January 2001),
    p. 20.
55 J. Corwin, RFE/RL, *Russian Federation Report*, 3 (2), 10 January 2001, as cited in
    Obshchaya gazeta, No. 52, 10 January 2001, p. 2.
56 'Full text of Putin annual state-of-the-nation address to Russian parliament', *BBC
    Monitoring*, as reproduced in *Johnson's Russia List*, 6195 (19 April 2002), p. 11.
57 RFE/RL, *Tatar-Bashkir Service*, 3 May 2002, p. 2.
58 Ibid., p. 4.
59 RFE/RL, *Russian Political Weekly*, 3 (17), 1 May 2003.
60 I. Rabinovich, 'Bashkortostan, Tatarstan Weaken Putin's Reforms', East–West
    Institute, *Russian Regional Report*, 8 (13), 23 July 2003, pp. 1–3.
61 Ibid.
62 R. Orttung, 'Putin's Governor Generals – Conference Analyses Impact of
    Federal Reforms (7–9 June 2002)', East-West Institute, *Russian Regional Report*,
    7 (20), 17 June 2002, p. 9.
63 RFE/RL, *Russian Political Weekly*, 3 (12), 19 March 2003.
64 V. Filippov, 'Forthcoming Reforms of Russian Federalism: Will They Face the
    Opposition in Parliament', in R. Khakimov (ed.), *Federalism in Russia* (Kazan:
    Kazan Institute of Federalism, 2002), p. 197.
65 Elazar (1987), p. 78.
66 G.A. Gadzhiev, V.L. Lazarev, B.B. Pastukov and I.G. Shablinskiy, *Establishing
    Constitutional Democracy in Russia: The Present Phase* (Moscow: Institute for Law
    and Public Policy, 2002), p. 47.
67 Filippov (2002), p. 190.

8   What is to be done?

Bicommunalism, federation and confederation in Cyprus[1]

Michael Burgess

Introduction: taking out insurance policies

Since 1974 the island of Cyprus has been divided into two territories between the Greek Cypriots in the south and the Turkish Cypriots in the north. This is a de facto reality. I wish to take this practical reality as the point of departure for my argument in this chapter simply because it is tantamount to an insurance policy that enables me to avoid disputes about history, purported legalities and illegalities and the concomitant blame culture that almost always accompanies this approach and has the combined effect of obstructing dispassionate analysis, enlightened discussion and open debate. In this particular respect, the Cyprus conflict is rather like that in Northern Ireland where the interpretation and the teaching of history have become weapons of competing partisan loyalties that have legitimised communal identities and rival views of partition. In other words, history itself has become part of the problem. It, too, is a prisoner of the past. Consequently we must distinguish scholarly historical analysis from the political uses of history. As Francis H. Hinsley remarked, 'people often study history less for what they might learn than for what they want to prove'.[2] Just as it seems impossible today to liberate Irish history from what is a particularly sterile and suffocating form of imprisonment, so it is instructive for both Greek and Turkish Cypriots to avoid carrying this kind of ideological baggage with them into the seminar room and to the negotiating table. And, for what it is worth, the Irish Question (which is really a British Question) has recently demonstrated that a new *modus operandi* can be made to work if a new political will, incorporating the spirit of mutuality and reciprocity, can be forged from changing circumstances.

Mindful of this intellectual contamination, it is much more profitable to begin with what already exists. This does not imply that Greek Cypriots should legitimise the Turkish occupation of the north by its official recognition. Rather it is to confront and deal directly with the political and military reality that exists. It is, in other words, a political and military definition of reality. But it is crucial to engage that reality in order precisely to change it. The fundamental question is to decide what is possible. And what is *possible* is determined ultimately by what is *acceptable* to both sides of the Green Line. This brings us, in turn, to the basic problem: how to accommodate the political aspirations of both communities within the same polity. The politics of accommodation, however, can succeed only if the different interests, anxieties and perceptions of the two antagonists can be openly addressed. Each community has to acquire an empathy for the other in order to enable it to appreciate more fully the sensitivities of the other. Each must, as it were, stand in the shoes of the other. From the perspective of would-be reformers, then, the possible future scenarios are dependent upon the current point of departure. Without either accepting or recognising the legitimacy of the present status quo, the fundamental *sine qua non* of practical progress in 'talks about talks' is to recognise that the concepts, language and discourse of the politics of reunification are ultimately contextual. Terms like federal, federalism, federation, confederation, partition, sovereignty, neo-federal, neo-confederal, consociationalism and bicommunalism make conceptual and empirical sense only when located in context. Meaning, in short, derives from context. There are clearly Shakespearian echoes in the terms of the political discourse; 'What is in a name? A rose by any other name would smell as sweet.' But in contemporary political discourse in Cyprus there is *everything* in the name. In reality definitions of federalism and federation allow for huge variations in their interpretation and practice. Shorthand definitions like 'self-rule and shared rule' and 'unity in diversity' convey important moral and political values and principles, but they can often play out very differently in different circumstances and surroundings. To use the word 'federalism' in India, for example, is to emphasise disunity and even fragmentation, which is partly why the constitution is silent about it. Conversely in the United Kingdom, the British perception of a 'federal' Europe has the opposite connotations to those in India, conveying instead the centralisation of power in Brussels that is a source of much anxiety and hostility, while in Canada the province of Quebec tends to construe the hallmark of 'federalism' to mean genuine provincial autonomy within the federation.

It is important at the outset therefore to take out insurance policies when wrestling with a conflict that is as complex, contentious and passionate as that of Cyprus. Concepts and terminology have their own history. We have to be very careful how we intend to use them. Discussants do not always declare their interests, unquestioned assumptions are sometimes unintentionally smuggled into the discourse and it is easy for commentators and observers to be oblivious of the consequences of their own choice of words. The purpose of these introductory remarks, then, is to serve as a warning that one man's 'freedom fighter' is another's 'terrorist'. Conflicting perspectives mean that for the Turkish Cypriots the events of 1974 were a legitimate and constitutional *intervention* justified on the emergency grounds of protecting a vulnerable minority culture, while for the Greek Cypriots it was an unjustified *attack* or *invasion* by Turkey that resulted in an illegal *occupation* of 37 per cent of the island. We will not make any practical progress unless we can avoid bringing selective historical and ideological baggage to the public debate. Even if United Nations (UN) endorsement of the Greek-Cypriot interpretation of these events remains the correct one, it matters not a jot to the current political and military reality. In any future negotiations Greek Cypriots will still have to confront the Turkish presence on the island as the unwelcome departure point for conflict management and resolution. We must begin, then, with what exists.

Consequently when we look to the future we must not forget the past nor must we necessarily sanction the status quo as an option. But we must approach the present primarily as another opportunity to change the context of the problem. It is possible to look at the conflict in a different way. Clearly the basis for the new political strategy must be that of the application in 1990 of Cyprus formally to join the European Union (EU). This signifies the process of 'changing the circumstances' that Jean Monnet referred to when he sought to overcome a particularly intractable problem in the building of Europe: 'change the context and the problems themselves are changed'.[3] The introduction of the EU as a formal player in the Cyprus conflict has the possibility to change the old dynamic of relations between peoples and states. A new conceptual and institutional space has been created that could conceivably furnish more room for manoeuvre. The chapter will address these new circumstances later, but first we must briefly return to the roots of the conflict that are located in the constitutional foundations of the Cypriot state that came into being in 1960. It is important to remind ourselves of where the contemporary story began.

The Cyprus Constitution of 1960: the politics of recognition

In the mainstream constitutional and political literature about Cyprus, a broad academic consensus seems to have emerged about 'the failure' of the 1960 Constitution. Indeed, there appears to be agreement among scholars that it was, at the outset, foredoomed to failure. Its destiny was sealed as soon as the ink was dry on the paper. While not wishing to challenge the accumulated wisdom of the expert eye contained in this literature, it is nonetheless worth pausing to take another look at those parts of the Constitution that might still have a residual significance for the contemporary debate about what is to be done in the future.

Constitutions are emblems of values, beliefs and interests and they incorporate the living breathing tissues of the polity itself. In the context of the new Republic of Cyprus in 1960 the Constitution incorporated a series of consociational principles that could be accurately construed as 'the politics of recognition'. In particular, it was founded upon the notion of bicommunalism whose logical corollary was the following set of enlightened liberal democratic principles; proportionality, power-sharing, collective identity, bilingualism, fundamental individual and collective rights, the veto and concurrent majority, and minority representation. These principles were firmly institutionalised in a manner that formally recognised and reinforced the sense of two distinct cultural communities living together in a single polity on the island. The legal and political framework was specifically designed to accommodate the stresses and strains of the enduring bicommunal conflict so that a series of mechanisms and procedures would function as a basis for the resolution of outstanding disputes and the general management of conflict.

The set of principles identified above permeated the legislative, executive and judicial branches of government that effectively constituted a 'Presidential–parliamentary' political system centred around a Greek-Cypriot President and a Turkish-Cypriot Vice-President (loudly trumpeted in Article 1) with an executive Council of Ministers, comprising seven Greek ministers and three Turkish ministers, a House of Representatives (HR) composed of 50 elected representatives according to a 70:30 ratio of Greek to Turkish members (Article 62), and two distinct Communal Chambers elected by their own Greek and Turkish communities, separate from the HR, with limited taxing powers and responsible broadly for all cultural affairs. Matters relating to the Greek Communal Chamber would be subject to the general oversight of the Greek President while corresponding affairs of the Turkish Communal Chamber would fall within the jurisdiction of the Turkish Vice-President. Article 133 established the Supreme Constitutional Court composed of a Greek, Turkish and a neutral judge who would be the President of the Court appointed for six years, all other judges being permanent but retiring at the age of 68 years old.[4]

This very brief skeletal outline of the structural composition of the state institutions and their relationships had, in hindsight, one outstanding characteristic, namely, its almost obsessive emphasis upon the bicommunalism of the polity. In retrospect, it had the unfortunate consequence of emphasising, to the point of exaggeration, the 'separateness' of the two communities. As we will see in the next section of the chapter, bicommunalism is a double-edged sword; it must strike an extremely delicate balance between the centrifugal and the centripetal forces immanent in the polity. The Constitution of 1960, however, seems to have been the result of negotiations that strode far too forcefully in one direction. This march towards the politics of constitutional recognition tended to place too much emphasis upon institutional separation, parallelism and the reciprocal veto so that it created a polity with too few powers, functions and relationships that overlapped, intermingled and dovetailed together to furnish the basis for cementing and bonding the two communities in an overarching sense of national state unity. The character of the new republic tended to overstate its 'checks and balances' – the politics of restraint – at the expense of those institutional relationships, mechanisms and procedures that might conceivably have had a binding effect designed to energise the forces for unity and union. Such a constitution had no possibility to forge a new sense of comity, trust and reciprocity.

For the political scientist who attempts a textual exegesis of the Constitution of 1960 and tries to reassess and reappraise its goals, strengths, weaknesses, anomalies and its widely acclaimed failure, it is impossible to detach it from the circumstances of its time. The product of a set of extremely complex factors – domestic politics, international and bilateral relations, bicommunal interests, strategic and economic considerations and sociopsychological matters – it bears the indelible imprint of a particularly hazardous epoch in the history of Cyprus.[5] This is nowhere more clearly substantiated in Cyprus than in the meaning of the term 'constitution' itself. After all, what other country would include in the term 'constitution' a Draft Treaty of Guarantee between three foreign powers (the United Kingdom (UK), Greece and Turkey) and another Draft Treaty of Alliance between Greece, Turkey and the Republic of Cyprus? The interlacing of a complicated set of relationships that yielded, and continues to yield, a constitutional deadlock frozen in time includes the following overlapping dimensions: the elemental bicommunal conflict between Greek Cypriots and Turkish Cypriots; Greek-Cypriot–Greek relations and Turkish-Cypriot–Turkish relations; Greek–Turkish relations; and an ever-changing international context involving the UN, intermittent British and American influences and now the EU. Small wonder that the so-called 'Cyprus conflict' has been so intractable and small wonder that a constitutional politics of recognition that can work has been so elusive.

Separateness, then, can easily lead to separation. But constitutions are not panaceas. Many critics of the Constitution of 1960 claim that it was found wanting because it not only repeated many of the errors that had been exposed before and simply failed to bring about the resolution of the conflict, but it also exacerbated the problem. Nonetheless, constitutions – however complicated and difficult to implement and operate – cannot by themselves be held responsible for bicommunal failure. They are merely products of a particular, momentary political will. The seeds of failure were sown at the Zurich Conference of 1959 and by the Joint Commission established to draft a constitution in 1960. The real blame for the failure of 1960–63 must lie in the nature of the negotiations that preceded the introduction of the constitution; constitutional negotiations that did not allow for the participation of the people of Cyprus, either indirectly through representatives or directly via referendum. Historians naturally focus upon the key *dramatis personae* and there is no doubt that many hidden agendas existed that favoured different conspiracy theories, but the upshot was a failure of political will.

It is now time to turn our attention away from the constitutional foundations of failure in Cyprus and look toward the conceptual basis of a possible federal future.

Federalism, federation and confederation

Before we can consider the possibility of Cyprus having a federal future, it is imperative that we first confront the conceptual basis to any new constitutional foundation. Here I want to make a firm conceptual distinction between federalism, federation and confederation. Moreover, it is also vital that we remember the emphasis made earlier in the chapter about the importance of context, perception and the point of departure because concepts do not operate in a vacuum. On the contrary, they themselves have a history and they entertain rival constructions.

Concept and definition

Let us begin by using a modestly revised version of Preston King's definition of federation as the basis for our survey. King's definition of federation suggests that it is: 'an institutional arrangement, taking the form of a sovereign state, and distinguished from other such states solely by the fact that its central government incorporates' constituent territorial units into its decision-making procedures 'on some constitutionally entrenched basis'.[6] This definition is both precise and comprehensive, and it broadly reflects the current scholarly thinking about the subject.[7] The term 'federalism' in this context, however, is much more difficult to conceptualise because it is homonymous. It is less tangible than federation because it is a term that expresses more than one distinct meaning. Let us look a little closer at federalism.

Federalism is the driving force that informs federation and can be construed in three separate ways as ideology, philosophy and/or empirical fact. This means that it can be a body of ideas that actively promotes federation in the way, for example, that federalists seek a federal Europe, or it can be a philosophy of federal ideas that prescribes or recommends federation as the good life, the best way to organise human relations. But it can also be construed as something much more prosaic. Federalism can be viewed simply as an empirical reality that recognises social life as intrinsically federal, that is, something which corresponds to and recognises the innate complexity of human life: the different roles that we play and our sense of ourselves as bundles of identities. In a nutshell, it refers to different ways of life and the everyday routine practice of how we live our lives. This, in turn, suggests that it is quintessentially a multidimensional concept, having facets that are *inter alia* historical, social, economic, political, cultural–ideological, intellectual and philosophical. And these facets underline a natural social reality expressive of multiple roles, aims and identities.

The key to understanding the significance of this conceptual distinction is to appreciate that federalism informs federation and vice versa. As King has put it, 'although there may be federalism without federation, there can be no federation without some matching variety of federalism'.[8] But this statement signals the complexity of our subject rather than its simplicity. It is therefore an over-simplification to suggest that federation logically follows federalism or that an elementary causal relationship between them exists. It does not. In practice the relationship is symbiotic: federalism is the driving force of federation, but federation as a tangible structural and institutional set of mechanisms and procedures also impinges upon federalism, canalising and channelling it along different pathways that help to reshape, reform and revitalise it. Federalism, in other words, does not always lead to federation.[9]

What, then, do we understand confederation to be and how is it related to federalism and federation? The first observation to make is that in order for us to enter the conceptual world of confederation we must move the discussion from the sphere of *intrastate* domestic affairs to the external sphere of *interstate* relations. The former has as its principal focus the internal affairs of domestic state politics – relations *within* the state – while the latter shifts our attention to the realm of international relations (IR) – relations *between* states. In his *Unions of states: the theory and practice of confederation*, first published in 1981, Murray Forsyth defined confederation as 'a federal union' that constituted 'the spectrum between inter-state and intrastate relations'. It was, he argued, the 'intermediary stage between normal inter-state and normal intrastate relations'. It was not a state because it was 'not a union of individuals in a body politic, but a union of states in a body politic'. He summarised it as:

> the process by which a number of separate states raise themselves by contract to the threshold of being one state, rather than the organisation that exists once this threshold has been crossed [it occupied] the intermediary ground between the inter-state and the state worlds, of going beyond the one but of not unequivocally reaching the other.[10]

In other words, it is the 'bodies politic' rather than 'individual persons' that become the 'citizens' of the confederation.

Concept, context and Cyprus

History teaches us that federations have typically emerged in the past via two distinct processes, namely, aggregation and/or devolution, decentralisation and disaggregation. The former refers to the historical processes of state building and national integration whereby previously separate states, territories or communities joined together and merged their status to form a new, larger state, while the latter alludes to former empires or unitary states that have devolved power and authority to constituent territories thereby conferring independence upon previously subordinate communities. Examples of the former are the United States and Switzerland while in the latter case(s) of devolution Canada, Australia, India and Malaysia possessed common historical origins in the British Empire. However, it is important to note that the genesis of federations has often resulted in practice from the coexistence of these two processes rather than from one or the other, as the examples of Germany and Austria testify. It all depends upon which particular point of historical departure is used. The federal idea is extremely flexible and highly circumstantial so that it could conceivably be put into practice as an instrument of reunification that might facilitate the restructuring of a state where the former parts, such as the five new German *Lander* from the earlier German Democratic Republic (GDR), or Flanders, Wallonia, Brussels and the German-speaking area of Eupen and Malmedy, construed as the four constituent cultural-linguistic parts of Belgium, could be effectively reordered and refashioned to suit different circumstances. Cyprus constitutes a unique example of an independent state founded upon republican principles with a bicommunal polity that is constitutionally based but which is territorially divided between a legitimate liberal democratic regime in the south and an illegitimate regime propped up by the military force of a foreign country in the occupied north. A military definition of reality has produced a stalemate between two distinct communities for a little over 30 years.

In these peculiar circumstances, what relevance do the concepts of federation and confederation have for the constitutional and political reunification of the island of Cyprus and how could they be utilised in practical terms? It is here that context and the point of departure loom large in the minds of the would-be reformers and the practitioners of federal and confederal principles. Let us begin this short survey by looking at how and why a federal Cyprus might work in practice. We are compelled in these circumstances to examine the motives for such a union harboured by the principal protagonists in the conflict and, as we have already noted, there are many different interests involved and several different dimensions to be considered. We will look first at federation, but simultaneously underline a crucial preliminary caution. This is that movement of any kind from the current illegitimate reality of a divided island must not under any circumstances facilitate the official recognition of the Turkish north. There can be no movement in any direction that serves, even indirectly, to legitimise the division of the island. 'Division', in other words, must not become 'partition'.

Proposals for a federal Cyprus during the last two decades seem to have been especially popular with the Greek-Cypriot community in the south. Their principal motives for federation have included *inter alia* the following reasons: to remove foreign armed forces; to re-establish freedom of mobility; to reintroduce the freedoms of settlement and property; property restitution; repatriation of Anatolian Turkish settlers; to promote foreign, public and private investment and greater overall economic integration; and to recognise a particular conception of political equality of the two principal communities based upon a federal system of shared communal representation. The upshot of these motives would have resulted in the reunification of the island with a single sovereignty, an international personality, a single citizenship and its independence and territorial integrity guaranteed. Consequently, from the broad Greek-Cypriot perspective, the reunification of the island had to be founded upon the official recognition by the two communities that the Republic of Cyprus still existed, that the existing government was the legitimate and lawful authority and that the various UN resolutions on the question of Cyprus would be respected.

Conversely the view from the other side of the divide was very different in certain important respects. The overwhelming concern of the Turkish-Cypriot community has always been and remains today that of physical and economic security. Clearly any type of federal arrangement would have to address this overriding question, but there are also other benefits that must be included in their motives for reunification: greater economic integration would bring a faster convergence of the incomes of both communities; they could gain autonomy from Turkey; the concomitant autonomy might enable them to develop their own independent cultural and educational projects consistent with their own historically distinct identity; the cessation of Anatolian Turkish immigration and settlement would no longer be an unrelenting political and sociological threat to the Turkish-Cypriot community; and they would achieve official recognition in a bicommunal federal arrangement based upon a form of bicommunal political equality that might attract exiled Turkish Cypriots back to the island.

It is obvious from this very brief sketch outline that the crux of the matter – the real sticking point – would be precisely what kind of federal arrangement might be acceptable in order to facilitate practical negotiations. The two main protagonists might agree upon basic federal values and principles, but not their structural and institutional implications. Recent history illustrates this dilemma and underlines the persistence of divergent perceptions of the federal idea. While the Greek-Cypriot perception of a reunited Cyprus springs from a conception of federation that suggests what might be called a 'strong federal republic' that emphasises a distribution of powers between the federal government and the constituent units facilitating central control of foreign affairs, budget and taxation, customs and international trade, immigration and citizenship, the Turkish-Cypriot understanding of the federal idea indicates something much more akin to a 'loose federal republic' or confederation where much greater autonomy would be ascribed to the constituent units.[11] But what is at stake here is more than just divergent perceptions. Here we return to the two observations that we made earlier in the chapter, namely, context and the point of departure.

The particular conception of a federal Cyprus is shaped and determined by which particular Cyprus we have in mind. For example, the Turkish-Cypriot position springs from the military reality that has existed since 1974. This means that most elites take the Turkish invasion, occupation and subsequent events as their starting point for negotiations. The implicit assumption built into this particular discourse is that the Republic of 1960 has already been dissolved, that two separate Communal Administrations exist and that these have usurped the full authority and jurisdiction of the previously existing Republic. From this perspective, it is easy to understand how and why they believe that they can claim that negotiations for a new federal republic should be conducted by and premised upon the existence of two distinct and separate Turkish-Cypriot and Greek-Cypriot Administrations. This false premise was identified many years ago in previous discussions about the federal idea:

> the Greek Cypriot side, starting from the premise of the continued existence and validity of both State and Government, has taken a completely different line. It has described the Turkish Cypriot allegation as 'deceptive'. The so-called Turkish Cypriot Administration was imposed by and is functioning under the force of arms and it cannot be maintained that it constitutes a true and free Administration. On this view, the attempted equation of the 'two Administrations' is false in as much as a comparison is being made between 'two things dissimilar and unequal', i.e. the Government of the Republic of Cyprus and the so-called Turkish Administration which is not exercising any state functions at all and which is not recognized as a separate state. The organization of the federal system, ... cannot be based on the pre-existence of the federal states, because such do not exist, but must instead be viewed and considered as an attempt to make a federation out of a unitary State, the federalization, in other words, of an integral State entity.[12]

The constitutional and political implications of this correct juridical interpretation, if not exactly suggesting that the new federation should necessarily be centralised, were that this was an example of 'federation by devolution', as identified in the above survey. However, if we try to stand in Turkish-Cypriot shoes, it quickly becomes clear that their own point of departure – notwithstanding 1974 – could also be the legitimacy of the bicommunal state, the Republic of Cyprus, established by the Constitution of 1960 that their political elites formally endorsed. It was this very constitution, after all, that granted them communal as well as individual rights, the original safeguards that they still cherish. The federal reconstruction of Cyprus therefore will be firmly rooted, shaped and moulded according to both context and point of departure. Neither federation nor confederation is a panacea for every form of human conflict.

Negotiations for a federal Cyprus, then, must not include the legitimation of the status quo either by default or sleight of hand. It would be preposterous for a divided Cyprus to be legitimised, as it were, by absent-mindedness. But what is clear is that if the federal idea is to have any relevance at all to the future of Cyprus, it must have the possibility to work. In other words, 'securing a settlement without the voluntary endorsement of both of the communities runs the risk of repeating the failure of the 1960 settlement'.[13] The Cyprus conflict is an international and a geopolitical question, but the domestic dimension suggests that ultimately there must be some form of political will strong enough to overcome the deep-seated mistrust and animosity that still exists between Greek-Cypriot and Turkish-Cypriot communities walled off from each other for over a quarter of a century. It may be that a new type of federal arrangement of an unprecedented kind might be forged from an essentially fragile political will that insists upon the 'separateness' of the distinct identities rather than upon their 'unity'. The dogged stalemate between the Greek-Cypriot 'federalists' and the Turkish-Cypriot 'confederalists' – the clash between conflicting conceptions of the polity – might conceivably be broken if a new dynamic could be introduced into this uncompromising zero-sum game. It might mean that political trust can be built up only by beginning with a form of arrangement, however loose, that is deliberately designed to keep the communities apart in certain important respects while bringing them together for other, less contentious activities so that closer relations – perhaps even political legitimacy – could evolve, as it were, naturally out of performance. In this almost Monnet-type of approach to human relations, the subjects themselves would be the judges of whether or not new forms of association were working.

Let us turn now to look at another aspect of this complex 'Rubik's Cube' that is the Cyprus question, namely, bicommunalism.

Bicommunalism reviewed

In 1988 Ivo Duchacek edited a special issue of *Publius: The Journal of Federalism* which had as its principal focus the question of bicommunalism and federalism, and briefly surveyed the broad area of bicommunal politics, intercommunal conflicts and cooperation and federalism.[14] What is interesting for our purposes is the preliminary discussion of the conceptual and terminological meanings that were used to refer to particular types of human conflict, cooperation and association. In view of these findings, it is important for us very briefly to review some of this literature in order to explore its relevance to the Cyprus conflict. Consequently I have divided this section of the chapter into two subsections that I take to be separate but interrelated dimensions to the Cyprus problem. We will look first at the conceptual and terminological aspects of the subject before looking a little closer at the vexed question of identity.

Bicommunalism and federal forms

Duchacek began his own contribution to the debate on bicommunalism by recognising that it concerned 'societies and polities in which two distinct communities clearly dominate the political arena'.[15] But he also acknowledged that the very notion of a 'bicommunal polity' was 'an analytical construct, not a statistical fact'. In reality there was no bicommunal configuration in which only two communities were present. There were, he claimed, 'always some other communities, however small each may be in numbers, economic resources and political strength'. Moreover, what he called bicommunal 'dyads' were not symmetric. The communities differed in many important respects: 'political clout; ambitions and anxieties; access to resources; location; date of arrival; quality of leaders; culture or simply numbers'.[16]

These observations remain important in the context of Cyprus. And of particular significance is Duchacek's implicit reference to bicommunal dyads that are 'asymmetrical'. At what point does a society and/or polity become bicommunal and at what point does an essentially bicommunal society and/or polity cease to be bicommunal? What kind of yardstick do we use in order to answer these questions? Is it a sense of national identity, simple numerical criteria, or is it just political expediency? Is it accurate to portray Cyprus as multi-ethnic or multinational? Clearly there are still more questions than answers. No two cases are the same. But can a Greek Cypriot cast legitimate doubt upon the viability of, and the moral basis to, a bicommunal Cyprus on the grounds that 'no society four-fifths of whose population belong to one ethnic group should be designated as a bicommunal one'?[17] Furthermore, there are tensions and anxieties above and beyond the question of birth rates. Mindful of the asymmetrical trends in the birth rates of the respective Israeli and Palestinian peoples during the late 1980s, Duchacek noted that 'if the majority's birth rate is dramatically lower than that of the minority, the fear of being out bred in a not too distant future tends to destabilise the polity'.[18] This has also been a political anxiety – the revenge of the cradle – in Northern Ireland. But in the Cyprus context the reverse is the case. Greek Cypriots are concerned not about the sudden explosion of an indigenous Turkish-Cypriot birth rate, but the long-term impact of a deliberate, consciously-pursued policy of incessant immigration and settlement patterns of Anatolian Turks in the north.

Linked to this problem of the 'numbers game' in Cyprus is what Duchacek has called 'the near immutability of the numerical imbalance' by which he means the psychological perception of a permanent minority that confronts a permanent majority. This is reminiscent of the *Quebecois* whose population of seven million (83 per cent of whom are French-speaking) continues to search for a new constitutional accommodation with the 24 million Anglophone Canadians that dominate the federal institutions. In cases such as these, he argued, numerical immutability 'endows an intercommunal conflict with inflexibility and bitterness'.[19] However, this difficult predicament has not prevented Belgium from achieving its own *modus operandi* with 58 per cent Flemish and 32 per cent Walloons in 1993 when it became a federation. Phrases such as 'two scorpions in a bottle' or 'two solitudes' that vividly express the form of relations between two communities in a single state that do not speak to each other, either because they cannot or simply do not want to, does not necessarily mean that they cannot live together. But it does mean that they have to use imaginative mechanisms, techniques and procedures in order to reconcile their differences peacefully. Consociational techniques involving overarching elite accommodation in segmented and vertically plural societies have been utilised for many years in a wide variety of countries, such as Canada, Switzerland, Belgium, the Netherlands, Lebanon and Austria.[20] Moreover, to constitutionalise difference does not mean that structures and institutions have to be constructed in such a rigid and uncompromising way that is so protective that it stifles debate, undermines trust and limits different forms of contact and cooperation between the elites and mass publics of the two communities.

So where did Duchacek's conception of dyadic or dual federations and confederations take him? What conclusions did he draw from his conceptual, terminological and comparative empirical survey? In accentuating the positive, Duchacek claimed that federal, confederal and consociational forms of association for communal dyads could be considered but only if the following four features were present: the territorial diffusion of power; pluralistic democracy; the commitment to establish or maintain a composite nation; and compound majoritarianism. It is worth noting that different combinations of these characteristics have been found to be perfectly viable in different countries experiencing seemingly intractable conflicts at different times. There is no simple, ready-made formula for particular types of conflict, but different combinations of the four identified above have a good track record. The notion of a composite nation, for example, has worked very well in Switzerland and in Belgium while compound majoritarianism has also dampened down conflict in these two federations and is used for constitutional amendment in Australia and Canada. But these examples, while encouraging a certain modest guarded optimism, have only very limited significance for an essentially 'two-state' resolution in Cyprus. The particular form of bicommunalism that appears now to be so entrenched in the public mind in Cyprus brings us inescapably to the question of identity. Let us look briefly at this problem as it is clearly related to the federal idea.

The problem of identity

Questions of identity are notoriously difficult to conceptualise in the social sciences. The construction of different forms of identity gives rise to huge intellectual debates about how we define ourselves, 'who' we think we are, how others perceive us and how we think that others perceive us. It is the kind of debate about which it is not possible ever to be on a firm footing. Nonetheless, we cannot avoid it as a problem in the context of Cyprus simply because the problem of identity lies at the root of what is to be done. What are the assumptions that we make when we consider the alternative futures for what seems to have been accepted in polite society as a 'bicommunal polity'? We should not assume what needs to be proved.

In this part of the chapter I want to place the microscope upon these bicommunal assumptions in order principally to expose the deeper complexities that exist in the two distinct communities that are separated politically, militarily and territorially. This exposure is obviously important if we are to try fully to understand and appreciate the subtleties that inhere in what we might term broadly as a bifocal Cyprus, but it is also of critical significance to the construction of a federal Cyprus. In the first place it is important for us to look closely at how the last quarter of a century of the division of the island into two separate territorial spaces, together with the occupation and settlement of the north by the Turkish military and Anatolian Turkish settlers, has impacted upon questions of identity among the Turkish-Cypriot community. Many commentators and observers of eastern Mediterranean affairs have referred to what might be called the 'Turkification' of the north, partly reinforced by a conspicuous exodus of young indigenous Turkish Cypriots from a community that provides them with few sophisticated employment prospects and partly accentuated by the attendant ageing population. There are important implications here, too, for the sense of space and territorial identity. Older members of the community might have strengthened their sense of spatial and territorial self-identification while younger Turkish Cypriots living abroad might conceivably have a much weaker conception of spatial awareness though not of their homeland.

Recent research on the question of self-definition in the north confirms that the dominant factors that characterise the identity of most Cypriot-born Turkish Cypriots are strong combinations of Turkish/Cypriot/Muslim.[21] And the complexity of this identity interestingly indicates a strong Turkish-Cypriot differentiation from Turkish immigrants along the political cultural lines of language, history and social culture/ways of living. Indeed, among some Turkish Cypriots it has been observed that increased contact with Anatolian Turkish settlers has even 'created tensions between Turkish immigrants and native Turkish Cypriots' some of whom consider 'the large presence' of these people 'a real threat to Turkish-Cypriot identity'.[22] But this sense of self-differentiation might have little relevance to the federal idea in Cyprus and has, indeed, already been dismissed by the political leadership as of no significance all. Rauf Denktash, the former Turkish-Cypriot leader, is the best-known advocate of an ethnic-based conception of Turkish-Cypriot identity that emphasises Turkish roots and Turkey as the natural guardian of Turkish-Cypriot interests. His opinion about Turkish-Cypriot identity was recently put on record in the following way: 'there is no "Cypriot nation". Turkish Cypriots on Cyprus have established a state. It cannot be a nation state, because there is no Turkish-Cypriot nation'. And for good measure he added the following:

A Turkish Cypriot is the extension of Turkey in Cyprus. So we are Turks, of Cyprus. Journalists ask us, are you a Turk first or a Cypriot? – The answer is: are you a Londoner first or an an Englishman? One is geography, the other is nation. We are Turks, as Turks of Anatolia are; but because our geography is Cyprus, we are Turkish Cypriots. If you were to organise Turkey on a geographical basis, you would call a Turk from Erzurum an 'Erzurum Turk'.[23]

This conception of Turkish-Cypriot identity clearly reflects divergent self-perceptions in the north and conveniently ignores an alternative vision of the historical emergence of a distinct people with a polity that reflects a composite nation and a distinct political culture. Moreover, it overlooks those aspects of domestic life and cultural elements that might be shared in common with Greek-Cypriot perspectives.

However, if the Greek and Turkish cultural–ideological origins both loom large in the respective identities of Greek Cypriots and Turkish Cypriots what about the circumstances of the so-called small 'minorities'? These small communities that include mainly Maronites, Armenians and Latinos are virtually invisible when both academics and practitioners consider the various future scenarios for a reunited Cyprus. Yet they, too, maintain religious, linguistic and other cultural distinctions albeit without having significant political salience. The importance of these small but distinctive identities for the federal idea in Cyprus might lie in their ability to assist with plans to disaggregate the state into more than just two units. Belgium managed to do just this by dividing competences between Flanders, Wallonia and Brussels for economic affairs (making three separate units) but recognising Flanders, Wallonia, Brussels and the German-speaking community for cultural–ideological matters (making four distinct units).[24] This facilitated a form of cross-cutting cleavages in decision making whose primary purpose was to break down the familiar zero-sum equation of bipolarity that had come typically to characterise Belgian government and politics.

Let us summarise this section in the following way. First it is useful to point up the existence of socio-cultural differences within the Turkish-Cypriot community. This largely sociological perspective stresses the heterogeneity rather than the homogeneity of the Turkish Cypriots as a majority in the north but the largest minority community in the Republic as a whole. But the question that must be answered when looking to the future is: does this heterogeneity have any political significance for federation and confederation? In other words, could it have any political uses when seeking to construct a new federal model in Cyprus? Second, can the commitment to a bizonal, bicommunal, federal future in Cyprus satisfy the divergent imperatives of the preservation of the Hellenic identity of the island for Greek Cypriots while simultaneously guaranteeing the security of the Turkish Cypriots? Since the recent turbulent history of Cyprus is littered with different kinds of constitutional proposals, we can bring this section to a convenient close by suggesting that the only way for reactivated talks, possibly leading to fresh negotiations for a federal settlement, to be successful is if something distinctly new and different can be introduced into the stalemate that might change the dynamic in these fossilised relations. In a nutshell, is it possible to change the context of the relations between the two principal communities in order for the conflict itself to be changed? This is very much Monnet's 'method' of problem solving and it is construed in the manner of finding another way – a different context – in which it might be possible to approach the conflict. We will turn now to explore this change in the equation that could conceivably reorder the priorities of the principal actors in the process of rebuilding the state of Cyprus.

Changing the dynamic: Cyprus and the EU

The formal application of Cyprus to join the EU in July 1990 confirmed that 'the Cyprus problem is basically an international question and a geopolitical issue'.[25] In practice it is not possible to separate and compartmentalise these international and geopolitical questions from the purely domestic aspects of the conflict. We can conveniently summarise the tangled skein of relationships that characterise this conflict in the following rather cumbersome way:

- bicommunal Greek-Cypriot and Turkish-Cypriot relations
- bilateral Greek-Cypriot and Greek relations
- bilateral Turkish-Cypriot and Turkish relations
- trilateral Republic of Cyprus, Greek and Turkish relations
- quadrilateral Republic of Cyprus, UK, Greece and Turkey relations
- bilateral Greek and Turkish relations
- the United Nations' role.
- British, Greek and Turkish relations as guarantors
- the strategic interests of the United States and NATO
- the role of the European Union.

Even put in this somewhat simplistic way, we can appreciate the multifarious relations that are the hallmark of the conflict and which in a sense render the notion of 'bicommunalism' something akin to a platitude. It is impossible to predict with any certainty either how any single variable will impinge upon another or how any particular combinations of variables will interact with others. Nonetheless, a body of opinion does appear to have emerged during the last decade that construes the EU as having the potential to be a catalyst in leading to a possible federal settlement.[26]

The strategic thinking that lies behind this body of opinion presents a rather optimistic scenario and is based upon what Thomas Diez has recently identified as three distinct, if overlapping, pathways of how membership negotiations or EU membership itself could positively influence the Cyprus problem and defuse the mutual sense of threat experienced by the leading protagonists. These three pathways are presented as the *carrot* catalyst, the *stick* catalyst and the *subversion* catalyst, and they represent, respectively, a policy of largely economic cost-benefit analysis that would entice the north into the EU; a strategy that would put pressure on Turkey by threatening to marginalise it if it continued to obstruct and delay negotiations for a settlement; and finally an approach that would utilise primarily technical matters related to the EU's *acquis communautaire* to promote 'non-political' functional cooperation as a form of conflict avoidance.[27] It should be noted that these three different versions of the catalytic effect of the EU upon the Cyprus conflict have not been portrayed as mutually exclusive, but nor was the author at all optimistic about their positive impact largely because the EU 'is not the third party to the conflict that it may wish to be', given that EU officials have themselves made significant statements regarding the resolution of the conflict.[28] In short, neither Turkish-Cypriot nor Turkish officials perceive the EU as a neutral outside actor. Indeed, they construe it as being 'part of the conflict' so that 'the problem-solving attitude accordingly is misplaced'.[29]

On 1 May 2004 the whole of Cyprus entered the EU as part of the latest enlargement negotiations that welcomed ten new members into an increasingly federal Europe of 25 constituent states. However, while the *de jure* implications underlined the legal unity of Cyprus, the de facto military reality meant that the new EU border ran along the so-called 'Green Line' dividing the country between the Greek-Cypriot south and the Turkish-Cypriot north. As we shall see, this unprecedented set of circumstances was the direct consequence of domestic referendum arrangements in both parts of the divided island. But it serves to buttress the observation that nothing can ever be taken for granted in the domestic politics of Cyprus. We can expect only the unexpected. There is no way of knowing precisely how a way forward can be found with any major degree of confidence. However, it would certainly be misguided to expect the EU dimension to the conflict to facilitate a ready-made solution. The grounds for optimism that EU membership will *necessarily* furnish security guarantees for both communities, offer seductive economic benefits for Turkish Cypriots and guarantee the future of a decentralised conception of Cyprus based upon respect for the independence, unity, territorial integrity and sovereignty of the United Cyprus Republic (its new name) need to be examined very carefully. Membership of the EU does change the dynamic – it alters the context – of the conflict but it is not by itself the answer. We have to make a pivotal distinction between process and substance. Those who want to see a federal Cyprus in a federal Europe will first have to succeed in the *process* of hard bargaining and negotiation before they are likely to have the *substance* of an agreement. As we will see in the next section, that process has so far yielded the eponymous Annan Plan of the UN which required the approval of both island communities. It was and remains the only political basis for the constitutional reconstruction of Cyprus. In other words, it is currently the 'only game in town'.

In summary, the EU does represent new hope and a fresh opportunity to arrive at a new *modus operandi* in Cyprus. It is quite rightly depicted as a new form of political union that is unprecedented, one that has the virtue of accommodating different but overlapping conceptions of authority and legitimacy, but the Helsinki decision of the EU meeting in December 1999 (which Turkey also agreed to sign in order to facilitate its own candidacy aspirations) that resolution of the Cyprus question would not be a precondition for its accession had the effect of muddying the waters even further. Turkey has never accepted the link between these two things. But inertia – the maintenance of the status quo – also has consequences. Accordingly the question that emerges from the recent accession negotiations and current bicommunal discussions is what the precise nature of this relationship is and whether or not, once unravelled, it could lead to some new kind of federal arrangement that might be sufficiently flexible and innovative to go beyond the traditional nation-state projects. This brings us to the Annan Plan that was officially published on 1 April 2004 and to which we now turn.

The Annan Plan

The Annan Plan that was subject to a referendum in both parts of the divided island on 24 April 2004 was the fifth version of a UN sponsored proposal for the reunification of Cyprus dating back to 2000. When 64.90 per cent of those who lived in the north voted in favour of the plan and 75.83 per cent of those who lived in the south opposed it, the plan effectively became null and void. The implications of this outcome were, once again, complex and multifaceted, but they have equally not halted political discussions. These will continue as long as the EU Commission and European Parliament (EP) together with UN input and British, American, Greek and Turkish voices keep the door to compromise and conciliation open. But what is interesting for our purposes here is not only the *process* of negotiations but also the *substance* of the Annan Plan. A quick glance at the terminological basis and constitutional discourse of the Plan is revealing for what it tells us about the federal, confederal and bicommunal nature of the proposed reunification.

A 'Foundation Agreement' that contained 14 articles setting out the principal commitments and goals of the reconstructed state preceded the proposed formal constitution of the new United Cyprus Republic. The fundamental basis of the reunification was reaffirmed as the two communities of Greek Cypriots and Turkish Cypriots that claimed to be 'co-founders' of the Republic established in 1960. Acknowledging each other's 'distinct identity and integrity', the relationship between them was 'not one of majority and minority but of political equality where neither side may claim authority or jurisdiction over the other'. The bedrock of the country was construed as a 'partnership' but importantly a 'bizonal partnership' to ensure 'a common future' in 'an independent and united Cyprus' in which 'democratic principles, individual human rights and fundamental freedoms', as well as respect for 'each other's cultural, religious, political, social and linguistic identity' would be recognised. Special ties of friendship with Greece and Turkey were emphasised (along with the Treaties of Guarantee and Alliance) and remarkably the latter's ultimate membership of the EU was officially welcomed. These so-called 'main articles' were reflective of the 'constitutive power' of the two communities, their 'separately expressed common will'.[30]

The status and relationship of the new state, its federal government and its constituent units were 'modelled on the status and relationship of Switzerland, its federal government and its cantons'. As an independent state in 'the form of an indissoluble partnership, with a federal government and two equal constituent states', the Constitution incorporated the basic principles of the rule of law, democracy, representative republican government, political equality, bizonality and the equal status of the constituent states. Constitutionally all sovereign powers not vested in the federal government would be exercised by the constituent states, thus confirming the thrust of the original American federal model that residual powers would reside in the states. Particularly interesting was the reference to the rights of the constituent states to participate in the formulation and implementation of external relations policy and EU relations 'in accordance with Cooperation Agreements modelled on the Belgian example'. The separate Greek-Cypriot and Turkish-Cypriot communities in their respective constituent state capacities could have 'commercial and cultural relations with the outside world in conformity with the Constitution'.[31]

The concept of citizenship was also intriguing. Following the Swiss example, all Cypriot citizens were also to enjoy 'internal constituent state citizenship status' that would complement but not replace Cypriot citizenship. The implication of this was that political rights at the federal level would be exercised according to 'internal constituent state citizenship status' while political rights at the constituent state and local levels would be exercised at 'the place of permanent residency'. Finally, for our purposes in this brief survey, constitutional amendment was to be by the 'separate majority of the voters of each constituent state in accordance with the specific provisions of the Constitution'.[32]

The concepts, terminology and discourse that characterised the Foundation Agreement's summary of the key features of the new constitution posed a series of extremely difficult questions surrounding the disputed history and highly contentious constitutional past of Cyprus. One example of this was the reference in the 'Main Articles' of the Foundation Agreement to Cyprus as constituting 'our common home' established by the two communities which were 'co-founders' of the Republic originally established in 1960. This statement reignited the old controversies associated with the Constitution of 1960 in the extent to which its critics deemed it unworkable, inherently divisive and foredoomed to failure. The 2004 proposals explained neither why a new constitution was needed nor what the reasons were for the failure of the old constitution. After 30 years of de facto partition, how far had so-called 'distinct identities' changed? Were the new proposals based upon accurate social assumptions about contemporary Cyprus or were they likely to be equally as divisive as 1960 in aggravating the sense of two solitudes? In short, was the Annan Plan in danger of merely repeating the mistakes of the past?

A second example of conceptual controversy was the general use of the term 'partnership' and the specific reference to a 'new bi-zonal partnership' that was selective in omitting the term 'bicommunalism'. This omission was highly significant and obviously deliberate but in the absence of a clear explanation it left the impression that there had been a real, if unacknowledged, radical departure from the High Level Agreements of 1977 and 1979 and every UN resolution since 1990 that called unequivocally for a bicommunal, bizonal federation. The important point here was that the Constitution of 1960 defined the term 'bicommunal' in a *non-territorial* sense: Greek Cypriots and Turkish Cypriots together with Armenians, Maronites and Latinos could live together anywhere on the island. Consequently, the omission of this term lent an exaggerated significance to the avowedly *territorial* meaning of the word 'bizonal' and allowed anxieties to emerge about a new partition of Cyprus along ethno-religious lines. In summary, it is not obvious that this ambiguous phraseology was at all helpful in the current context of the Cyprus conflict. There are clearly circumstances in politics when deliberate ambiguity is strategically both astute and wise because it can promote unity, but in this particular case it could very easily have the opposite effect. It could lead to further mistrust, confusion and misunderstanding, as, indeed, some observers might regard the referendum result.

There is no space in this chapter to provide an in-depth analytical survey of the Annan Plan in its entirety, but this brief reference to some of its conceptual omissions and ambiguities suggests that it remains in some important respects a work in progress. There is still much to be done.

Conclusion: imagining the future

Let us go back to the future. This chapter has sketched out the complexities of the bicommunal and bizonal configuration of the Republic of Cyprus and demonstrated that the stalemate of the last 30 years on the island has been as much due to international factors as to domestic bicommunal politics on the island. In practice the predicament of contemporary Cyprus is the result of the interaction of both domestic and international relations. But imagining the future has to take into account very different circumstances today. We must begin with what constitutes contemporary reality so that a feasible political strategy must start with what already exists.

Conflicting interpretations of the past can never be completely erased, but they must not be allowed to obstruct forward thinking. Since the end of the Cold War and the tragic events of 11 September 2001, the international pressures that impinge upon the Cyprus conflict have changed. Membership of the EU suggests that Cyprus will be pulled along in Europe's future quest for new relations both with Russia and the independent republics of the former Soviet Union and with the Arab states of the Middle East and, indeed, the wider Islamic world. An EU–Mediterranean axis that looks both to the north-east and to the south-east is a credible agenda.

These shifting geopolitical and international EU imperatives interact with the changing domestic perceptions of both Greek-Cypriot and Turkish-Cypriot communities in a complex way that might conceivably furnish the basis for a new constitutional and political rapprochement having the possibility to satisfy the security and territorial integrity concerns of both parties. Notwithstanding some of the negative aspects of the Annan Plan identified above, the omens in certain important respects seem conducive for a new constitutional settlement. Some outstanding questions remain to be negotiated and we must remember that even if the idea of a bizonal, bicommunal federal Cyprus, as agreed according to UN Resolution 649 (1990), is ultimately accepted, it will not be without its own problems. It is not a panacea.

It is imperative that neither Greek nor Turkish Cypriots should be confined in a narrow conceptual straitjacket with respect to their perception and understanding of the traditional terminology of *federation* and *confederation*. The EU itself combines both federal and confederal principles and the federal model for a future Cyprus will have to be fashioned largely though not solely by the two communities alone and, rather like the EU, tailored to the needs of its own governments and citizens. This means that practical progress towards a stable settlement can ultimately be achieved only if there is a conceptual shift from a bicommunal, bizonal federation to the empirical reality of a multi-ethnic federation. Cyprus must find its own federal model in a larger federal Europe.

Notes

1 This chapter draws significantly on a previously published paper by Professor Michael Burgess, which was initially published in Cyprus in the journal *Fidere*, Vol. 1 – October 2003, pp. 7–27. This was the first volume of an annual publication by the Cyprus Centre of Federal Studies and Local Self-Government. This chapter is reprinted with the kind permission of Sotiris Drakos (Editor-in-Chief of *Fidere*).

2 F.H. Hinsley, *Power and the Pursuit of Peace*, (Cambridge: Cambridge University Press, 1980), p. 13.

3 J. Monnet, *Memoirs* (New York: Doubleday, 1978), pp. 37, 76, 87 and 511.

4 I have used an original copy of the 1960 Constitution and would like to thank Sotiris Drakos of the Centre for Federalism and Local Government in Nicosia for very kindly providing me with it.

5 There are many conflicting historical interpretations of critical junctures in contemporary Cypriot politics, but 1959–60, 1960–63, 1968–74, 1974, 1977–79 and 1990 are certainly among the most widely acknowledged of these turning points, depending upon what case is being made.

6 P. King, *Federalism and Federation* (Beckenham, Kent: Croom Helm, 1982), p. 77.

7 It is important to note that not every scholar of the subject has adopted this conceptual approach, but it has proved to be highly useful for facilitating comparative analysis. See M. Burgess and A.-G. Gagnon (eds), *Comparative Federalism and Federation: Competing Traditions and Future Directions* (Hemel Hempstead: Harvester Wheatsheaf, 1993).

8 King (1982), p. 76.

9 I have developed this discussion at length in M. Burgess, *Federalism and European Union: the Building of Europe, 1950–2000* (London: Routledge, 2000).

10 M. Forsyth, *Unions of States: the Theory and Practice of Confederation* (Leicester: Leicester University Press, 1981), pp. 2–3, 6.

11 These are the terms used by F. Guven-Lisaniler and L. Rodriguez in their survey entitled 'The Social and Economic Impact of EU Membership on Northern Cyprus' in T. Diez (ed.), *The European Union and the Cyprus Conflict: Modern Conflict, Postmodern Union* (Manchester: Manchester University Press, 2002), Chap. 10, pp. 181–202.

12 P.G. Polyviou, 'The Problem of Cyprus and Constitutional Solutions' Chap. 9. Part IV, 'The Future', p. 228 in M.A. Attalides (ed.), *Cyprus Reviewed* (Nicosia, Cyprus: Jus Cypri Association, 1977).

13 T. Bahcheli, 'Searching for a Cyprus Settlement: Considering Options for Creating a Federation, a Confederation, or Two Independent States, *Publius: The Journal of Federalism*, 30 (1–2), Winter/Spring 2000, p. 213.

14 *Publius: The Journal of Federalism*, 18 (2), Spring 1988.

15 I.D. Duchacek, 'Dyadic Federations and Confederations', *Publius: The Journal of Federalism*, 18 (2), Spring 1988, p. 5.

16 Duchacek (1988), p. 5.

17 See Polyvios G. Polyviou (1977), p. 215.

18 Duchacek (1988), p. 5.

19 Duchacek (1988), p. 12.

20 See A. Lijphart, *Democracy in Plural Societies* (New Haven, CT: Yale University Press, 1977) and his *Democracies: Patterns of Majoritarian and Consensus Government in Twenty-one Countries* (New Haven, CT: Yale University Press, 1984).

21 See Guven-Lisaniler and Rodriguez (2002), Chap. 10, pp. 183–7.

22 Guven-Lisaniler and Rodriguez (2002), p. 184.

23 Quote taken from J. Pillai, 'A Conversation with Mr. Rauf Denktash, President of the Turkish Republic of Northern Cyprus', *Journal of Cyprus Studies*, 5 (1–2), pp. 7–48 in Guven-Lisaniler and Rodriguez (2002), p. 183.

24 Recent developments however have confirmed the persistent tendency towards bipolarity in the Belgian polity with the merger between the Flemish Regional and Community Councils. For an up-to-date general survey of the Belgian case study, see J. Fitzmaurice, *The Politics of Belgium: A Unique Federalism* (London: Hurst & Co., 1996).

25 A. Theophanous, 'Prospects for Solving the Cyprus Problem and the Role of the European Union', *Publius: The Journal of Federalism*, 30 (1–2), Winter/Spring 2000, p. 218.

26 See T. Diez, 'Last Exit to Paradise? The European Union, the Cyprus Conflict and the Problematic "catalytic effect"', Chap. 8, pp. 139–62 in T. Diez (ed.), *The European Union and the Cyprus Conflict: Modern Conflict, Postmodern Union* (Manchester: Manchester University Press, 2002).

27 Diez (2002), pp. 144–6.

28 Diez (2002), p. 147.

29 Diez (2002), p. 147.

30 For references to the Foundation Agreement and the Constitution of the United Cyprus Republic, I have used the following website address: www.argyrosargy-rou.fsnet.co.uk/annanplan/english/FoundationAgreement.htm.
31 Ibid.
32 Ibid.

Federalism, nationality, statehood

The problem of the European Union

Murray Forsyth

The overall political structure of the European Union, as it exists at the moment, is not that of a federation. Federalism, however, is intimately bound up with the Union, which cannot be fully understood except in relation to it.

The process of European integration since 1950, for example, of which the Union is the product, has been at heart a federalising process. The structures which have evolved to represent the unity that has been formed by this integration process, while they may not resemble those of a fully fledged federation, do resemble those of a federal union – indeed the very name union, which has been deliberately adopted by the European institutions, is federal through and through. Federalism is also closely bound up with the Union, because the formation of a fully fledged federal state, or a European federation, is implicit in the very steps towards unity that have been taken so far. Federation is the telos, that is to say, the implicit aim, of the whole enterprise.

In this chapter I hope to substantiate and fill out these rather bald assertions, before broaching the huge, unspoken question that lies behind them, namely, is it possible for the European Union to achieve or fulfil its telos? Can the Union become a federation, or is this goal necessarily beyond its reach, a utopian dream? As will be seen, the answer to this fundamental question involves a clarification not merely of the concept of federalism, but of the meaning of state and nation as well.

The federal component of the Union

Most people would probably agree with the proposition that the European Union is not a fully fledged federation. What makes us so sure of this? We feel instinctively that a federation is a form of state, and the European Union is not a state, despite its extensive legislative powers and its impressive control over the money circulating within its borders. Why is it not a state? The fact that strikes the eye most immediately and forcibly is that in the established federal or unitary states of today the central government possesses the right and power of making war and peace and all the critical rights and powers that follow from this. It is one of the attributes of a state properly so called that it participates as a full member in the world of international politics. Conversely, the member units, or subunits, of states have lost the key rights and powers that would enable them to do this – if they ever had them. The member units of a federal state may indeed be called states, but they lack these critical rights and powers.

In the European Union the nation states have not lost these rights and the Union does not possess them. The recent crisis in Iraq revealed with startling clarity how firmly the member states have retained their independence in this area. The use of the word 'sovereignty' is sometimes condemned in academic circles as being old fashioned and metaphysical, but here national sovereignty is surely a very real fact.

One could, of course, point to other striking gaps in the sphere of competences wielded by the European Union when it is compared to a typical federation. The lack of a substantial and autonomous money-raising power is one of these. The absence of the right and power of making war and peace, however, makes particularly obvious the fact that we are dealing with entities that differ in kind.

Having said this, it is worth observing that in the past federal unions of states tended to be formed primarily for reasons of defence and security, and possessed more rights and powers in this area than the European Union, without being fully fledged federations. One thinks of the United Provinces of the Netherlands, or of the Confederation of the United States of America. Clearly the European Union could develop further capacities in the field of defence and security without automatically becoming a federation. Conversely, some federations that were formed as self-governing parts of an empire – such as Canada and Australia within the British Empire – possessed substantial powers relating to defence and security, but did not win the ultimate right to make war and peace independently until well after they were created.

Less obvious, but equally profound, contrasts can be made when one turns to the internal structure of a body like the European Union and compares it with that of a federal state or federation. In a state the constitution does not take the form of a pact or treaty between the different members of the body politic itself, even if it may have been interpreted in this way in the early years of such bodies. The constitution is the act of a single will, the act by which a single political unit gives itself (or is given) shape and form. This shape and form may be federal or it may be unitary. The point is that it is a decision and a statute – a 'basic law' – and not a pact between two or more partners.

It is true that in a federation the idea of a basic pact between the members may linger on de facto in the background of the constitution as a norm to which appeal is sometimes made. This seems to be particularly the case, for obvious reasons, when there are two leading cultural units in the federation. I am thinking here of the long-lived notion among French

Canadians that Canada is founded on a pact between two cultures, one English and one French. I have little doubt that the present Constitution of Belgium is looked upon likewise by many Belgians as 'essentially' a compact between Flemish and Walloons. It should also be remembered that, even in the United States, the notion that the Constitution framed in Philadelphia in 1787 was a compact between the states, was asserted repeatedly right up until the Civil War, and was indeed the main legal justification for the act of secession that ignited the struggle. Those who asserted the idea could point in particular to the way the Constitution had been ratified under Article V11. It took the Civil War itself to eliminate the idea.

Apart from these special situations, there is one further, and more fundamental sense in which the idea of a compact lives on in a federation. It is sometimes expressed as the principle of 'federal loyalty' or 'solidarity'. This means that there is in a federation, alongside the formal stipulations of the constitution, a tacit understanding between the central and regional governments to respect each other's status and power as established by the constitution. It is the most important carry-over of the idea of *foedus* into a federation. Without it we tend to think of a federation as a 'sham', or as a formal apparatus rather than a living reality.

The fact that a federal constitution no longer takes the form of a treaty between the members, but a law 'over' them, has implications for the much debated right to secede, which has already been touched upon. It means that the right of one or more member units to judge unilaterally when the others have breached the provisions of the treaty, and to consider themselves freed from it if they judge that they have, can no longer be legitimately claimed. (Still less, of course, do they have the right to withdraw unilaterally from the federation simply when they judge that it is no longer beneficial to them!)

However, it would be naive to think that this magically conjures away the claim of a right to secede. The idea that the tacit or implicit pact on which the federation rests, of the two kinds that have been outlined above, has been broken by one side, may still be strong enough to make the other side claim a right to denounce it. It should also perhaps be noted that the very fact that in a federal state, as distinct from a unitary one, the local units possess substantial governmental structures and organisation, makes secession a less impracticable alternative than it might otherwise be.

In contrast to the situation in a federation, a constitution that takes the form of a treaty between the members, or, more precisely, of a treaty between members that is constituent in nature, is a leading characteristic of a federal union of states. We may prefer to use the terminology of 'confederal', 'confederation', 'confederacy', when we refer to such unions, but it is not essential, and because these terms have tended to become petrified into schematic definitions which confuse rather than clarify, I shall not use them here.

Again, in contrast to the situation in federations, treaties form the very heart of the European Union. The Paris Treaty, the Rome Treaties, the Treaty on the Fusion of the Executives, the Single European Act (despite its imposing name), the Maastricht Treaty on European Union, the Amsterdam Treaty, the Treaty of Nice, have followed one another over the past 50 years. These treaties should not of course be dismissed as 'mere' treaties. They are intended to be permanent, and their constitutional significance is recognised by the frequent practice of submitting them to national referendums. They affect the very status of the signatories.

From time to time efforts have been made to simplify and 'consolidate' this accumulation of pacts. As a result there are in 2004 essentially two basic treaties: the consolidated version of the Treaty of Union and the consolidated version of the Treaty Establishing the European Community.

This account of the successive treaties that lie at the heart of the Union demonstrates incidentally why it is right to call the integration process an essentially federal process, because federalism in the old original sense of the term was not an internal differentiation of a given political unit, but a permanent binding together through treaties, or *foedera*, of political bodies external to one another. As Lasserre remarks, commenting on the long Swiss experience, the word federalism has come to signify in Switzerland the absence of solidarity, it has become synonymous with cantonal egoism, 'alors qu'il exprime tout d'abord, par son origine etymologique comme dans la realite historique, une solidarite consentie et codifie'. He then points to the 'reseau des pactes' which formed the 'substance meme' of the old Swiss Confederation, against which the 'cantonalistes' so frequently chafed, but which gradually resulted in the growth of the Swiss nation.[1] We shall refer back again to the Swiss example; it is enough here to see the parallel with the network of pacts that form the very substance of the European Union.

The most recent pact, the 'Treaty Establishing a Constitution for Europe', which was drafted during the years 2002–03 by a special Convention, and which failed initially to gain acceptance by the member states, though it may yet do so, deserves further comment. In retrospect it can be seen to have been in part the victim of its own ambiguities, ambiguities which are directly relevant to the subject of this chapter. These ambiguities grew out of an initial lack of clarity over what the Convention and the treaty were intended to achieve. The speech in 2000 by the German Foreign Minister, Joschka Fischer, which gave the initial impetus to the whole exercise, represented the maximalist aspiration. His speech bore the significant title: 'From Confederacy to Federation: thoughts on the finality of European integration.'[2] He wanted to move beyond federal union to a federation – what he, to be sure, called a 'lean' federation, but a federation nonetheless. The minimalist aspiration did not envisage a qualitative leap of this kind. It sought something much more limited and practical: to give a sharper and more coherent definition of the existing Union.

Looking at the final text of the draft treaty, as it was presented in July 2003, one can see that it reflects quite clearly the minimalist approa~¹

It does not attempt to found a federation, but essentially reconstitutes the existing Union – consolidating, clarifying and systematising the fundamental provisions that are scattered in the existing treaties, and that are all too often obscured by technical matters.

Above all it seeks to systematise the distribution of powers between the Union and the member states drawing a clear distinction between competences exclusively exercised by the Union, and competences shared between the Union and the member states, with additional provisions regulating when and how the Union may act in the sphere of shared powers. It makes plain that competences not conferred on the Union in either of these ways will be explicitly reserved to the member states. In this way it seeks to incorporate in the Union the triadic distribution of powers typical of many federations, and rationalises its structure logically and convincingly.

This will not transform the Union into a federation, however. Nor will the various changes in the structure, procedures and powers of the institutions of the Union that the treaty at present envisages make a qualitative difference, significant as they are. The existing competences of the Union will be slightly enlarged. Its capacity to act with flexibility and discretion within its existing areas of competence will almost certainly be enhanced. Internally its structure will take on more the characteristics of a 'government'. Its external profile will also become rather sharper.

It will, however, remain a 'Union' established by a treaty between its members, a Union moreover that was still far from wielding decisive power in the area of defence and security. The provision that 'any Member State may decide to withdraw from the European Union in accordance with its own constitutional requirements', with which the draft constitution concludes, makes its treaty character unmistakable.

Unfortunately the limited, practical thrust of the Convention's work was obscured. The idea that it was making a brand new constitution *tout court* 'for Europe' still hung round its deliberations, and was given credence by the very title of the draft treaty, and the *fanfaronnade* of the preamble. It was little wonder that in the public debate constant parallels were made with the constitutions of existing states, usually with a view to heaping scorn on the new European venture.

Having distinguished the European Union from a federation in terms of its powers and its basis, it is worth considering more closely its institutional structure. How far is this similar to that of a federation? More broadly, is it possible to make useful distinctions between federations on the one hand and unions on the other? I think one can, as long as one is alive to the sheer range of possible institutional permutations in these bodies, and of the overlapping between them. If one says simply that in a federation internal sovereignty belongs to the centre, then one draws the line, in my view, too absolutely, and misses the nuances. The difference between a federal state and a unitary one shrivels into nothingness. There can be no doubt that, in time of emergency, the difference between a federal state and a unitary one

can often shrivel in practice to nothingness, but the norm is surel
been stressed already – that there is in a federation a kind of tac
which the centre respects the status and authority of the member
vice versa. Dictation or coercion by the centre is consciously (
sciously avoided.

One must not be mealy-mouthed about this tacit pact. There will always
be conflicts, friction and rivalry. At the same time the history of federal
states provides remarkable evidence of a willingness on the part of centre
and members not to push a conflict too far; a willingness to make compromises; an *un*willingness indeed to invoke the ultimate right of sovereignty.
A federal union, such as the European Union, tends to live by a similar reti-
cence, but with much greater wariness shown by the centre.

The main difference between the institutional structures of a union and a
federation would seem to reside in the different weight which is accorded in
each to the diet, congress or council, that brings together the representatives
of the member states of the union as such. In a union of states such a council
of states represents so to speak the permanent pact that underlies it; it is the
quintessentially federal institution. It is not necessarily the only institution
in the union, but it is so to speak the keystone of the arch, or the sun around
which the other bodies revolve.

It is worth stressing that in a union a council of states is the quintessentially federal institution, because in the literature on the European Union it
has become an entrenched habit – for perfectly understandable reasons – to
refer to the various councils of states as being the quintessentially *non-federal*
institutions. They are merely 'intergovernmental'. The reasons for this shift
in terminology are interesting and will be touched on later.

The working practices of the councils of unions of states can vary widely.
Although they are endowed with the power of making what are in effect, if
not in name, 'laws' for the whole union, they are not to be confused with
parliamentary assemblies. Their meetings are rarely public. They are arenas
for diplomacy and bargaining. In the ideal type of such councils each
member state doubtless has equal status, an equal power of veto and equal
voting rights. In political reality such equalities can often buckle. How far
the veto power of each member state is entrenched or how far majority
voting is permitted, as well as how far the votes of the members in the
council are weighted – these are matters of circumstance. So are the number
and type of other institutions that surround or exist alongside the council or
diet.

When one turns one's attention from a union to a federation one can see
immediately that a shift in the institutional balance has occurred. The 'quintessentially federal' institution of the council of states has become hemmed
in, limited, squeezed into becoming the 'upper chamber' of a multi-
chambered legislative assembly. It is still a specifically federal organ, and a
highly important one, but it is now only a part of an overarching 'federal
government', which is distinguished from the 'state governments'.

In a federation the council is joined by 'monarchical' institutions, by which I do not mean offices occupied by royal dynasties, but simply offices held by one person, typically those of a Prime Minister, Chancellor or President. In parliamentary federations, such as the Canadian or German, the monarchic office will be responsible to, and lead, the lower house of the legislature. In federations where the separation of powers is maintained, such as the American, the monarchic office will be placed outside the legislature in the person of a President. Monarchic offices are not intrinsically federal. They do not embody 'shared' rule, but 'indivisible' rule, unitary rule. They represent unity and a capacity for effective decision which are both particularly essential in the foreign arena. Amongst the federations, only Switzerland, with its long tradition of neutrality and democracy, has held in check the growth of strong monarchical elements in the federal government. There the executive remains thoroughly collegiate.

In a federation the council is joined too by firmly established democratic institutions representing the whole population as one undivided people. Democratic institutions of this kind are also not intrinsically federal. They are intrinsically unitary, like monarchic ones. They are there to clamp the federal government to the people 'one and indivisible'. Consociational techniques can of course be used to counter and temper the unitary thrust of democracy, and make it more 'federal'. Switzerland is here again a good example, though of course Switzerland, while tempering democracy in its parliamentary system, brings it in again in a more direct form through referendum.

In the European Union, as is well known, the council representing the member states now manifests itself in two forms: at the lower level, the Council of Ministers, and at the higher level, the European Council, which brings together the heads of state or government, and the President of the Commission. This differentiation of the council, which began in the 1970s, can be seen as representing the determination of the representatives of the states not to relinquish their major role in deciding the legislation of the Union, within the fields ascribed to it, but at the same time to give themselves a distinct forum in which freely to consider and decide upon the overall development of the Union. It formalised a division of labour that had always existed.

The representatives of the member states, meeting in the two-level council, stand at the core of the European Union, but from the start of the process of integration they have been accompanied by other institutions, of which the two most important, from the point of view of this discussion, are a collegiate 'executive' – today's Commission – and a parliamentary assembly – today's European Parliament. Both these organs have a significant share in the law-making power of the Union. In other words the legislative power of the Council of Ministers in several areas is already shared with the Parliament, and these areas will increase if the draft constitutional treaty is adopted, while the Commission has a significant right of legislative initiative. I shall return to the role of the Commission later on.

The European Convention, in its draft constitutional treaty, in fact attempts to strengthen both the 'monarchical' and the democratic elements in the Union. It tries to enhance the 'prime-ministerial' character of the President of the Commission, and at the same time the 'presidential' character of the head of the European Council. These changes, if carried through, will doubtless give greater effectiveness to these two bodies. It is doubtful whether they will dislodge the European Council from its position at the apex of the Union. Apart from anything else, progress down the road to enlarging the scope of the Union, so that it becomes a union for defence and security, have so far been modest, and the heads of state and government will be loath indeed to relinquish the power to determine its pace and end point. It is interesting to note that the chairman of the Convention, Giscard d'Estaing, actually wanted to make the European Council explicitly the 'highest authority in the Union', though this proposal was not included in the final draft.

The draft provides for the election of the President of the Commission by the European Parliament, though the candidate for election will be proposed by the Council. It seeks to ensure that the Parliament in the future will be more accurately representative of Europe's people as one entity. It even makes a nod in the direction of popular 'initiatives' of the Swiss kind. A fully democratic parliamentary regime is, however, still a considerable way off.

This account of the European Union as a federal union, but not a federation, has focused on its powers, its treaty base and its institutions. It needs to be supplemented by at least a brief consideration of motivation. The creation of a federal union represents a step beyond the normal modalities of international relations: a new actor has been created. Several states have thrown a cordon around themselves, created a common, 'domestic' space within this boundary, and established institutions capable of expressing the will of this new entity within and without. It may not be a state but it is certainly not simply the practice of 'international relations'. What makes states act in this way?

That states will act in this way out of national interest goes without saying. States rarely if ever act in the external field purely to implement some abstract idea. The idea must be hinged to specific interests to be operative. That the national interests of the states making a union must converge also goes without saying. No treaties are made unless there is such a convergence. The real question is: why are treaties of *union* decided upon rather than treaties typical of international relations?

It is not possible to discuss this question more than briefly here. It is obvious that the countries that have created the European Union have had a vast range of interests in common – economic, social, technological, military and so on – over the past 50 years, and that these common interests would have created a huge web of liberalisation agreements, cooperation agreements, international agencies and so on, even if the European Union had not been established. If we ask why the specific path of union was followed, then one has to look for more all-encompassing factors.

The first is surely the presence, or at least the perception, of a common and urgent threat, and the will to ward it off. This is a factor which always has the capacity to push states beyond the 'normal', and in particular to combine very closely together. The paradox here is that the clearest and most blatant threat to the European countries, in other words the prolonged threat from the Soviet Union, had the effect of pushing the states of Western Europe, not into a European defence union, though extraordinary efforts were made to create one in the early 1950s, but of pushing them instead into an alliance, the closest form of international relations, with the United States. The reasons for this are fairly obvious and do not need to be entered into here. The main point is that, although NATO bore the brunt of the threat, the presence of the Soviet menace remained for decades an important propellant also towards European unification. External encouragement to union from the United States should also be mentioned in this context, though it scarcely had the compulsive effect of the Soviet threat. The latter has, of course, now disappeared, but there is no guarantee that another threat might not take its place. Indeed at the time of writing the common, though clandestine, threat from terrorist organisations seems to be tightening European cooperation significantly.

When one turns from the external propellants to the internal, it is clear that a decisive role has been played by the will of the European states definitively to exclude the possibility of war between themselves. When war between a particular group of countries has shown itself not once, but twice, to be horribly destructive to all concerned, and when the normal practice of international relations, combined with the construction of an ill-thought-through union for peace at the world level, i.e. the League of Nations, has blatantly failed after the first disaster to prevent the outbreak of the second, then it is wholly understandable that a powerful will to go beyond the normal modalities of international affairs arises within that group of countries. In the interwar years all manner of conventional pacts had been made between the European states in an effort to preserve peace; efforts had been made to preserve the balance of power between them, smaller states had made declarations of neutrality, nothing had been effective. A world league had also failed. In revulsion against all this, a will to create permanent peace between the countries concerned emerged after 1945. National self-interest coincided with idealism, and Kantian principles found root in reality.

It is one of the fundamental objectives of union – of all unions – to create an arena of permanent, definitive peace between the participants. The normal world of international relations, on the other hand, presupposes the possibility of war between the participants. A union thus sets out to transform the normal international relations between a given group of states into relations akin to those that obtain *within* a particular state.

This impulse to transform the international into the domestic runs through the whole history of the European Union. It can be seen at work with particular clarity in the early, critical years of European integration, when the line of future development was set. In the making of the European Coal and Steel Community, and above all in France's historic decision to change its traditional policy towards Germany and Germany's endorsement of this change, the will to go beyond the normal and to create the basis for definitive peace is crystal clear. It is implicit later in the decision to create a 'Community' with a 'Common Market', rather than a 'Free Trade Association'. Once again national interest was not obliterated but raised to a new level.

The final factor impelling specifically towards union has been the shared sense of belonging to one distinctive historical entity, Europe, and the shared wish to see this entity, which has been driven from its former prominence, restored, revived and vigorous. Whether one calls this entity a culture, a civilisation or a group of peoples whose history and whose future are inextricably bound up with one another – a 'community of destiny' – does not seem to matter too much. The important thing is that this wish to reassert a distinct, historically evolved community existed after 1945, and still exists in the very different context of today. It may not operate with the same intensity at all times or in all places, but it has undoubtedly been one of the motives that have inspired European statesmen to go beyond the international to union. I shall discuss it again when considering the national element within the European Union.

A will to ward off a threat, a will to make permanent peace, and a will to assert Europe's presence in the world, these three factors offer, if not a complete, at least a sufficient explanation of the determination of nation states to create a union, rather than a variety of other, more conventional, agreements and pacts, to reconcile their convergent interests. The federal outcome – because union, as I have tried to indicate, is a federal outcome – has to be seen primarily as the precipitate of a number of nation states pursuing their national interests in the context of these three common motivating elements.

How far federalism in and for itself has been a motivating factor depends on how one uses the term. If one means by it a belief that a fully fledged federal state, or some other model federal organisation, is the answer to all world problems, and that one only need 'apply' this type of organisation to Europe to resolve its problems, then it has played, in my view, a minor part. If one means a belief that the ultimate way to achieve the three specific ends indicated above is to establish a federal state, but that this can only be the culmination of a long process, then it has played a much more important role. It has provided an overall sense of direction, a means of maintaining some form of coherence along the way.

This belief has logic on its side too. To ward off threats from outside, to create an arena of permanent peace internally, and to give people with a sense of identity a capacity to act and make their presence felt in the world –

is that not precisely the aim and purpose of the state as a form of human organisation? A union can take one so far, but by its very structure it cannot fully achieve its ends. It is still, as it were, infected by international relations. The state as a self-constituted entity is its logical, if not necessarily its historical end point. Hence, as was mentioned earlier, a fully fledged European federation is the telos, or implicit aim of the integration process since the war.

This leads on to a final observation, which is that the European Union in its evolution and present structure also shows the impact of ideas which are not specifically federal, and these too have to be given due recognition when analysing it. These ideas may be categorised broadly as the 'technical' approach to integration, which can be seen at work very clearly in the structural development of the early communities. According to this approach, integration or federation in Europe was to be achieved by establishing a particular kind of 'decision-making technique' within any new joint bodies created by the states.

This technique centred on a collegiate body chosen initially by the governments of the member states, but detached thereafter from all national ties or obligations, which would thus be enabled to interpret and implement the 'general' or 'European' will of any new community. Such an 'authority' or 'commission' would be supranational in the sense that it would be detached from the nation states, and also in the sense that its task would be not merely that of administering any new community, but of presenting the council of the member states of the community with the material on which they must take decisions, of prodding the council into action wherever possible, and of watching over the way member states implemented their treaty obligations. This animated bureaucracy, alternating between politics and administration, was regarded as the hub of the 'community method', a method that can still be seen embedded in the structure of the European Union, and that has achieved almost sacral status.

Is the 'community method' federal? In the sense that it is a technique designed primarily to promote progress towards a future European federation it can be so described. In the sense that 'supranational' institutions have in practice pushed consistently for decisions that favour more integration and closer union, it can again be described as federal. But is it in its actual form, as a political mechanism, federal? It might be said that in so far as the Commission is composed of individuals drawn from each of the member states, it is federal, because it brings the member states into the orbit of the central institutions. This, however, is obviously false, because, as has already been indicated, the members of the Commission, once appointed, are expressly enjoined to act and to decide in complete independence from the member states, that is to say they are not bound by any instruction from the member states, and the member states are forbidden to try to influence them.

I think it has to be concluded that there is nothing *intrinsically* federal about the community method. It reflects rather the technological age in which we live. It also reflects, in part at least, the classic revolutionary idea of 'vanguard' or 'spearhead' bodies designed to inject new worlds into old – the new world here being federation and the old world being that of the nation states. The widespread tendency to refer to the Commission as 'Eurocrats' or 'Technocrats' is hence not far from the mark. They must surely be differentiated into the political and administrative branches of a responsible European executive as federalisation proceeds.

In this discussion I have tried to keep as close as possible to the irregular surface of reality and not to squeeze things into boxes where they do not fit. The European Union, like all other federal bodies, is unique, odd, peculiar and lopsided. But it can legitimately be called, and can legitimately call itself, a federal union of states, and can be seen as a staging post on a long, nay a gigantic, federal journey, towards a federal state.

The presuppositions of a European federation

The previous section has considered the European Union as federal union which has as its logical end point the creation of a European federation. It has touched on the underlying motives that have pushed the European states in a federal direction, and it has also indicated the radical change of constitution and structure that would be implied in the transformation of a union into a federation. This section will examine the two latter features more closely, with a view to giving at least a partial answer to the questions: how feasible and credible is the goal of a European federation, and what would be the essential precondition of its establishment? Can history and theory help solve these enigmas?

It is impossible to discuss the viability of Europe as a federalising entity without simultaneously discussing nationality and nationalism as well. Some would argue that it is necessary to discuss nationalism solely because it is the antithesis of federalism, the brake on the whole enterprise. 'Federalism versus Nationalism' makes a good slogan. It is, like most slogans, far too *simpliste*. Nationalism, in the limited sense of a strong attachment to the existing European nation states, has undoubtedly been a force which has often opposed itself to the federalisation of Europe, and will probably do so in the future. This should not, however, be taken to mean that the pursuit of national self-interest automatically runs counter to the federal impulse, nor that the federalising impulse itself has not been fuelled by a sense of common European nationality. The relationship between federalism and a sense of nationality cannot be summed up as a simple either/or. In the previous section I have already indicated this, and in this one I shall try to take the argument further.

The main reason why a discussion of Europe as a federalising entity must simultaneously embrace a discussion of nationalism is this: the transition from a federal union – as Europe is now – to a federation is at heart the transition from a non-state to a state. Whether the form of government of the new state is federal or unitary is really a secondary question. The crux is the establishment of a government which is recognisably the government of a state and not of some looser aggregation. The question of the form of government is secondary in another sense. *Should* Europe agree to constitute itself as a state, then there would surely be no disagreement that the new state should have a federal form of government, although the precise form of federalism would doubtless be a matter for debate. In other words, one cannot envisage a unitary form of government gaining much support, given Europe's history, size and variety. The key issue now and in the foreseeable future is not whether a European state should have a federal or a unitary form of government, but whether there should be a European state. Only if this objective is seen to be credible, logical, necessary and in keeping with the inner sentiments of the people at large, will the existing federal union be transformed into a federation.

It is at this point that the question of nationality and nationalism necessarily and naturally presents itself. It intrudes because when one considers the process of state building, or of state formation, above all when one considers how it has taken place in Europe, because that is the experience most relevant in this instance, we find that it has been intimately intertwined with nation building, or national formation. The two are like Siamese twins. The will to form a state and the will to be a nation coincide and interweave at innumerable points, both in theory and practice, and the very interchangeability of the two words in many contexts, only reinforces this fact.

As we have noted earlier, a state is intrinsically a body that participates in the international world with equal status to the other participants. It is intrinsically a body which marks off its own land and people and protects them against outside threats. The will to form a state is thus inherently a will to assert oneself against, and to match the 'foreigner'; it has an inevitable tinge of 'nationalism' in it.

To take another example, it is now also generally accepted in Europe, that when some sort of crisis or dislocation occurs, and a new state has to be constituted, or an old one reconstituted, then the only power that may confer legitimacy and authority on the new constitution is the nation, or, if one wishes to be more precise, a national assembly elected specifically to represent the people in its constituent role. It is taken for granted that a legitimate state is one constituted from below. Even the Belgian Constitution retains the clause that all power stems from the nation. The various rights that have been claimed to dispense a state's constitution from above, whether on behalf of a dynasty or of a privileged group such as the Communist party, have become things of the past. The nation is the generally recognised constituent power of the modern European state.

This links up directly with our earlier discussion of federal union. It was remarked there that the transition from a union to a federation in Europe would mean the change from a constitution that was a pact between states to a constitution that was a unilateral decision, a statute emanating from a single source, a law 'above' the states. From what single source could such a law, binding the states, emerge? In the name of what authority could the existing states of Europe be united in one state? There can surely be only one answer, and that is Europe considered as – or more importantly considering itself as – one people, that is to say, as a nation.

This leads on to the question: is it possible to conceive of Europe as a nation, or perhaps more pertinently could Europeans come to conceive of themselves as a nation? Clearly the answer depends on what one means by a nation. There are certain definitions of nation and its cognate terms that make it impossible for Europe to become a nation, or alternatively make it highly undesirable that it should do so. For example the tendency to see nations as groups that are permanently marked off from one another by fixed, scientifically ascertainable characteristics, primarily biological and linguistic, and to discount or belittle the contribution of dynamic factors such as politics, history or ideals and beliefs, in forming national consciousness, militates against the idea of Europe becoming a nation. It favours instead a vision of Europe that is politically subdivided even further than at present, so that each objectively ascertainable ethnolinguistic group is given a roughly equal political status. The linguistic heterogeneity of Europe is so pronounced that any equation of nation and language must lead to complete scepticism about a European national consciousness.

Similarly, those who see a sense of nationality as meaning exclusive attachment to *existing* nation states, as if such a sense could not widen to embrace the community formed by a number of nation states, or as if the sentiment of attachment to such a wider community could not possibly be termed nationalism, cannot conceive of Europe becoming a nation.

To see nationality as 'fixed' unalterably by size, however, seems as unrealistic as seeing it 'fixed' unalterably by language and biology. This is not to deny that national consciousness has often expressed itself as a passionate defence or assertion of a particular language or race. It is rather to deny that national consciousness is inalienably or exclusively wedded to language or to any other inherent group characteristic.

There is another obstacle to conceiving of Europe as a nation which deserves a brief mention. This is the tendency to see loyalty to the nation as implying necessarily the outright rejection of liberalism, and the complete subordination of the individual to the nation, however defined. If the development of Europe as a nation implies the emergence of this kind of anti-liberal ideology, then there will be few indeed who will endorse it. The sense of nationality, however, it cannot be too often emphasised, is not necessarily and irrevocably an anti-liberal ideology. On the contrary, it has been often intimately entwined with liberalism.

Rather than make a huge inspection tour of all possible meanings, it seems preferable to start from the sense of nationality that exists in most of the European states of today, and to keep this as a kind of benchmark.

The sense of community, identity and loyalty that binds together the peoples of the individual nation states of Europe, and to which one gives the name national consciousness, has been patently the product, in each instance, of a historical process. This process has been one of action and reaction rather than of unilinear development. Facts, to put it crudely, have impinged on group consciousness, and group consciousness has in turn impinged on facts. The facts in question have included shared language and common descent, but these have not always been the immutable or sole awakeners of national consciousness. 'Natural boundaries' have played a role. The shaping force of distinct historical events or vicissitudes – external threats, wars, conquests, victories, achievements, disasters, for example – has been huge. The impact of gradual historical developments, in particular economic and technical evolution, has been profound, if often ambiguous. Common institutions, whether political, dynastic, administrative, legal, military or educational, have always been of critical importance. Common doctrines, ideals, or beliefs, whether political or religious – even those that seem very 'international' in content – have contributed greatly. As we have stressed, national consciousness is not simply the passive product of these 'facts'; it reacts in turn to shape institutions, events, creeds and even language.

It is this action and reaction which has produced the polity characteristic of modern Europe – the nation state – and it is this interplay which could produce in turn a European nation state. Looking back, at the experience of the individual states, the process can be defined as one of progressive integration, and looking forward, at Europe as a whole, it can be defined in the same way. We think of European integration as unprecedented, and in a way it is; but in another way it is the repetition of the kind of process which has formed Europe's component units, albeit with a rather different mix of nation-forming 'facts'.

The integration which has formed the individual European nations, as Pomian has observed, has been a two-sided affair: a differentiation at the frontier, or a marking off of a particular segment of humanity against other, similar types of groups, or against other, more universal, groups; and a coalescence internally or vertically, from top to bottom.[3] This second development does not only mean that over time the people or society within the national boundary coalesces into one, it means also that political authority within the boundary comes to be tightly linked to the people. These two forms of internal integration are mutually reinforcing: the high degree of oneness, or the developed sense of identity of the people, makes the development of a representative system of government, or what we call democracy, possible.

It need hardly be emphasised that the tempo of this process of national integration, and its pattern, has differed widely within the continent. It has long been recognised, for example, that the pattern of national integration in the eastern part of the continent has diverged markedly from that in the west. The reasons for this are manifold and need not be discussed here. The significant fact is that despite the very different sequences and speeds of integration, the same forces, ideas, pressures, can be seen at work in the various states – albeit in different proportions and combinations – and that the end point striven for or achieved is recognisably similar.

Pomian has well summarised what he calls the 'trajectory' of the European nation. At the point of departure of each European nation, he writes, we find

> different ethnic groups, often hostile to one another, with their chiefs, their priests, their warriors and their plebs, their beliefs, their traditions, their customs; linguistic communities incapable of understanding one another, or only understanding each other with difficulty; categories differentiated by their juridical status, usually hereditary, and notably by the contrast between the slavery or dependence of some and the liberty of others.

At the point of arrival, he continues, we find

> a fairly large collectivity – several million people at least – which is distinguished from other similar collectivities by its traditions, its ways of life, its beliefs, its institutions, its symbols, its territory, its history inscribed in its often unconscious habits, its monuments, its landscapes, as well as its language, in the overwhelming majority of cases. A collectivity all of whose members have the same juridical status, that of citizen, and have thereby the same right to participate in public life, in ways defined by the laws in force, and the same duties adjusted solely in terms of age, sex, and state of health.[4]

Pomian's words convey succinctly the nature of the integration of which the European nation state is the outcome and embodiment. He also brings together quite naturally two components of nationhood which are well known to students of nationalism but which are often kept apart, as if one was true and the other false, or as if one was incompatible with the other. Perhaps one should say more explicitly that he touches on and combines two doctrines – two compelling visions – which have been of immense importance in shaping and 'integrating' the European nation state over the past 200 years: the idea of the nation as a distinctive historical entity, and the idea of the nation as a community of citizens with equal rights and liberties. These two ideas are of particular relevance to the question of the possible future development of the European Union, and I shall now try to indicate their significance in this regard.

The idea of the nation as a community of equal citizens may be called, with some caution, the 'rational' or the 'liberal-rational' vision. One calls it this not because all other versions of nationalism are 'irrational', nor because it appeals only to the intellect, and is incapable of rousing passion. History shows quite clearly that it is capable of arousing intense passion. One calls it rational because its image, its picture of what the nation should be is the product of a logical deduction from man's nature, that is, from man considered abstractly, of what the 'just state' should be.

This concept of the nation springs directly out of ideas about man and the state which developed gradually in Europe in the wake of the Reformation. It is a quintessentially European notion, albeit one that has spread to several other parts of the world. Its roots are to be found in the destruction of the medieval idea of political authority descending from above, which takes place in Europe in the sixteenth and seventeenth centuries, and its replacement by the idea of political authority being founded on a social contract. It is grounded on the notion of each human being possessing as such, equal freedom, and on the concomitant notion that political authority must, in order to be legitimate, spring from below.

In practical terms the rational vision seeks to replace one idea of the 'people' – those who make up the body politic – with another. In place of the people as a body criss-crossed and fractured by a host of artificial barriers, social, territorial and political, it seeks to create one people, with only one barrier, that at the external frontier. In place of the people as an aggregate of groups possessing differential rights – whether political or civil, territorial or hierarchical – it seeks one united people, sharing equal rights and liberties, under one government constituted by them. The evils it seeks to combat are essentially those of 'privilege', 'discrimination', 'monopoly'. One can see this impulse breaking to the surface with immense clarity in the early years of the French Revolution, before it was hijacked by the Jacobins. It can be detected, acting more gradually and cautiously, in Great Britain, from the Reform Bill onwards.

The ramifications of this idea among the different states of Europe in the nineteenth and twentieth centuries are indeed huge. Internal economic barriers are swept aside and replaced by a single uniform economic boundary enclosing the people as a whole. A 'national' economic system is established. A 'national' system of local government is set up. A 'national' transport system is inaugurated. A 'national' education system is introduced. A 'national' army is recruited. The law comes to apply equally to all. The courts protect the equal rights of each. The 'constitutional state' comes into being. Representative democracy spreads. The list of changes, slow or sharp, which the rational idea of the nation has produced in the states of Europe over the past 200 years, could go on for a long time. In one direction they represent a restriction on arbitrariness, in another a vast unleashing of 'national' power.

The rational idea of the nation does not stand alone. It grows up alongside another idea of the nation which relates to it in multifarious ways which range from near identity to outright opposition. I shall call it the 'historical' idea. Here the nation means a particular people marked off from others by historically evolved characteristics, or, more precisely, a people which has become conscious of its historically evolved, distinctive identity, and is determined to give this identity practical and effective reality. Whereas the first concept of the nation is the product of a will to implement a rational doctrine of 'man', the second is the product of the historical consciousness of collective identity, combined with a will to give this collective identity institutionalised form and power. While the first may occasionally be a focus of intense emotion, the second is intrinsically and continuously connected with feeling and emotion.

The assertion of nationhood in the historical sense leads typically to a range of demands, though not necessarily to an automatic sequence from one to the other. There is the demand for cultural autonomy. There is the demand for political autonomy. There is the demand that the state, or the overall political framework in which the nation finds itself, should be reformed so as to allow the nation to be represented within it. There is finally the demand that a new state, a new body politic should be created, which will henceforth represent the nation.

The specific nature of the historical consciousness, and the will, which creates the nation in this sense, needs emphasising. It is not to be confused with a rather cerebral awareness of similarity. It goes beyond this. Nor is it linked inexorably to one specific characteristic which marks the 'nation' off from others, for example language. As we have already stressed, a large number of factors have come into play historically in the creation of nations and national consciousness will typically place its emphasis now on one characteristic, now on another. It is also worth noting that in some instances a supposedly fixed characteristic such as language is artificially revived *after* national consciousness and will have been awakened.

National consciousness, at its most fundamental, would seem to be the consciousness of belonging to a historically continuing, distinctive unit of humanity, one that has played a role in the past (or could have done if it had not been held down), and one that has a role to play in the present and future. The assertion of one or more characteristics is the expression of this underlying sense of a community at a given moment, and the choice of characteristics is determined by the threats to which the community feels exposed, or the opportunities that are presented to it, at that moment.

In describing the emergence of 'historical' nations one is thus not talking primarily about people seeking pragmatic, utilitarian goals, but rather of people feeling themselves part of an unfolding destiny, something capable of evoking devotion and sacrifice. As a sensed historical reality that overarches the individual, preceding him and outliving him, the nation is able to give the individual's own short existence a direction and a meaning. It taps into one of the deepest needs of humanity, and in doing so generates the passion to selfless deeds.

It is important, however, not to underestimate the degree to which a sense of nationality, or of historical distinctiveness, can be engendered simply by the presence of an external threat, danger or invasion. Its first manifestation may be simply an instinctive attempt to ward off such menaces, which are recognised as 'alien' or 'foreign' without extended preliminary cogitation. The deeper sense of being part of a historical entity, to which reference has been made, may itself develop in the wake of such elementary confrontations, rather than before them.

This discussion of nationhood and nationalism, in their various forms, relates to the process of European integration in a number of significant ways. It has to be recognised that first, when one turns one's attention away from the political form of European integration – federalism and the ancillary mechanisms mentioned earlier – to the substance of integration, the thing of inherent value that is being constructed, or being encouraged to emerge, within the scaffolding of federalism, then one sees something that is best defined as an incipient European nation state, that is to say a continental nation state emerging alongside the 'national' nation states.

More specifically, when one looks at the substance of what has been achieved by and through the existing European Union and its predecessor bodies, one finds that it matches uncannily many of the things achieved by earlier 'liberal-rational' nationalism. The efforts in post-war Europe to eliminate all internal barriers to trade and economic movement, to abolish as far as possible all 'national' discrimination and monopoly, and to create a 'level internal economic playing field', while at the same time creating a common economic frontier at the periphery, are patently analogous to earlier movements within the various nation states. So are more positive measures like the gradual creation of a European 'economic system', of which the establishment of the European Central Bank is the most impressive manifestation so far, and the creation of a European transport system. Most important of all the analogies is the establishment very early on in the European process of procedures for making laws directly and equally applicable to all. With that innovation, it may be said, the first step in the creation of a European nation, in the sense of a community of citizens with equal rights and liberties, was made.

In contrast to the modest but real steps that have been taken to creating a European nation in the liberal-rational sense, the development of a consciousness of Europe as a nation in the historical or cultural sense, that is, as an historically evolved entity with a distinctive and invaluable role to play in the world, seems rather limited, and its contribution to the formation and progress of the Union hitherto can scarcely be called a major one. There is undoubtedly a widespread understanding that similarities exist between the European peoples. It is usually expressed by saying that we share a common heritage, in particular the heritage of the ancient classical world, and of Christianity. However, similarity, and even the consciousness of similarity, as I have tried to argue, is rarely sufficient to propel people to work selflessly to promote a new unity.

One important factor served until recently to hamper or weaken popular identification with Europe as a cultural entity, namely the Cold War. While Europe was divided into two opposing ideological blocs, to be supportive of Europe as a cultural whole meant ignoring the brute reality of Soviet power. It could also lead paradoxically, not to support for European integration, but to a questioning of the right of institutions confined to the western part of the continent to call themselves 'European'. With the collapse of the Iron Curtain, and the subsequent accession of so many countries of Eastern Europe to the European Union, what may be called the 'European' legitimacy of the Union has been immeasurably strengthened, and self-identification with historical Europe is freed from very practical constraints.

Is it necessary for this European sense of nationhood to develop further? It could be argued, and it is widely argued, that the main imperative at this moment is for the nation states to defend their distinctive ways of life against the unremitting quest for uniformity that is represented by the Union. Here, incidentally, we can see the 'rational-liberal' idea of nationality running up against, and provoking the 'cultural' idea of nationality. The clauses in the Treaty of Union and in the draft constitutional treaty of 2003 demanding that the Union respect the 'identities' of the member states were clearly intended to counter the resentment that has been stirred up. It might even be argued that here is the basis of an excellent federal pact – the Union dealing with the transnational technical–rational requirements of the modern age while the individual nation states protect areas of culture and individuality.

There can be no doubt that the prime reason why, if the step was taken to move beyond the existing Union towards the creation of a European state, a federal rather than a unitary system of government would be essential, is the need to protect the cultural individuality of the nation states. To this extent the division of powers suggested above has an element of validity in it. However it is difficult if not impossible to imagine a European state, whether federal or unitary, in which the central authorities are seen solely as the technical means to solve technical problems. Unions may be able to exist as 'useful mechanisms', but states are more than this. People must be able to identify with them.

In other words, if the telos of European integration is the creation of a European state, then the development of a sense of cultural and historical individuality, which critically involves education, cannot be seen as being completely divorced from the sphere of activity of the European institutions. A state may not presuppose a unitary form of government, but it does presuppose unity, a common will in place of a pact, and the history of state building in Europe tells us that one of the most important generators of this common will is a common sense of historical and cultural individuality.

The emergence of a European federation thus depends critically on the development of a stronger sense of Europe's cultural and historical identity. This does not imply the elimination of the cultural individuality of the existing nation states. The cultural diversity of the states gives Europe a distinctive character, and marks it off from the two great continental states that flank it, the United States and Russia. To destroy or uproot this diversity, whether in the name of technical progress, or of some 'new' European culture, would be to destroy part of Europe's own identity. The development of a stronger sense of European identity must clearly supplement, not supplant, the various national identities. More precisely it must retain them while transforming the way they are felt and understood. They must come to be seen for what they are: different manifestations of one culture, different branches of one tree and different children of one family. European culture has to be seen not as a discrete thing standing over or above or behind the individual nations but as working through their very history and being.

The immanence of European culture in its diversity – the innumerable cross-cuttings, continuities, analogies, cross-fertilisations, repetitions, borrowings – is something that good historians can and do portray, but it needs to be brought more energetically into the bloodstream of education in the various states. The prevailing vision of national histories in Europe as so many parallel lines that sometimes intersect has to be transmuted into a vision of them as so many branches of a larger network of tracks reaching back into the past and forward into the future.

Considerable work has been done in this area. The Council of Europe has a long record of encouraging the awareness of Europe as a cultural entity, and the European Commission has made several educational initiatives aimed at spreading knowledge of European integration. The College of Europe in Bruges and the European University Institute in Florence represent modest steps towards the founding of a fully fledged federal university for Europe. The European Union must identify itself much more vigorously with this kind of cultural and educational work, if a widespread sense of European nationality is to take root.

It has already been sufficiently emphasised that the growth of national consciousness has always been the resultant of many forces interacting. The will to counter and to match the powers that exist beyond one's borders is at once state and nation building, and it is obvious that the growth of such a will depends very largely on how these external powers develop and behave, which can never be wholly predictable. The simple existence of common institutions, such as now exist in Europe, may gradually form a common or 'national' consciousness. Most federal unions in the past have been 'incubators' in this way for the growth of national feeling. Time and habit and interaction are huge factors. Common symbols play an important role. These truths do not obviate the need for a more sustained effort within the existing Union along the lines mentioned. If further integration – in the form of the creation of a common European defence, for example, or the fuller democratisation of the institutions, or, looking further ahead, the attempt to pass beyond union to federation – is seen as a purely technical matter, without a profound psychological or spiritual dimension, then the danger of it backfiring increases simultaneously. People at large, and their leaders, will have to come to identify themselves as Europeans, and to see in Europe itself a value of transcendent worth, which demands full political embodiment, for these major steps to succeed.

Federation and nationalism: some historical analogies

Having argued that European integration is inherently a federal process which has as its logical end point the establishment of a federation, and having argued simultaneously that a federation is a state, and that the establishment of a state, in the modern world, is intimately and necessarily entwined with the creation of a nation, it is worth turning briefly to the history of the formation of some well-known federations to see if the way that they emerged supports these contentions.

In the case of the United States it is worth recalling first that in the Philadelphia Convention of 1787, that framed the federal constitution that has survived until today, the initiative was taken, not by a group who saw themselves as federalist, but by a group who expressly wished to replace the existing federal structure by a 'national' one. The 'national' party represented a movement of opinion that had developed in America well before the summoning of the Convention.[5] They had been dissatisfied from the start with the Confederation of 1781 (a classic 'federal union' in the sense that it has been defined earlier) and they wanted to replace it by something far stronger. Alexander Hamilton was their greatest spokesman, and in his letter to Duane in 1780 their policy is already clearly outlined.[6]

In the Philadelphia Convention their objectives are plain. In place of the existing treaty-based federal system they wanted one based on a constitution, and they recognised quite clearly the difference between these two things. In place of the existing Congress (or council of states, as we might call it) they wanted to create a 'National' Legislature, a 'National' Executive and a 'National' Judiciary. The separate states which together formed the Confederation, were to be transformed into the local government agencies of a single state.

If we ask what, in overall terms, the proponents of the national plan meant by it, we must answer that they wanted to replace the existing federal system by a single state, which would rest on the foundations of one American people, or on the citizens of the various states considered as one undivided body. The constitution of this new state would have to be approved by the people in this sense. The legislative and executive of the new state would have to be elected by the people, and the laws made by the legislature would in turn have to apply directly to the people and to be enforced directly on them. The word 'nation' here cannot be separated from the idea of a state. The national party wanted the American people quite simply to form a state, with all the unity, power and independence that this word implies. That they saw the people as having a collective identity almost goes without saying, it was an assumption inherent in their demands.

What deserves to be noted is that the widespread sense of a distinctive American identity in 1787 was not based on language. To be sure the fact that the Americans had a common language enormously facilitated their political integration. However the American sense of sharing a distinctive, historically evolved identity, which made them different from other peoples, and which indeed gave them a sense of mission in the world, was not founded by them on the fact that they all spoke English. That would scarcely have distinguished them from the enemy they had just defeated! It was founded primarily on the fact that, in a world of monarchies, they were republican – with all the emotive resonances of that profoundly ambiguous term – and that they had successfully asserted the validity of republican principles against those who wished to extinguish them.

This is why so many of the *Federalist Papers*, written to persuade the people of the State of New York to ratify the constitution that finally emerged from the Convention, are not devoted, as one might have expected, to an exposition of federal principles, but rather to a defence of the republican quality of the new government. As Madison wrote:

> The first question that offers itself is, whether the general form and aspect of (the new) government be strictly republican. It is evident that no other form would be reconcilable with the genius of the people of America; with the fundamental principles of the Revolution; or with that honourable determination which animates every votary of freedom, to rest all our political experiments on the capacity of mankind for self-government. If the plan of the convention, therefore, be found to depart from its republican character, its advocates must abandon it as no longer defensible.[7]

The national party, needless to say, met with opposition in the Convention. Seventeen days after the presentation of their plan, an alternative one was presented which was 'purely federal'. This proposed essentially a strengthening of the existing Confederation, not its transformation into a new state. It is not necessary to enter into the details of this plan. Suffice it to say that the national party acknowledged, in the course of the ensuing debate, the need to give the existing states, which formed the pillars of the old Union, an assured status within their new overarching polity: the 13 states could not simply be abolished, they had to be incorporated into the new structure. The political body that was finally agreed upon by the Convention, and was to become the prototype of a 'federal state' in the centuries that followed was the product of a strong drive to create a nation state accommodating itself to a conservative reluctance to go beyond a strengthened 'federal union'. Without the conservative element the new polity would not have been federal; but without the national element it is dubious if it would have borne any resemblance to a state.

The circumstances of the creation of the Canadian federation, or, to use the language of the time, the 'Confederation of the Colonies of British

North America as the Dominion of Canada', which took place in 1867, seem at first sight so remote from the situation that obtains in Europe today, or in America in 1787, as to make any parallels or 'lessons' unlikely. The units that were federated were colonies; the statute that created the federation was passed by the British Parliament; the context was imperial. Nevertheless, the fact that the Canadian federation embraced from the start communities differentiated by language, religion, civil law and social habit, makes it of peculiar relevance to a consideration of the prospects of European federation. Does the Canadian example contradict the argument that federation presupposes a national sentiment?

At the risk of simplification, it may be said that the linguistic, religious and cultural nationality of the French Canadian population was the main (though not the only) factor which ensured that the structure of the new Canadian polity would be federal and not unitary, or in other words, that the various provinces would retain real rights and powers and not be reduced to local government agencies. It is well known that Macdonald, who played such a vital role in the promotion, elaboration and adoption of the scheme of Confederation, was originally in favour of a unitary system of government, or what he called 'legislative union'. He admitted frankly that it was the determination of the French-speaking population not to lose their 'individuality', and a similar feeling on the part of the Maritime Provinces, that persuaded him to endorse a federal solution.[8]

When we change the question, and ask, not what ensured that the new political unity of Canada would be a federal one, but what made Canadians demand the creation of a new political unity, we find that nationality enters the picture again but in a different way. It is not my purpose here to rehearse all the factors, constitutional, political, economic, internal, external, immediate and long term, which led to the formation of the Confederation, something which has been done well many times. My purpose is at once narrower and broader: to try and define the 'national' assumption that ran like a thread through so many of these specific factors.

This is not to suggest that there was a broad-based national 'movement' in favour of the 1867 constitution. Confederation, at the time of its adoption aroused 'little if any popular enthusiasm'.[9] The group of able statesmen who framed and secured the adoption of the constitution had powerful backing in their respective provinces, but the constitution itself was never put directly to the people. Nevertheless the ideas of these men are highly significant. The leaders in the coalition government that pushed through the project of Confederation in the Province of Canada, both French speakers and English speakers, were in remarkable agreement on the need to transform the various colonies of British North America into a 'great nation' and to create a 'new nationality', alongside the United States, on the continent.

As early as 1859, George Brown, who at that time was only proposing a federation between the two halves of the Province of Canada – today's Ontario and Quebec – was asked if his proposed federation was a step towards nationality, and he replied: 'I do place the question on grounds of nationality. I hope there is not one Canadian in this Assembly who does not look forward with high hope to the day when these northern countries shall stand out among the nations of the world as one great confederation.'[10] Similarly Macdonald, arguing for federation of all the provinces in 1860, said:

> We were approaching to the population of the United States at the time they declared their independence; we were standing at the very threshold of nations, and when admitted we should occupy no unimportant position among the nations of the world.

In his great parliamentary speech of 1865, recommending the adoption of the new constitution, he made the same point. It seemed to him, as well as to all the statesmen who helped to frame the constitution, whether of French or English background,

> I think it will so appear to the people of this country, that, if we wish to be a great people; if we wish to form – using the expression which was sneered at the other evening – a great nationality, commanding the respect of the world, able to hold our own against all opponents, and to defend those institutions we prize ... this can only be obtained by a union.[11]

Most interesting of all were the opinions of the undisputed leader of the French Canadian community, George Etienne Cartier, expressed in the same debate. Time and again he reiterated that the time had come for all the provinces to form 'a great nation'. In ancient times, he said, nations had grown outwards from one centre.

> This is not the case in modern times. Nations now are formed by the joining together of various people having similar interests and sympathies. Such is our position at the present time. Objection is made to our project, because of the words 'a new nationality'. But if we unite we will form a political nationality independent of the national origin and religion of individuals. Some have regretted that we have a distinction of races, and have expressed the hope that, in time, this diversity will disappear. The idea of a fusion of all races is utopian; it is impossibility. Distinctions of this character will always exist; diversity is the order of the physical, moral, and political world.[12]

Cartier, in other words, had no wish to fuse or abolish the different ethnic communities that existed in Canada. He strongly opposed a unitary system of government such as Macdonald originally wanted. He wanted a federal system of government precisely to accommodate 'the differences in races and local interests'. At the same time he wanted no mere 'federal union' of the type that has been defined earlier in this discussion; he wanted the new Confederation to be the foundation of a new nation, by which he meant in essence a new state, a new power on a level with the other powers that made up the international world, a state that would enable the provinces of British North America to transcend 'a mere provincial existence',[13] and would enable Canadians as Canadians, rather than as French- or English-speaking Canadians, to gain a voice in the world.

This leads one of course to ask what characterised Canadians as Canadians. What was *their* individuality, to use Macdonald's term? Cartier said that modern nations were founded by 'various' people having 'similar interests and sympathies'. That the provinces of British North America had similar interests – particularly economic interests – may be readily accepted, but what did Cartier mean by similar 'sympathies'? Did Cartier perceive a common ethos permeating Canadians irrespective of their racial origins and religious beliefs? The same speech indicates that he did. In it Cartier reviewed the early history of the Province of Quebec, and he underlined the fact that at the critical time of the American Revolution, the French Canadians stoutly resisted the attempts of the Americans to wean them away from British rule and to incorporate them in the United States. 'The French Canadians refused to respond to an appeal which had for its object the complete overthrow of the monarchical system in America.' 'They understood that they would preserve intact their institutions, their language and their religion by adhesion to the British Crown.' As part of the United States, they 'would have seen their nationality disappear'.

These historical facts, he went on, 'teach us that French-Canadians and English-speaking Canadians should have for each other a mutual sympathy, having both reason to congratulate themselves that Canada is still a British colony'.

> The Americans united with the object of perpetuating democracy on this continent; we, who have had the advantage of seeing republicanism in operation for a period of eighty years, of perceiving its faults and its vices, have been convinced that purely democratic institutions cannot assure the peace and prosperity of nations, and that we must unite under a federation so formed as to perpetuate the monarchical element. The difference between our neighbours and ourselves is essential. The preservation of the monarchical principle will be the great feature of our confederation, whilst on the other side of the line the dominant power is the will of the masses, of the populace.[14]

'The difference between our neighbours and ourselves is essential.' As we have seen, American national sentiment at the time when their federal constitution was framed was entwined with republicanism; Canadian national sentiment at the time when their federal constitution was framed was entwined with adherence to the monarchical principle. Adherence to monarchy in this context must not, however, be seen in a narrow way as if it meant simply support for a particular organisation of the executive power (though this was undeniably important). It encompassed a whole range of attitudes about society and its proper ordering which have lived on in Canada to the present day.[15] The desire of the political leaders of British North America to create one powerful Canadian state or nation was rooted in a deep seated will to resist annexation, assimilation or absorption by the United States, whether economic, political or cultural. The great power of the United States on their border was seen as threatening and dangerous because the United States represented a radical, levelling, homogenising and seemingly anarchic democracy that was antipathetic to the sentiments of most Canadians, whether of French or British extraction.

Turning finally to Switzerland, the transformation there from federal union to federal state in 1848 is again instructive about the interrelationship of federalism, nationality and statehood. It is particularly instructive for Europeans because, of course, Switzerland is a European country, and in its religious, linguistic and ethnic diversity mirrors in miniature the diversity that exists in Europe as a whole.

The movement that transformed Switzerland into a state in 1848 was a national one. The framing of the new constitution, which was for the first time a genuine constitution, that is to say a statute endorsed by the people, and no longer merely a pact between the cantons, was the culmination of a dynamic movement for the regeneration of the country that had welled up in 1829–30 and that had flowed at an irregular pace throughout the land in the ensuing two decades. This movement was powerfully stimulated by the French Revolution of 1830, and like this revolution it represented a resurfacing of the 'ideas of 1789' after the period of reaction that had followed the defeat of Napoleon. Its leaders called themselves liberals, progressives or radicals, and they sought change first at the level of the cantons and then at the level of the Confederation. Their extremism provoked a very short civil war in 1847, in which the opponents of reform were routed. In the calm aftermath the radicals were able to draft the new constitution.

The ideas and aims of the progressives were national in two senses. On the one hand they embodied the 'rational-liberal' variety of nationalism that has been defined earlier. They wished to sweep away the economic and political privileges and barriers that had hitherto fragmented the Swiss people and to assert their rights as one body of equal citizens, able to go about their business within one national economy, and governed by one representative national assembly. Undoubtedly the more extreme radicals wanted to change Switzerland into a unitary state. What distinguished the Swiss constitutional transformation, however, was that the leaders of the victorious radical movement realised that the cantons, who were the pillars of the existing federal system, and who represented the religious, linguistic and ethnic distinctions amongst the people, could not simply be thrown into the melting pot and reconstituted as departments *à la française*, but had to be found a place in the new political structure. As in the United States of America, it was the incorporation of the old federal structure into the new overarching national structure, by means primarily of an upper legislative assembly representing the states or cantons as such, which created the new federal state.

The ideas of the progressives were national in a second, more obvious sense. They wanted Switzerland to be able to stand up henceforth to the powers that encircled it and that were constantly intervening or threatening to intervene in its affairs. They wanted Switzerland to be one in the conduct of foreign affairs and to have an army of its own capable of guaranteeing its security. They wanted it to have equal status to the states that surrounded it. Given the humiliations that the country had recently suffered this appeal for strength and independence vis-à-vis the foreigner struck a chord in all segments of the population, and gripped even the conservatives. To be a nation in this context meant to be a full participant in international politics.[16]

Was there also a consciousness of the Swiss as a 'historical' nation in the sense that was outlined earlier, that is to say as an historically evolved community with a distinctive character and role in the world? It would be misleading to claim that national feeling of this kind was a major motivating force in the revolution that took place in 1848. The latter was above all forward-looking. However it is important to realise that such a feeling had been maturing in Switzerland since at least the middle of the eighteenth century. The foundation of the Helvetic Society in 1762 was an important milestone. Bringing together German and French speakers, and Catholics and Protestants, and aiming at the 'enthusiastic awakening of the consciousness of Swiss interdependence',[17] it worked as a leaven amongst the intellectual classes of the country during the remainder of the century. Then there were the path-breaking historical works of Muller, starting in 1780, and culminating in his monumental *History of the Swiss Confederation*. Muller strove to create and instil a sense of the great past achievements of the country as a whole; to the surprise of the educated reading public, as one historian has put it, 'he showed them Switzerland as a nation'.[18] The ambitious educational ideals of the short-lived Helvetic Republic (1798–1800), and the idealistic vision of Helvetia's mission in Europe and the world, as a uniter and mediator of people of different race and language, that was propagated at that time, deserve also to be mentioned. Finally in the peaceful period of the Mediation (1802–13) interest in Swiss history, geography and culture in all its forms blossomed as never before, and made its impact at all levels of society. In a word, although the sense of the Swiss as a distinct historically evolved community may not have played a separate operative role in the constitutional transformation of 1848, it was something which had grown up and taken root in the country well before that. This sense was not based on the possession of a common language, but on a dawning realisation that common experiences reaching back far into the past, common institutions and a common geographical ambience, had welded together one people with a common way of doing things and of viewing the world, and with a common role to play within it.

Conclusion

It is time to draw the threads together. The European Union, it has been argued, is a federal union. Its historical evolution, and the ends that are implicit in it, suggest that it will, at some future date, seek to transform itself into a federation. That is its logical destiny.

The changes that this transformation would imply in the base and super-structure of the Union have been outlined. In trying to gauge the possibility of such a transformation I have stressed that the making of a federation is first and foremost the making of a state, and that the making of a state, in the modern world, is entwined with the assertion of nationhood, or, to put it at its bluntest, that the modern state is the resultant of a people's will to enjoy a political existence, that is to say, to defend, govern and assert itself in the world. That there are important variations in the meaning of the word 'nation' has not been denied – they have been described at some length – but the variations are not seen as invalidating these general propositions.

The transformation of the European federal union into a federation thus implies the presence of a sense of European nationhood and the will to estab-lish a state to represent, in the fullest sense of the word, that nation. This state will be specifically 'federal' not because it will abolish the existing 'nation states' – France, Germany and so on – but because it will incorporate them as living units into its own national structure, just as the existing states, provinces and cantons were incorporated into the national structure of America, Canada and Switzerland when they became federations. The crux is that it is the sense of being or becoming – we must allow the language to be flexible here – one nation that provides the dynamic, the motor, for this kind of transformation; federalism denotes the tempering, moderating impulse which ensures that existing structures, existing communities, exist-ing nationalities, are embedded firmly in the new state. In the move beyond union to federation, federalism is, so to speak, the snaffle, bit and rein; the will to be a nation-cum-state is the horse.

It might seem as if this deduction rules out the possibility of Europe ever becoming a federation, given that the people of the continent, and of the newly enlarged Union, are divided by so many linguistic and ethnic bound-aries as to make the concept of a pan-European nation unimaginable. However this, it has been argued, is not the case. A sense of nationhood is intimately entwined with a sense of belonging to the same historically evolved community; there can be no question about that. Those who lightly accept that Turkey, for example, should be a full member of the European Union, must, if the analysis which has been presented here is correct, think the matter through again, because it is loaded with implications for the future. At the same time the sense of belonging to one historically evolved community is not necessarily or exclusively the prerogative of those who speak the same native language or have the same lineage or descent. There is no inherent reason why, under the pressure and influence of innumerable factors, operating both within and without the European Union, the sense of belonging to one European people should not generate the will to form one state for Europe as a whole.

Notes

1 David Lasserre, *Etapes du Federalisme: L'Experience Suisse* (Lausanne: Editions Rencontre, 1954), p. 180.
2 Peter Norman, *The Accidental Constitution: The Story of the European Convention* (Brussels: EuroComment, 2003), p. 11. In the discussion that follows I have relied mainly on Norman's account of the Convention, and on the text of the Draft Constitutional Treaty that he appends to it.
3 Krzysztof Pomian, *L'Europe et ses Nations* (Paris: Gallimard, 1990), p. 156.
4 Pomian (1990), p. 157.
5 See especially Merrill Jensen, *The New Nation: A History of the United States during the Confederation 1781–1789* (New York: Vintage, 1950), p. 43ff.
6 Jensen (1950), p. 50.
7 *The Federalist*, No. XXXIX.
8 Speech of Attorney-General Macdonald on the Confederation of British North America, 6 February 1865. Reprinted in A.P. Newton (ed.), *Federal and Unified Constitutions* (London: Longmans, 1923), pp. 177–90.
9 John Boyd, *Sir George Etienne Cartier, Bart.: His Life and Times* (Freeport: Books for Libraries, 1971, a reprint of the original edition of 1914), p. 276.
10 Boyd (1971), p. 184.
11 Boyd (1971), p. 182.
12 Boyd (1971), pp. 222–3.
13 Boyd (1971), p. 222.
14 Boyd (1971), pp. 221–2.
15 J.L. Morton spells out the full meaning of the emphasis on monarchy at the time of Confederation in his book *The Canadian Identity* (Toronto: University of Toronto, 1972), pp. 104–7, though his argument that the Fathers of Confederation did not consider that the new political structure was federal hardly squares with their express statements.
16 The internal and external aspects of the national movement in Switzerland at this time are well described by Edgar Bonjour in his address '*Die Errichtung des Schweizerischen Bundesstaates*', included in *Die Schweiz und Europa* (Basel: Helbing and Lichtenhahn, 1958), pp. 381–94. See also the volume of which H. Bonjour, S. Offler and G.R. Potter were joint authors: *A Short History of Switzerland* (Oxford: Clarendon, 1952), pp. 243–73.
17 Karl Dandliker, *A Short History of Switzerland* (London: Swan Sonnenschein, 1899), p. 196.
18 Bonjour *et al.* (1952), p. 238.

10 Federation and managing nations[1]

John McGarry and Brendan O'Leary

Federalism is a normative political philosophy that recommends the use of federal principles, i.e. combining joint action and self-government (King 1982). 'Federal political systems' is a descriptive catch-all term for all political organizations that combine what Daniel Elazar called 'shared rule and self-rule'. Federal political systems, thus broadly construed, include federations, confederations, federacies, associated states, condominiums, leagues and cross-border functional authorities (Elazar 1987). Federations are very distinct federal political systems (Watts 1998; Watts 1987), distinguished from both union states and unitary states – where central institutions claim a monopoly over sovereignty. In a genuinely democratic federation there is a compound sovereign state, in which at least two governmental units, the federal and the regional, enjoy constitutionally separate competencies – although they may also have concurrent powers. Both the federal and the regional governments are empowered to deal directly with their citizens, and the relevant citizens directly elect (at least some components of) the federal and regional governments. In a federation the federal government usually cannot unilaterally alter the horizontal division of powers: constitutional change affecting competencies requires the consent of both levels of government. Therefore federation automatically implies a codified and written constitution, and normally is accompanied at the federal level by a supreme court, charged with umpiring differences between the governmental tiers, and by a bicameral legislature – in which the federal as opposed to the popular chamber may disproportionately represent the smallest regions. Elazar emphasized the 'covenantal' character of federations, i.e. the authority of each government is derived from a constitution and convention rather than from another government.

Federations vary in the extent to which they are majoritarian in character, but most constrain the power of federation-wide majorities. They constrain the federal demos, though there is extensive variation in this respect (Stepan 2001: 340–57). The United States, Australia and Brazil allow equal representation to each of their regions in the federal chamber, which means massive over-representation for the smaller ones. Other federations also over-represent less populous units, but not to this extent. Federations differ additionally in the competences granted the federal chamber. Some, such as the US Senate are extremely powerful and is arguably more powerful than the House of Representatives because of its special powers over nominations to public office and in treaty making; others, including those in Canada, India and Belgium are weak (Watts 1999: 93–4). Constitutional change can be blocked by individual regions in some instances, although normally a veto requires a coalition of regions. A federation is majoritarian to the extent that it lacks consociational practices of executive power-sharing, proportionality principles of representation and allocation, cultural autonomy and veto rights; and it is majoritarian to the extent that it lacks consensual institutions or practices – such as the separation of powers, bills of rights, and courts and monetary institutions insulated from immediate governing majorities. A majoritarian federation concentrates power resources at the federal level and facilitates executive and legislative dominance either by a popularly endorsed executive president or by a single party premier and cabinet.

The federal principle of separate competencies says nothing about how much power each governmental level enjoys. Regions in some federations may enjoy less de facto power than those in decentralized unitary states. Moreover the constitutional division of powers (even as interpreted by the courts) is not always an accurate guide to policy-making autonomy and discretion enjoyed by different tiers. Some powers may have fallen into abeyance, or the superior financial and political resources of one level (usually the federal) may allow it to interfere in the other's jurisdiction. A better indicator of the degree of autonomy enjoyed by regions may be the proportion of public spending that is under the control of the respective levels (for such measurements see Watts 2001: 29 and Lijphart 1979: 504).

A key distinction for our purposes is that federations can be multinational/multi-ethnic or mono-national in character.[2] In the former, the boundaries of the internal units are usually drawn in such a way that at least some of them are controlled by national or ethnic minorities. In addition, more than one nationality may be explicitly recognized as co-founders and co-owners of the federation. The first such federation was Switzerland, established in its current form in 1848 – though its status as a multinational federation is debated: Swiss typically insist they share a common nationhood while recognizing the languages, religions and historicity of its multiple cantons. The second, Canada, was established in 1867, and was regarded – at least in francophone eyes – as a binational, bilingual and bi-religious federation. The Indian subcontinent was divided after decolonization into the two multi-ethnic federations of India and Pakistan. Africa has two official federations, Ethiopia and Nigeria, while South Africa is also federal except in name. Ethiopia is officially multinational; whereas Nigeria and South Africa are national federations which recognize multilingual and pluralist social facts. The communist Soviet Union, Yugoslavia and Czechoslovakia were organized as multinational federations, and the Russian Republic (RSFSR), one of the constituent units of the Soviet Union, was itself organized along multinational federal lines. These communist federations did not bestow genuine democratic self-government on their minorities, and fell apart in the early 1990s, though Yugoslavia continued as a dyadic federation incorporating Serbia and Montenegro until 2003, when it was transformed into a confederation renamed Serbia and Montenegro that later dissolved into two independent states. Bosnia became a multinational federation under the internationally enforced Dayton Agreement of 1995, with one of its units itself being another binational federation of Bosnians and Croats. Belgium has recently evolved into a binational federation, and both Euro-optimists and pessimists think that the European Union (EU) is moving toward a federation. Multinational federations have been proposed for a significant number of other divided places, including Afghanistan,[3] Burma, China, Cyprus, Georgia and Indonesia.[4] Iraq has become one (O'Leary *et al.* 2005).

National federations may be nationally homogeneous (or predominantly so), or they are organized, often consciously, so as not to recognize more than one official nationality. Often this happens in such a way that the state's national and ethnic minorities are also minorities in each of the constituent units. The official goal behind national federation is nation building, the elimination of internal national (and perhaps also ethnic) differences. The founding and paradigmatic example of a national federation is the United States. Its model was adopted by the Latin American federations of Mexico, Argentina, Brazil and Venezuela. Germany, Austria, Australia and the United Arab Emirates are also national federations. American and American-educated intellectuals often propose national federations as a way to deal with ethnic heterogeneity in post-colonial and post-communist societies.

Federations can also be distinguished according to their level of democracy. Some, such as Canada, the United States and Belgium should be seen as maturely democratic; others, such as Malaysia and Nigeria, as partially democratic; and still others, such as the communist federations of the Soviet Union, Yugoslavia and Czechoslovakia as undemocratic. But there is an increasingly popular view in the academic literature on federalism that this distinction is unimportant. A number of prominent American academics interpret the failings of the communist federations as an indictment of (multinational) federalism per se (Brubaker 1996; Bunce 1999; Leff 1998; Roeder 1991). This book is, however, about democratic federations; and one of our arguments is that democracy matters, crucially, as does the type of democratic system. Indeed, there is not yet an example of an established democratic multinational federation – though Nigeria had to be rebuilt after a major civil war, and the jury is out on the fate of Iraq.

This chapter is primarily concerned with multinational (and multi-ethnic) federations because we regard national federations largely as devices associated with integrationist or assimilationist politics – which are not the subject of this volume. We shall first discuss the debate on the value and

Table 10.1 Examples of national and multinational or multi-ethnic federations

National federations	Duration	Multinational or multi-ethnic federations	Duration
Argentina	1853–	Belgium	1993–
Australia	1901–	Bosnia-Herzegovina	1995–
Austria	1920–	Burma	1948–
Brazil	1891–	Cameroon	1961–72
Germany	1949–	Canada	1867–
Mexico	1917–	Czechoslovakia	1968–92
United Arab Emirates	1971–	Ethiopia	1992–
United States	1789–	India	1947(50)–
Venezuela	1960–*	Iraq	2005–
		Malaya	1957–63
		Malaysia	1963–
		Mali	1959–60
		Nigeria	1960–66; 1969
		Pakistan**	1971–
		Russia	1993–
		Soviet Union	1918–91
		St Kitts-Nevis	1983–
		Switzerland	1848–
		West Indies Federation	1958–62
		Federal Republic of Yugoslavia (Serbia and Montenegro)	1992–2003***
		Yugoslavia (Communist)	1953–92

Notes
*   Venezuela abolished its Senate in 1999.
**   Pakistan (before the secession of Bangladesh).
***   The Federal Republic of Yugoslavia (Serbia and Montenegro) was transformed into the confederal union of Serbia and Montenegro in February 2003 but dissolved into two independent states in June 2006.

feasibility of federations as management devices for ethnic and national differences, then the track record of multinational federations in mitigating conflict, and conclude with an analysis of the factors that contribute to their success and failure.

Nationalism and federalism in practical political design and argument

There are four important positions on the value of federation as a method of accommodating national and ethnic minorities, all of which have been articulated by intellectuals, constitutional lawyers and political scientists, and have had an effect on the design of particular states.

Jacobin unitarism: federation as state destroying

In the French revolutionary tradition, associated with the Jacobins, federalism was regarded as part of the counter-revolution, hostile to the necessity of linguistic homogenization, a road block in the path of authentic, indivisible, monistic popular sovereignty. Rather than accommodating minorities through self-government, the Jacobins sought cultural assimilation; they were determined to make peasants into Frenchmen; and therefore they were deeply hostile to all forms of accommodation that inhibited this goal, including federalism. The Jacobin response to diversity was a strong unitary state and one French nation. This tradition survives in contemporary France, where it is central to the myth of the French Republic (Hayward 1993).[5] Federalism, with its multiple governments, is seen by those in the Jacobin tradition as incompatible with equal citizenship and a sovereign people. This is not just a concern about regional governments creating uneven ('patchwork quilt') public policy provisions. Latter-day Jacobins cannot accept the federal principle that allows citizens in regions with small populations to be over-represented at the expense of those in more populous regions, and they have difficulty with the federal idea of a judicial umpire who can overrule the people's elected representatives. Both facts explain the reported French astonishment at George Bush Jr being elected US President in 2000 with fewer popular votes than his opponent (a result of the disproportionality inherent in the Electoral College, and a partial by-product of the US's federal system), and the incumbency being effectively decided by the federal Supreme Court (Ferenczi 2001).

Modern Jacobins think that the political recognition and accommodation of minorities and ethnocentrism go together. If minorities do not want to promote ethnocentrism, the argument goes, why do they seek self-government? Jacobins think that political recognition of multiple nations or ethnic communities leads to regressive government and discrimination against minorities dominated by local regional majorities, and institutionalizes and reinforces divisions, endangering unity. These views are shared on the left and right. Communists claimed that Paris's proposals to give self-government to Corsica would undermine 'solidarity between Corsican and French workers, who can only defend their interests by working together', and would lead to discriminatory measures against those on the island who are not of Corsican descent.[6] The then French Interior Minister, Pierre Chevenement, resigned over the proposals, protesting that they would lead to an 'island ruled by an underworld that spends three-quarters of its energy settling accounts and internal battles'.[7] While the proposals for Corsica fall short of federation, both Chevenement and the French President, Jacques Chirac, attacked them as leading in that direction: Brittany, Alsace, Savoy, as well as French Basques and Catalonians, would allegedly follow Corsica's lead (Ferenczi 2001: 42).[8] Ultimately, in this view, federation promotes state break-up, with the attendant risks of ethnic cleansing and Matryoschka-doll secessions emerging as ethnic nationalism takes hold.

The Jacobin view that unitarism is needed for unity, if not always its support for civic equality and popular sovereignty, is replicated throughout the world. It was the dominant view in Great Britain until recently, particularly among Conservatives. Most ex-colonies in Africa, Asia and the Caribbean have shunned federation as an obstacle to economic development, political stability and state unity. Post-colonial state builders' antipathy to federalism is now matched amongst the intellectuals and governing elites of Eastern Europe, who regard it as a recipe for disaster, given the Czechoslovakian, Yugoslavian and Soviet experiences. Federalism is their 'f' word. The recent emergent principle of international law, stemming from the report of the Badinter Commission on the former Yugoslavia, that permits the disintegration of federations along the lines of their existing regional units, has strengthened the belief that federation should not be considered a desirable form of multinational or multi-ethnic accommodation (Horowitz 1998; Weller 1992). Several Eastern European states have moved in the opposite direction in recent years. They seceded from multinational federations and replaced them with what Brubaker calls 'nationalizing' states, that is, states that are tightly centralized and controlled by their dominant national community.

Ironically, the Jacobin argument that federation is incompatible with nation building is shared by 'hard-line' nationalists trapped inside states controlled by other nations. They concur that nation and state should be congruent, although they disagree on the appropriate boundaries of the state. This has been the position of Quebec's *Parti Quebecois*, particularly the faction around the ex-Premier, Jacques Parizeau, and of Basque Nationalists in Batasuna. It was also the view of the Turkish-Cypriot leadership under Rauf Denktash, the Chechens and, until very recently, the Liberation Tigers of Tamil Eelam. Such hardliners seek independence as unitary, sovereign and indivisible nation states, though some are prepared to consider confederation.[9]

Federalism as nation building

Unlike the Jacobins, who see (state) nationalism and federation as inconsistent, some exponents of federalism think that (state) nationalism and federation go together. The earliest federalists in the German-speaking Swiss lands, and in what became the Netherlands, the USA, and the second German Reich were 'national federalists', i.e. they saw the prime function of federalism as being 'to unite people living in different political units, who nevertheless shared a common language and culture' (Forsyth 1989: 4). They maintained that only an autonomous federal government could perform certain necessary functions that confederations or alliances found difficult to perform, especially a unified defence and external relations policy (Riker 1964). They advocated federation as a tool for nation building and sometimes saw it as a stepping stone towards a more centralized unitary state.

The USA is the paradigm national federation. Americans now equate 'national' and their 'federal' government. Americans have little difficulty with what Jacobins consider the 'demos-constraining' features of federalism: autonomy for regions or states (non-centralization); the over-representation of small states in upper chambers; electoral colleges; and constitutional amending formulas which require widespread consensus among states. In fact, Stepan has argued that the United States competes with Brazil for the title of the world's most demos-constraining federation (Stepan 2001: 334). The attractiveness of demos-constraining institutions reflect the historic stress of some Americans on liberty rather than equality. The American founding myth is of colonies that won independence from empire. Many Americans reject the strong state favoured by French republicans and praise federation precisely because it diffuses power to multiple points. American exponents, such as Riker, have argued that the demos-constraining features of American federalism are liberal because they protect individuals from populist majorities (Riker 1964). Americans insisted on a federation for post-war Germany, because they were convinced it would make a resurgence of fascism less likely. The view that federation is essential to liberty is central to American discourse, in spite of the chequered history of federation in Latin America, as well as in Pakistan, Nigeria and the USSR.

But America's makers and their celebrants have taken the position that federation is antithetical to nation building if it is multinational, multi-ethnic, or 'ethnofederal'. As the United States expanded south-westward from its original largely homogeneous (except for African slaves) 13 colonies, it was decided that no territory would receive statehood unless minorities were outnumbered by White Anglo-Saxon Protestants (WASPs) (Glazer 1983). Sometimes, the technique employed was to gerrymander state boundaries to ensure that Indians or Hispanics were outnumbered, as in Florida. At other times, as in Hawaii and the south-west, statehood was delayed until the region's long-standing residents could be swamped with enough WASP settlers. American authorities were even sceptical of immigrant groups concentrating in particular locations lest this lead to ethnically-based demands for self-government, and grants of public land were denied to ethnic groups in order to promote their dispersal; William Penn dissuaded Welsh immigrants from setting up their own self-governing barony in Pennsylvania (Gordon 1964: 133). In consequence, the US federation shows 'little coincidence between ethnic groups and state boundaries' (Glazer 1983: 276). We submit that it is no accident that National federation was part and parcel of American nation building, aiding the homogenization of white settlers and immigrants in the famous melting pot of Anglo conformity (Gordon 1964). Celebration of the homogeneity of the founding people is evident in *The Federalist Papers* (see especially John Jay's assumptions in Madison *et al.* 1788/1987: paper II).[10]

America's experience has informed an integrationist argument on how federalism can be used to manage divisions in contemporary ethnically heterogeneous societies. Donald Horowitz (1985: chs 14 and 15) and Daniel Elazar (Elazar 1994: 168), building on earlier work by S.M. Lipset (1960)[11], suggest that federations can be partly designed to prevent ethnic minorities from becoming local provincial majorities. The strategic thinking here is to weaken potentially competing ethno-nationalisms: federalism's territorial merits are said to lie in the fact that it can be used as an instrument to prevent local majoritarianism with its attendant risks of tyrannies of the local majority, or of secessionist incentives. The provincial borders of the federated units on this argument, should be designed on 'balance of power' principles – proliferating, where possible, the points of power away from one focal centre, encouraging intra-ethnic conflict, and creating incentives for inter-ethnic cooperation (by designing provinces without majorities), and for alignments based on non-ethnic interests. The argument is that the boundaries of federal units should precisely not allow any minorities to become majorities in control of states. This logic is interesting, but empirical support for it seems so far confined to the rather uninspiring case of post-bellum Nigeria (Suberu 2001: 4–6). In most existing federations efforts to redraw regional borders deliberately to achieve these results would probably require the services of military dictators or one-party states. Historically mobilized ethno-national groups do not take kindly to efforts to disorganize them through the redrawing of internal political boundaries. Belgium may, however, become an interesting exception to this scepticism: the Brussels region, created in the new federation, is neither Flemish or Wallonian, and perhaps its heterogeneity will stabilize 'international' relations in Belgium, because Flanders will not secede without Brussels and there is presently little prospect of Brussels obliging Flanders.

American republicans, with a small 'r', have shared with Jacobins the view that minority nationalists are backward, in 'revolt against modernity' (Lipset 1985) or people who 'tend to subordinate all free government to [their] uncompromising position' (Elazar 1994: 128–9, 163–4). They think that it is both counterproductive and unnecessary to accommodate minority ethnicities or nationalities. This view has been strengthened by America's own experience, in the Deep South, of southern whites using their control of state governments to oppress blacks. America's experience with a disastrous civil war also attuned its intellectuals to the centrifugal potential of federalism, particularly when regions are controlled by distinct cultural communities. Eric Nordlinger, one of the first contemporary American political scientists to take an interest in ethnic conflict regulation, rejected the use of federation because he feared it would lead to state break-up and the abuse of power by ethnocentric minorities (Nordlinger 1972: 32–3; see also Tarlton 1965).

Reflecting these sentiments, a number of American academics have argued that the break-up of the former communist federations and the accompanying chaos, can be traced squarely to their 'ethno-federal' structures (Brubaker 1996; Bunce 1999; Leff 1998; Roeder 1991). Rogers Brubaker maintains that the Soviet regime went to 'remarkable lengths, long before glasnost and perestroika, to institutionalise both territorial nationhood and ethnocultural nationality as basic *cognitive* and social categories. Once political space began to expand under Gorbachev, these categories quickly came to 'structure political perception, inform political rhetoric, and organize political action' (Brubaker 1996: 9). The implication is that (at least some of) these divisive identities did not exist before the Soviet Union federated, and would not have come into play had it not federated. In Jack Snyder's view, 'ethnically based federalisms ... *create* political organisations and media markets that are centred on ethnic differences' (Snyder 2000: 327, our italics). According to him, the decision to establish ethnofederations in the Soviet Union, Czechoslovakia and Yugoslavia was *unnecessary*: 'Arguably, ethnofederalism was a strategy of rule actively chosen by its Communist founders not a necessity forced upon them by the irresistible demands of ethnic groups' (ibid.).[12] The results of ethnofederation in his view were straightforward: only the communist federations broke up and 'nationalist violence happened *only* where ... ethnofederal institutions channelled political activity along ethnic lines (USSR and Yugoslavia)' (2000: 252, our italics).

Cosmopolitans: federation as a stage in nation-transcendence

A third perspective holds that federation is capable of dissolving all national allegiances, including minority and majority nationalisms. It comes in two different variants. The first is represented by several nineteenth century anarchist and liberal federalists, notably Joseph Proudhon and Carlo Cattaneo, who were resolutely hostile to nation-state nationalism (Majocchi 1991: 162), and by many twentieth century liberal federalists, notably within the European movement (see e.g. Bosco 1992: Part Three). Such federalists have been, and are, resolutely anti-nationalist, associating both state and minority nationalisms with ethnic exclusiveness, chauvinism, racism and parochially particularistic sentiments. For them federalism belongs to an entirely different cooperative philosophy, one that offers a non-nationalist logic of legitimacy, and an antidote to nationalism rather than a close relative. This viewpoint was most clearly articulated by Pierre Trudeau – educated by Elie Kedourie at the LSE – before he became Canadian Prime Minister.[13] Thinkers like Trudeau regard federalism as the denial of and the solution to nationalism, though occasionally they adopt the view that federation must be built upon the success of nationalism which it then transcends in Hegelian fashion (Majocchi 1991: 161). In effect they echo Einstein's reported remark that nationalism is the measles of mankind.

A different perspective was articulated by the Austro-Marxists, Karl Renner and Otto Bauer, in the last days of the Habsburg empire (see e.g.

Bauer 2000; Hanf 1991; Pfabigan 1991). For them nationalism had to be accommodated en route to a global socialist and communist order. They thought it was feasible to combine national autonomy in federal and consociational formats. Lenin and Stalin pressed their arguments, in an adapted format, into service in the Soviet Union. Federation was to be used to offer a limited accommodation to minority nationalism, but solely towards the end of building a universal socialist society. Minorities were to be offered the fiction, but not the fact, of national self-government.[14] While this policy was superficially similar to that of multinational federalists (to be discussed below), Marxist–Leninists were, of course, formal cosmopolitans, committed to a post-nationalist global political order. However, pending the world revolution, they maintained that federal arrangements, 'national in form, socialist in content', were the optimal institutional path to global communism.

Multinational federalists: multinational maintenance engineers

Multinational or multi-ethnic federalists, by contrast, advocate federation 'to unite people who seek the advantages of membership of a common political unit, but differ markedly in descent, language and culture' (Forsyth 1989: 4). They seek to express, institutionalize and protect at least two national or ethnic cultures, on a durable and often on a permanent basis. Any greater union or homogenization, if envisaged at all, is postponed for the future. They explicitly reject the strongly integrationist or assimilationist objectives of national and/or post-national federalists, and see these as nation destroying rather than nation building. They believe that complementary dual or multiple national loyalties are possible, and indeed desirable. Multinational federalists represent a third branch of liberalism, distinct from the Jacobin (federalism breaches civic equality) and American varieties (national federation promotes individual liberty by blocking centralized power). For multinational liberals, a proper understanding of liberal individual rights requires respect for the culture of individuals, and this means allowing minorities the power to protect and promote their culture (Kymlicka 1995; Stepan 1999: 31–2). Unlike unitarists and national federalists, multinational federalists reject the a priori view that minority-controlled governments are more backward or illiberal in their treatment of their own minorities than majority-controlled central or federal governments. Minority nationalisms are as likely to be of the civic variety as dominant nationalisms according to these liberals; indeed, Keating argues that contemporary minority nationalisms are strongly modernist, responding to the shift in power from the state to the global marketplace (Keating 2001; Kymlicka 1995).

Multinational federalism has considerable, albeit critical, support among contemporary academics (Hechter 2000; Linz 1997; Keating 2001; Kymlicka 1995; Moore 2001; Stepan 1999; Watts 1999; McGarry and O'Leary 1993; O'Leary 2001). But some supporters make quite remarkable claims for federalism. Von Beyme, referring to Western democracies, argued in 1985 that 'Canada is the only country in which federalism did not prove capable of solving ... ethnic conflict' (von Beyme 1985: 121).[15] Others are more modest. Kymlicka supports multinational federalism normatively, while acknowledging it faces considerable difficulties in practice (Kymlicka, 2001). Multinational federalists have been influential in the development of federations in the former British Empire, notably in Canada, the Caribbean, Nigeria, South Africa, India, Pakistan and Malaysia. Austro-Marxists and even some Marxist–Leninists were multinational federalists, albeit the transitional kind, and have had an enduring impact in the post-communist development of the Russian Federation, Ethiopia and even in the rump Yugoslavia. While unitarists have presently been in the ascendancy in Eastern Europe, multinational federalism has become more popular in Western Europe, both among proponents of the federalization of the European Union, and amongst power holders in established states – as the decision to create a federation in Belgium attests. We should also note the novel and more decentralized devolutionary, regional and potentially federal institutions of Spain, the United Kingdom, France and Italy. Multinational federalists are often *soft* minority nationalists, but also include governing elites who believe that accommodating national minorities holds the key to overall stability and unity. They include the Quebec Liberal Party, the Basque Nationalist Party (PNV) and the Catalan *Convergencia I Unio*. Contemporary Euro-federalists might be thought to be the most ambitious multinational federalists of our age, but judging by their institutional proposals their sympathies in fact lie more in the direction of making the EU into a national federation.

Plainly the multinationalists' defence of federation as a way of managing nations – to each nation let a province be given – is not able to accommodate those minorities that are so small in number or dispersed that they cannot control federal units or provinces. This includes francophones who live outside Quebec, Flemish-speakers in Wallonia, francophones in Flanders; and small and scattered indigenous peoples in Australia, India and the Americas. Multinational federalists reject the view that every minority must inevitably seek its nation state, and maintain that even among those that do they may settle for their own region instead. They argue that if the provincial borders of the component units of the federation match the boundaries of the relevant national, ethnic, religious or linguistic communities, i.e. if there is a 'federal society' congruent with the federating institutions, then federation may be an effective harmonizing device. That is precisely because it makes an ethnically heterogeneous political society less heterogeneous through the creation of more homogeneous subunits. Multinational federation thus involves an explicit rejection of the unitarist and national federalist argument that self-rule for minorities necessarily conflicts with the territorial integrity of existing states. It is also a *prima facie* challenge to the tacit Gellnerian notion that in modern times the equilibrium condition is one sovereign state, one culture (or nation) (Gellner 1983). If we treat broadly the 'political unit' in Gellner's definition, to encompass regional or provincial units in a federation, then his theory can accommodate such arrangements, but at the significant concession of recognizing that federal systems are compatible with dual and possibly multiple nationalities.

National minorities within a multinational federation often argue that they should have powers beyond those enjoyed by the federal units dominated by the national majority: they may support asymmetrical federalism, insisting that their distinct status be officially recognized and institutionalized. They may seek to share in powers that are normally the prerogative of the centre or federal government. Some minorities seek a role in federal foreign policy, or to be directly represented in international organizations. This may not mean the same as supporting confederation, because the minorities may be content for most purposes to remain part of a federation, but they are clearly stretching the limits of traditional federations, and moving in the direction of confederation.[16]

Multinational or multi-ethnic federations may originate from the union of previously self-governing communities, as happened in the case of Switzerland. However, in other cases, multinational federalists may engage in deliberate democratic engineering to match certain ascriptive criteria with internal political borders. This occurred at Canada's founding, when the province of Canada was divided largely along linguistic lines into Ontario and Quebec. It also happened in post-independence India, but not until Nehru was forced to concede reorganization of internal state borders along linguistic boundaries (Arora and Verney 1995; Brass 1990).[17] Nigeria has reorganized its internal boundaries on several occasions, to the advantage of certain minorities. Whereas its original tripartite federation was dominated by the Ibo, Hausa and Yoruba groups, its current 36 state structure includes 14 states that are dominated by other groups (Suberu 2001: 5). Switzerland carved a new canton of Jura (largely French and Catholic) out of the mostly German-speaking canton of Berne in 1979.

Weighing the evidence

On first glance, it would seem that there is considerable evidence for the French and American republican argument that multinational federalism has, as Snyder puts it, 'a terrible track record' (2000: 327). However, multinational or multi-ethnic federations which have either broken down, or failed to remain democratic, have been largely in the communist world or the post-colonial world. The federations of the Soviet Union, Yugoslavia and Czechoslovakia disintegrated during or immediately after their respective democratizations. Indeed, of all the states in the former communist bloc of Eastern Europe, it was only federations that irretrievably broke apart, and all of them did.[18] The last victim is the formal dissolution of Serbia and Montenegro. Of all these states, the federations experienced the most violent transitions. In the post-colonial world multinational or multi-ethnic federations failed, or failed to be successfully established, in the Caribbean, notably in the West Indies Federation. Even the miniature federation of St Kitts-Nevis recently faced the prospect of break-up (Premdas 1998). Multinational or multi-ethnic federations have failed in sub-Saharan Africa, in francophone West and Equatorial Africa, in British East Africa (Kenya, Uganda and Tanganikya) and in British Central Africa (northern and southern Rhodesia and Nyasaland), or have failed to remain durably democratic (Nigeria and Tanzania). The break-up of the Nigerian federation between 1966 and 1969 was only prevented after a secessionist conflict that caused approximately one million deaths. In the Arab world, only the United Arab Emirates has survived, but it is a national federation and hardly democratic. The new multinational federal experiment in Iraq is experiencing a civil war within its Arab core. The Mali and the Ethiopian federations in independent Africa broke up, too; while Cameroon experienced forced unitarism after a federal beginning. In Asia there have been federative failures in Indochina, in Burma, in Pakistan (the secession of Bangladesh) and in the union of Malaya (the secession of Singapore). In short, new multinational federations appear not to work as conflict-regulating devices – even where they allow a degree of minority self-government. They have broken down, or failed to be durably democratic, throughout Asia, Africa and the Caribbean. India stands out as the major exception in Asia, but it has important constitutional characteristics of a union state rather than a federation.[19]

It also seems clear that multinational federations make it easier for groups to secede should they want to do so. Federalism provides the minority with political and bureaucratic resources that it can use to launch a bid for independence. Giving a minority its own unit makes it possible for it to hold referendums on secession, which can be useful for gaining recognition. Multinational federations implicitly suggest the principle that the accommodated minorities represent 'peoples' who might then be entitled to rights of self-determination under international law. It is far more likely that, as the Badinter Commission on the former Yugoslavia confirmed, the international community will recognize a bid for independence from a federal unit than from a group that lacks such a unit. This is why all of the full constituent units of the Soviet Union, Yugoslavia and Czechoslovakia that broke away are now seen as independent states, whereas breakaway regions that were not constituent units, such as Abkhazia, Trans-Dniestria, the Turkish Republic of Northern Cyprus and Kosovo, were not recognized. To this extent, unitarists and national federalists have a point – though it is a point that multinational federalists have little difficulty conceding.[20]

But this bleak assessment of the track record of multinational federations has to be qualified in five important ways. First, the major federal failures, including the Soviet Union, Yugoslavia, Czechoslovakia and Nigeria were or have been, to a significant extent, sham or pseudo-federations. In several cases, they were forced together. The constitutional division of powers and the rule of law were often ignored in practice and they were not authentically representative (i.e. democratic). There was, therefore, no possibility of genuine dialogue, never mind cooperation, among the different national communities involved. In sum, these states had weak or no overarching identities to begin with, and no democratic mechanism for developing them. While the United States can be seen as the paradigmatic example of national federalism, the Soviet Union is the most prominent case of pseudo-federalism. Territorially it consisted of those remnants of the Tsarist Empire that the Red Army was able to subjugate after the October Revolution, plus those countries (Estonia, Latvia, Lithuania and Moldova) it conquered as a result of the Ribbentrop–Molotov pact (1939) and its victory in the Second World War. While its state structure was federated from the beginning, real power lay in the tightly centralized Communist Party (the CPSU), which operated according to the principle of 'democratic centralism' (Lieven and McGarry 1993). The union republics were therefore not autonomous in any meaningful sense. Moreover, their legislatures (the Soviets), although in theory elected by local populations, were in fact rubber-stamp bodies nominated by the CPSU. Key institutions, including the army and police, were controlled by Moscow. No effective judicial review existed to decide on the division of rights and functional spheres between the centre and the republics. And while it is true that Yugoslavia was more decentralized than both the Soviet Union and Czechoslovakia, at least after reforms in the late 1960s, it was no less undemocratic, and was held together by the League of Communists.

The colonial federations arose out of colonies that had been arbitrarily consolidated by white imperialists. Even the decision to federate at independence was made in some cases by the departing metropolitan rather than the colony's indigenous elites. Nigeria's original three-unit federation, which collapsed in the mid-1960s, was 'bequeathed' by the vacating British (Suberu 2001: 4). The Cameroon federation was a construct of British and French colonialists (particularly the latter), who wanted to preserve the dual personality they thought they had created (Elazar 1987: 240). It was converted into a unitary state by military strongmen soon after independence, while Nigeria has been ruled by centralizing military dictators for more than two-thirds of its post-independence history – and its presidential contenders in recent times have all been ex-generals. Even under democratic conditions, Nigeria is so centralized that it has been described as a 'hollow federation' and 'a unitary state in federal guise' (Suberu and Diamond 2000: 8) [21] Corruption and abuse of power are so pervasive that the rule of law can hardly be said to exist (Suberu 2001). [22]

These communist and post-colonial federations were additionally burdened by economic systems that were incapable of providing a reasonable or growing standard of living for their citizens. In each case, this caused resentment, not least among minorities in relatively enterprising regions of the state who saw their inclusion in the federation as a drag on their enterprise.

It was therefore not surprising that when the communist planning system became discredited and collapsed in the late 1980s it produced a legitimacy crisis.

Second, the case against multinational federalism would be stronger, if it could be shown, as critics claim, that it was unnecessary to accommodate national minorities, and that there were democratic civic nationalist (unitarist or national federalist) alternatives that would have worked better if not much better. Once this counterfactual test is probed the critics' position looks less credible. The decision to create both the Soviet and Yugoslav federations was taken in the midst of bitter civil wars and external invasions, when parts of both states had seceded (Connor 1984, 198; Woodward 1995: 30). The decision was regarded as essential for restoring unity and luring breakaway regions back into the state, and was taken in both cases by socialist internationalists, neither of whom was ideologically committed to multinational federalism. Before he assumed power, Lenin had expressed his vehement opposition to federalism and his clear preference for unitary structures.[23] Tito, before taking power, appeared to be a conventional Leninist. If federalism was unnecessary, we must conclude that both Lenin and Tito were extraordinarily incompetent from their own perspectives. Moreover, the thesis that communist multinational federalism 'created' divisions cannot adequately explain why strong ethnic identities exist among groups that were not accommodated through federal institutions, such as the Chechens or Crimean Tatars.[24] Similarly, while some have argued that Nigeria's divisions at the time of independence reflected British divide and rule strategies, few think that the state could have been (or could be) held together without some form of federation structure.[25] When an Ibo leader, General Ironsi, tried to convert Nigeria into a centralist state in 1966 it led to his downfall. Even though the Nigerian federation witnessed a failed and bloody bid for secession in Biafra (1967–70), the victors were careful to retain federal structures, albeit reformed, with new internal boundaries.

One reason to doubt the feasibility of civic nationalism, French or American, as an alternative to multinational federation is that it has not been particularly successful when it has been applied, under more propitious circumstances, in multinational states. Turkey still faces a large dissident Kurdish minority despite eight decades of oppressive 'Kemalist' civic nationalism. British civic nationalism within a tightly centralized union at the centre of a global empire could not prevent the breakaway of Ireland in 1921 (McGarry 2001; O'Leary and McGarry 1996: Chapter 2).[26] Irish nationalists mobilized successfully without the advantages of their own self-governing institutions. They were able to establish democratic legitimacy by winning the overwhelming majority of Ireland's seats in every election between 1885 and 1918. Britain's civic and unitary state proved incapable of preventing a nationalist rebellion in Northern Ireland from the late 1960s, or of preventing the resurgence of Scottish and Welsh nationalism. Even the home of Jacobinism that was able to turn peasants into Frenchmen in the nineteenth century has been unable to erode Corsican nationalism. The failure of unitarist or national federalist forms of civic nationalism may explain why all Western multi-ethnic democracies, including the United Kingdom, Spain, Belgium, France and Denmark are now more disposed towards decentralized autonomy regimes if not full-blown multinational federation.

Third, if one accepts that federalism was necessary for stability in the failed federations, the focus of blame for the violence accompanying their break-up can be shifted from multinational federation per se. One can argue that secession – and violence – followed from attempts by certain groups to centralize these federations, i.e. to move away from the spirit of multinational federalism. Yugoslavia's break-up, including the de facto breakaway of Kosovo, followed successive Serbian-dominated moves against the autonomy of Yugoslavia's republics.[27] The Soviet Union broke up after an abortive reactionary coup within the communist party aimed at repudiating Gorbachev's decentralizing initiatives. Violence was also caused by the centre's unwillingness to permit secession. That is, one can argue that democratic and federal constitutions with procedural and negotiable secession rules might have avoided violence better.[28] There was no violence in Czechoslovakia because mutual secession was agreed. In the territory of the former Soviet Union, the worst violence was (is) in Chechnya, a region that did not have the status of a 'union republic' within the Soviet Union throughout its history; and even though it acquired this status when autonomous republics were granted the same rights as union republics the Russian successor regime to the USSR has refused to recognize this last moment change of status. Had Chechnya's last moment rights within the USSR been recognized then it would have been able to secede with the union republics. In many cases, one might argue that post-communist violence has resulted from the *absence* of ethnofederalism, i.e. from the lack of congruency between constituent unit and ethnic boundaries. In the case of Yugoslavia, Slovenia's secession was relatively peaceful because it was homogeneous. The 'velvet divorce' in Czechoslovakia was facilitated because there were few Czechs in Slovakia and few Slovaks in the Czech lands.[29] War started in Croatia in 1991 largely because Croatia had a significant Serb population that wanted to stay united with Yugoslavia, and spread to Bosnia because it had Croats and Serbs who also wanted to stay linked to their respective ethnic kin. These groups were aided and abetted by Serbia and Croatia, respectively. Bosnia, the most multi-ethnic republic, was perhaps destined to be the most violent.[30] In 2001, violent conflict broke out in Macedonia, whose significant Albanian minority resented the dominance of Slavs. War between Armenia and Azerbaijan was largely fought over the inclusion of an Armenian ethnic enclave (Nagorno-Karabakh) in the latter. In Georgia, two conflicts broke out between Georgians and South Ossetians cut off by Georgia's secession from their kin in North Ossetia (within Russia), and between Georgians and Abkhazians – who baulked at being included in what they saw as a Georgian state. The only other violence was in the Trans-Dniestrian region of Moldova, where Ukrainians and Russians resented their inclusion in Moldova. Just as communist federal break-up was fuelled by centralizing measures, the same could be said of the violence that arose in the newly-independent, still heterogeneous, but unitary, republics. The wars in Croatia, Macedonia, the South Ossetian and Abkhazian regions of Georgia and Trans-Dniestria were all influenced by the majoritarian policies of the states' dominant groups. In Croatia, a minority rebellion broke out after the newly independent Croatian regime adopted a flag that resembled that of the war-time Croatian Ustashe regime that had committed genocide against the Serbs, and after it moved to disarm its Serbian policemen (Hayden 1992). In this perspective, these conflicts have been similar to those in Kurdistan in Turkey or Iraq, or the Basque region of Spain under Franco, i.e. reactions to centralization and coercive nationalizing assimilation programmes. It is unreasonable simply to attribute them to multinational federation per se.[31]

Fourth, while it is true that *only* federations broke apart in communist Eastern Europe, this glosses over the more basic fact that the states that broke apart were also the most ethno-nationally diverse states – which, of course, explains why they were federations.[32] In the case of the Soviet Union, Russians had a bare majority of the total population (51 per cent), while in Czechoslovakia and Yugoslavia, the largest groups had 63 and 39 per cent respectively. In none of the communist unitary states, did the total minority population constitute more than 17 per cent. The largest single minority group was the Turks of Bulgaria, with roughly 8 per cent of the population. It makes at least as much sense to argue that the instability of the communist federations resulted from their ethno-national diversity as their ethnofederal structures. In other research O'Leary has shown that national federations that are durably democratic and majoritarian have a *Staatsvolk*, a dominant people (O'Leary 2001). While lacking a *Staatsvolk* does not guarantee political instability in a federation, it makes it more likely and makes consociational arrangements more urgent. The United States, built around an historically dominant nationality of WASPs, proved more stable than Nigeria – which clearly lacks a numerically dominant people. The same comparison helps suggest why the Russian Federation is more stable and secession-proof, thus far, than the Soviet Union. Russians have a majority of 81.5 per cent in the Russian Federation; they had only 51 per cent in the USSR. The unitary states of Eastern Europe may have held together, in other words, not because they were not federations, but because each of them has a dominant community able to hold their state together if they had wanted to (see Table 10.2). Conversely, it is not at all certain that if, counterfactually, Yugoslavia had been a unitary state when it democratized that it would have stayed together. Ireland was able to secede from the much less diverse but unitary United Kingdom after the first universal male suffrage elections held in 1918.

Lastly, it is simply wrong to claim, as Snyder and others do, that

Table 10.2 The largest community's proportion of the population in the communist states of Eastern Europe

	Largest community	*Percentage of population*
Communist federations		
Yugoslavia	Serbs	38.9
Soviet Union	Russians	51.0
Czechoslovakia	Czechs	63.0
Communist unitary states		
Bulgaria	Bulgarians	83.0
Albania	Albanians	95.0
Romania	Romanians	89.5
Hungary	Hungarians	89.9
Poland	Poles	97.6

Sources: CIA World Factbook 2001, www.cia.gov/cia/publications/factbook/index.html (information for Bulgaria, Albania, Romania, Hungary, Poland); Library of Congress Country Studies, lcweb2.loc.gov/frd/cs/cshome.html#toc and www.kakarigi.net/homeland/maps/nations.htm.

'ethnofederalism' is unworkable. Two of the worlds' oldest states, Switzerland and Canada, are ethnofederations. They have endured from 1848 and 1867, respectively, and both demonstrate that the accommodation of ethnic minorities through ethnofederalism is consistent with prosperity and the promotion of basic individual rights. India, the world's largest democracy and most successful post-colonial democracy also has important practical ethnofederal characteristics.[33] Belgium, while of more recent vintage, has adopted successful ethnofederalist structures, and so has Russia, if Chechnya is left aside. Only a multinational federation would have been agreed by Kurdistan in Iraq. Within each of these states, there is plenty of evidence, including polling and electoral data and the positions of their political parties, that minorities may be content with less than a sovereign nation state (Keating 2002: 7–9). Together, these qualifications question the assumption that multinational federalism is bound to fail. Our next task is to inquire into the conditions that make success more or less likely.

Explaining success and failure

The five conditions that facilitate, but do not guarantee successful multinational federations are implicit in the preceding discussion. Here we spell them out.

The presence of a Staatsvolk

Table 10.1 suggests that national federations are more stable than multinational federations. The latter appear more likely to fail or break-up.

The reason often proffered is straightforward: national federations are generally nationally homogeneous, or virtually so. However, O'Leary's data suggests that a *Staatsvolk* can feel secure – and live with the concessions attached to multinational federation and, *ceteris paribus*, has the demographic strength and resources to resist secessionism by minority nationalities. Multinational federations without a *Staatsvolk* are more likely to be unstable, face secessionism or break-up, because minorities are more likely to think they can prevail (O'Leary 2001). Russia's future cannot be extrapolated from the experience of the Soviet Union, because Russians are far more dominant within the former than they were within the latter.[34] The same argument implies that Nigeria and a future European federation will, *ceteris paribus*, be relatively unstable, as neither possesses a *Staatsvolk*. What must be considered in our 'ceteris paribus' clause? We hypothesize as follows:

a   Multinational federations without a *Staatsvolk*, if they are to survive as democratic entities, must develop consociational practices, especially within the federal government, that protect the interests of all the encompassed national and ethnic communities with the capacity to breakaway.

b   The existence of a *Staatsvolk*, or the existence of consociational practices, will not by themselves assure the stabilization of a multinational democratic federation, though they will separately or conjointly increase its survival prospects.

c   Other conducive external and internal political, economic and social relationships may decide the fate of a multinational federation. The character of multinational power-sharing, whether a national minority has backing from a powerful neighbouring state, and whether its region is on the border of the federation will assuredly matter, as will the democratic and legal character of the federation, its mode of formation and its prosperity.

The federation's national communities should not only have self-government, there should also be consociational government at the centre

When federation is defended as a method of conflict regulation, the emphasis, as we have seen, is usually on how it can provide minorities with guaranteed powers of territorial self-government. Sometimes it is also argued that it has the virtue of avoiding the 'winner takes all' outcome associated with Westminster-type regimes: a group that is excluded at the centre may be able to console itself with regional power.[35] However, federalism is about 'shared rule' as well as 'self-rule', and national minorities are likely to want a federal government that represents them, that is inclusive and, indeed, we would say, consociational. National and ethnic minorities excluded from the federal government will have a reduced stake in the federation and the federal government will be less inclined to promote their interests. It is not surprising, then, that all of the durably democratic multinational federations have practised consociational forms of democracy within the federal government. Such arrangements involve four features: cross-community executive power-sharing, proportional representation of groups throughout the state sector (including the police and judiciary), ethnic autonomy in culture (especially in religion or language) and formal or informal minority veto rights (Lijphart 1977; O'Leary 2005). Consociational practices within the federal government are relatively undisputed in the case of Canada, Switzerland and Belgium (see Noel 1993; Steiner 1989; Hooghe 1993), and Lijphart has recently claimed that India had effective consociational traits during its most stable period under Nehru (Lijphart 1996; Adeney 2002). Since Congress's decline, India has been governed by a broad multiparty coalition representing its diversity. Even if one does not count India as consociational in respect of having cross-community executive power-sharing in New Delhi, it has usually had descriptively diverse representation of religious, ethnic and linguistic groups in the cabinet and civil service.

We can see the stabilizing importance of consociational organization in the federal government in the case of many of the failed federations, where centrifugal pressures were often exacerbated by unrepresentative federal governments. In Pakistan, before the secession of Bangladesh, a crucial federal agency, the army, was dominated by the West (Nasr 2001). Punjabis were over-represented in the core federal institutions. In Yugoslavia, the army, one of the most important federal institutions (absorbing two-thirds of the federal budget), was dominated by Serb officers, many of them from Serbian minorities in other federal units, who shared Milosevic's vision of a recentralized state. The Yugoslav Federal Council, the most important political institution, and one based on (non-democratic) consociational principles, was subject from the late 1980s to an undisguised takeover by Serbian politicians. Having suspended the autonomy of Kosovo and Vojvodina, the Serbia–Montenegrin alliance gained control of four of the Federal Council's seven seats, plunging the federation into crisis. The Soviet Union broke up after an abortive takeover of the central government by conservatives opposed to decentralization and secession. The episode undermined Gorbachev's attempt to reorganize the federation in ways that would have given the republics more self-government *and* better representation in Moscow. The breakdown of the Nigerian federation in 1966–67, which included anti-Ibo violence in the northern Hausa region and the bloody Biafran war of secession, arose after a coup which led to the centre being dominated by Ibo officers and a counter-coup in which these officers were overthrown (Suberu 2001).[36] Much of Nigeria's post-1970 conflict, including sectarian warfare between Muslims and Christians and the rise of violent separatism in the oil-rich Delta area, has also been traced to the lack of inclusiveness at the level of the centre (Suberu and Diamond 2002: 6–7, 13).[37] The breakdown of the West Indian federation was linked to Jamaicans' lack of representation and influence at the centre, and in the case of the federation of Nyasaland, northern and southern Rhodesia, it was black Africans who were under-represented (Watts 1999: 111).

This evidence suggests that it will not be sufficient for the Nigerian, Ethiopian and Pakistani federations or any prospective Iraqi federation to practise democracy. Past evidence suggests they will need to adopt and maintain consociational governance at the federal centre.[38] It also suggests that calls to have a fully fledged European federation, with the classic bicameral arrangements of the USA, to address the so-called 'democratic deficit' in the European Union will fail *unless* such calls are accompanied by strong commitments to consociational devices. Consociational governance would imply strong mechanisms to ensure the inclusive and effective representation of all the nationalities of the European Union in its core executive institutions, proportionate representation of its nationalities in its public bureaucracies and legal institutions, national autonomy in all cultural matters deemed of profound cultural significance (e.g. language, religion, education) and, last, but not least, national vetoes to protect national communities from being out-voted through majoritarian rules. In short, many of the current consociational and confederal features of the EU which some federalists want to weaken or temper in their pursuit of formal federation are in fact required to ensure the EU's prospects as a multinational democratic federation. The EU's greatest current danger stems from its ardent majoritarian federalists.

This argument about the importance of accommodation through consociational devices is different from that put forward by Linz and Stepan (1992). They put their faith in the ability of federation-wide political parties to win support from all groups, to balance majority and minority concerns, and to build what Linz calls '*bundestreue*', an overarching loyalty to the state (Linz 1997). In their view, the key reason for the disintegration of the Yugoslav and Soviet federations was that the first democratic elections were held in the republics rather than the state (whereas in post-Franco Spain it was the other way around). In Yugoslavia this sequencing gave divisive republican elites the resources and space to promote break-up, and obstructed the organization of federation-wide parties with an interest in holding the state together. Had federal elections been held first, federation-wide parties would have been able to act as unifying forces.

This reasoning is, however, questionable. State-wide parties may well be likely to do *better* in state-wide elections than in regional elections, but there is no guarantee, or even likelihood, that they will do *well* at any level in societies with noticeable national divisions. In the United Kingdom's first democratic elections, in the mid-1880s, the overwhelming majority of Irish seats were won by Irish nationalist parties.[39] The fact that they were elected in state-wide elections, as opposed to regional elections, does not appear to have coloured their view of the UK, or their ability to secede from it, and they won despite the presence of competitors from state-wide parties. Czechoslovakia's first democratic elections, which involved concurrent state-wide and regional elections, produced no state-wide parties at the state-wide (federal) elections other than the discredited communists, who won 23 of the country's 150 seats. They even subsequently divided into Czech and Slovak factions. All of the other parties that won seats were based on either the Czech, Slovak or Hungarian populations (Leff 1998: 98). Perhaps this political party fragmentation into ethno-national blocs was due, as Leff claims, to the simultaneity of elections at both levels (ibid. 97), i.e. to the fact that the federal election was not held in advance.

But how, then, are we to explain the first democratic election returns in the *unitary* states of Eastern Europe, where there were no regional elections? In these cases, party support still broke down almost exactly along ethno-national lines (see Table 10.3), with little evidence of integrative vote-pooling activities by either party elites or voters. These results are difficult to square with Linz and Stepan's assumption that Yugoslav state-wide elections would have produced strong Yugoslav state-wide parties, unless one is to assume that Yugoslavia was a good deal less divided than its neighbours. Given that it was the only state in Eastern Europe whose major communities had persons who had butchered each other within living memory (1941–45), this assumption is implausible. This comparative evidence suggests that state-wide elections in Yugoslavia would have resulted in elections that reflected its national divisions. Hoping for state-wide parties to hold Yugoslavia together was probably wishful thinking. Stability would have required successful bargaining among the different minority nationalist parties on a new consociational and confederal constitution. Such bargaining as there was on this agenda did not succeed.

Table 10.3 Support for minority political parties in the first post-communist elections in the unitary states of Eastern Europe

State/year of election	*Minority/proportion of state's population*	*Support for minority party as a proportion of votes cast*
Bulgaria/1990	Turks/8.5	6.0[a]
Romania/1990	Magyars/7.8	7.2
Poland/1991[b]	Germans/1	1.2

Sources: Centre for the Study of Public Policy, 'Mass Behaviour in New Democracies', at www.cspp.strath.ac.uk/index.html?bulgelec.html; the University of Essex's Project on Political Transformation and the Electoral Process in Post-Communist Europe, at www.essex.ac.uk/elections/; Elections in Central and Eastern Europe at www2.essex.ac.uk/elect/electer/pl_er_nl.htm#pl91.

Notes
a The 1990 election was to elect a constitutional assembly. The first parliamentary elections took place in 1991. The Turkish minority party, the Movement for Human Rights and Freedoms, won 7.5 per cent on this occasion.
b These were the first parliamentary elections. Presidential elections were held in 1990.

Authentic (democratic) multinational federations are more likely to be successful than pseudo-(undemocratic) federations

An authentic multinational federation is democratic. It allows the representatives of its respective national communities to engage in dialogue and open bargaining about their interests, grievances and aspirations. Such democratic dialogue is a prerequisite for the development of cooperative practices. Democratic multinational federalism may help to preclude the systematic transgression of individual and group rights It can prevent minority (secessionist) elites from exaggerating support for their preferences (Linz 1997). An authentic multinational federation is also based on the rule of law, law that recognizes national, ethnic or communal rights, a constitutional division of powers, and legal powers that approach those of impartial umpires. There is not yet an example of an established democratic multinational federation failing (though the number of cases is small), although there are, as we have seen, numerous examples of democratizing federations that have not worked. The evidence, limited as it is, suggests that we should not automatically assume that Canada, Switzerland, Spain, India or Belgium will go the way of the flawed communist or post-colonial federations.

'Voluntary' or 'holding together' multinational federations are more likely to endure under democratic conditions than those that are coercively constructed after modern social mobilizations

Stepan distinguishes between three types of federation (Stepan 1999: 19–34):

a   those that voluntarily come together from distinct polities/colonies, like the Swiss and Canadian federations;
b   those that are created from unitary states in an attempt to 'hold' the polity together, such as Belgium and, one might argue, India; and
c   those that are forced together (or 'put' together) by a dominant group, such as the Soviet Union.[40]

Federations that are consensually established as a result of elite bargaining, whether of the holding or voluntary variety, are more likely to be considered as legitimate by their citizens, and are more likely to survive than those that result from coercion. A foundational act of cooperation is also more likely than one of coercion to promote traditions of accommodation. Canada's success is owed in part to the fact that it originated in 1867 from a compact between anglophone and francophone elites led by John A. Mac-Donald and George Etienne Cartier. The Swiss federation was also the result of different groups agreeing to 'con-federate' in the historic past, even if the 1848 constitution was written by the victors of a civil war. While the Belgian federation emerged from a unitary state, it too was based on agreement between representative elites. India, which stands out as one of the few post-colonial democratic success stories, is also one of the few where indigenous elites took the decision to federate by themselves – albeit reluctantly, and albeit after prior British tutelage (Adeney 2002). Most of the failed federations, on the other hand, were put together without the consent of minority leaders.[41] This does not augur well for Bosnia-Herzegovina, which exists as a federation because of the internationally-imposed Dayton Accords.

Prosperous multinational federations (or states) are more likely to endure than those that are not

Walker Connor has correctly counselled us against exaggerating the importance of materialism when questions of national identity are at stake. Prosperity should not be considered a sufficient or even a necessary condition (as the example of India shows) for holding a multinational federation together (Connor 1994: 145–64). Nonetheless, *ceteris paribus*, prosperity – and distributive fairness – may matter. The plight of the communist federations and post-colonial federations was plainly exacerbated by their inability to provide materially for their citizens and by the discrediting of communist central planning. In the Ukraine and the Baltic republics, even Russians voted for the break-up of the USSR. In both Yugoslavia and the Soviet Union, the catalyst for break-up was necessary economic reforms, and the charge was led in both cases by those republics (Slovenia and Croatia in the case of Yugoslavia, the Baltic republics in the case of the Soviet Union) which had the most to gain materially from going it alone. We need not labour the obvious point that distributive fiscal and expenditure issues are the meat and drink of political controversy in those federations which do not use equitable formulae for fiscal equalization.

Conclusion

We have attempted to offer a more balanced and nuanced assessment of the value and durability of multinational federations than that put forward by critics of 'ethnofederalism'. Democratic federalism did not cause the break-up of the communist states, as these were not authentic democratic (or economically efficient) federations. Not all multinational federations have failed. There are a small number of remarkable success stories. We have tried to identify conditions that are conducive to the success of multinational federations. It is imperative that they be democratic and that they respect the rule of law. It helps if they are prosperous. It helps if they came together voluntarily. If federations develop from a unitary state, our arguments suggest that early and generous responses to expressed demands for minority self-government will work better than delayed and grudging responses. The demographic composition of the federation matters: a federation that has a dominant ethno-national community is likely to be more stable than one that does not. Lastly federation is usually not enough: where there is no *Staatsvolk*, consociational practices, particularly at the level of the federal government, are very important to the success of multinational federation.

Notes

1 John McGarry is the Canada Research Chair in Nationalism and Democracy in the Department of Political Studies, Queen's University, Ontario (email mcgarryj@post.queensu.ca). Brendan O'Leary is the Lauder Professor of Political Science at the University of Pennsylvania (email: boleary@sas.upenn.edu) where he directs its Solomon Asch Center. A number of organizations have funded our joint and individual research. Both of us thank the United States Institute of Peace. John McGarry thanks the Social Sciences and Humanities Research Council of Canada and the Carnegie Corporation of New York. Brendan O'Leary thanks the Lauder endowment.

2 This is a simple but important contrast. In subsequent work we distinguish between *national federations* in which there is but one official nationality and the *Staatsvolk* dominates in every federative unit; *national and multi-ethnic federations* in which there is again one official nationality but ethnic, linguistic or religious minorities may dominate some federal units (e.g. Switzerland and Nigeria); and *pluri-national federations* which recognize multiple nations, grant partner nations self-government, and have consensual or consociational governing arrangements in the federal government.

3 See www.forumfed.org/Publications/afghan/bria.pdf.

4 Multi-ethnic federalism was once suggested for the United States as a way of giving self-government to southern blacks. The idea of creating a black state in the south was supported by the American Communist Party in the 1930s and various black power organizations in the 1960s. It is no longer discussed, primarily because of black migration into northern cities.

5 Article 2 of the Fifth Republic's Constitution declares that 'France is an indivisible, secular, democratic, and social Republic'.

6 'Partial autonomy for Corsica splits French government', *World Socialist Web Site*, 5 September 2000 (www.wsws.org/articles/2000/sep2000/cors-s05.shtml).

7 'Corsica: The perils of devolution', *Economist*, 7 July 2001, p. 49.

8 Chevenement claimed that self-government for Corsics would be as contagious as the 'I love you' computer virus, 'Partial autonomy for Corsica splits French government', *World Socialist Web Site*, 5 September 2000 (www.wsws.org/articles/2000/sep2000/cors-s05.shtml).

9 Confusingly, hardline minority nationalists sometimes say they support federation when they mean confederation, as in the case of the former Turkish-Cypriot leader, Rauf Denktash. The *Parti Quebecois* does not commonly use the term confederation, but offers a synonym, 'sovereignty-association'.

10   Providence has been pleased to give this one connected country to one united people – a people descended from the same ancestors, speaking the same language, professing the same religion, attached to the same principles of government, very similar in their manners and their customs, and who, by their joint counsels, arms and efforts, fighting side by side throughout a long and bloody war, have nobly established liberty and independence.
      Publius [John Jay], in Madison *et al.* 1987 [1788], paper II: 91.

11 Lipset (1960: 91–2) argues that federation may create cross-cutting cleavages, but it can only do this if internal federal boundaries and ethnic boundaries intersect. Federalism 'increases the opportunity for multiple sources of cleavage by adding regional interests and values to the others which crosscut the social structure'.

12 Snyder says the decision to create ethnofederations was 'often' needless (p. 327), but does not specify where it was needless. The argument throughout his book suggests that he thinks it was always needless.

13 In an article entitled 'Federalism, Nationalism and Reason' Trudeau squarely associated federalism and functionalism with reason, and nationalism with emotions (Trudeau 1968 (1965)). Trudeau's anti-nationalism was directed at what he considered 'ethnic' nationalism, particularly that associated with his home province of Quebec. He had less difficulty with civic nationalism, of the Canadian variety. For a critical reading of Kedourie, see O'Leary (2002).

14 In the authoritative words of Walker Connor, Lenin's second commandment on the management of nationalism was strategically machiavellian: 'Following the assumption of power, terminate the fact – if not necessarily the fiction – of a right to secession, and begin the lengthy process of assimilation via the dialectical route of territorial autonomy for all compact national groups' (Connor 1984: 38).

15 The normal claim is that Canada is the only country, or Canada, Switzerland and Belgium are the only countries, where federalism has been successful in inhibiting conflict.

16 For an account that is sympathetic to the claims of national minorities for asymmetrical federation and for an international role, see Keating (2001). He argues that, particularly within the European Union, new post-sovereigntist institutional arrangements are taking shape in which national minorities seek to exercise power within several different forums – the state, the (transborder) region, the European Union and the world.

17 Ironically, the redrawing of new boundaries to accommodate minorities is easier if the federal centre has more power. In India, officially a union state rather than a federation, the central government has been able to create new boundaries without the approval of the state governments concerned. In Canada, by contrast, the federal government is unable to alter boundaries without the consent of the affected provinces. It cannot even create a new province out of federal territories without the consent of existing provinces, which is one reason why Nunavut is a federal 'territory' rather than a province.

18 The latest victim is the Federal Republic of Yugoslavia which was converted into a loose confederation known as Serbia and Montenegro in 2003, and then dissolved into the two separate states of Serbia and Monetenegro in 2006. Wits were vindicated in their judgement that no state with 'S & M' as an acronym could be stable.

19 Art. 249 of the Indian Constitution allows the federal parliament, by a two-thirds vote in the upper house, to resolve that parliament can make laws in the national interest with respect to any matter enumerated in the States List. Such a resolution remains in force for a year, but can be extended. Art. 250 allows the union parliament to make laws on any item included in the States List during an 'emergency', the existence of which is determined by the federal government under Art. 352. These provisions mean that there are, constitutionally, no exclusive state jurisdictions in India. Art. 250 has been used by parliament on several occasions to shift powers from the states to the concurrent list and 'Union' or federal list. Art. 356, 'President's Rule' allows the central government to take over the government of a state, a provision that has been used 100 times since 1950 (Mathew 2005: 169). These provisions help explain why India has been described as a 'federation without federalism' (Mattew 2005: 168).

20 Stepan, who supports multinational federalism and argues that the US (national) federal model has little relevance for multinational societies, concedes that the 'greatest risk' posed by federalism is that it can 'offer opportunities for ethnic nationalists to mobilize their resources' (Stepan 1999: 19).

21 Nigeria's hyper-centralism is a function of Abuja's control of oil revenues, but it also has a basis in the 1979 and 1999 constitutions. According to Joye and Igweike, under the new constitution (which largely copies the old one), there 'are few, if any ... areas in which state governments can act independently of the Federal Government' (cited in Suberu and Diamond 2000: 15). The existence of such separate competencies, as we have pointed out, is an essential hallmark of an authentic federation.

22 Unitarists often claim that decentralization leads to corruption and inefficiency, but contemporary Nigeria demonstrates that corruption and centralization can go hand in hand. Supporters of anti-corruption reforms in Nigeria argue that this requires 'power and resources [to be] shifted downward, to levels of authority that are closer to the people and more visible' (Diamond 2001: xviii).

23 In 1913, before he had responsibility for governing the Soviet Union, Lenin made clear his contempt for federalism and his preference for unitarism:

> We are in principle against federation. It weakens the economic connection and is inappropriate for a unified state. Do you want to separate? we say. Then go to the devil and cut yourself off altogether ... You don't want to separate? Then, please, don't decide *for me*, don't believe you have the 'right' to federation.
> (italics and grammatical errors in original) (Connor 1984: 217)

As Connor notes, Lenin dropped his opposition to federalism upon assuming power in order to ensure those nations that had seceded 'that reunion would not result in political subservience' (ibid.: 218).

24 There is an explanation for this implicit in the arguments of critics of multinational federations. It is that the decision to accommodate some national groups led those who were excluded to mobilize. We endorse this argument, but we think the way to deal with exclusion would have been to accommodate the excluded identity groups with their own federal units, rather than to refuse to accommodate all.

25
> As the rivalries among these three groups [Yoruba, Ibo, Hausa] crystallized into bitter political struggles during the late colonial period ... it became increasingly clear to all interested observers that only by some form of highly decentralized political arrangements could the main groups be accommodated within a single country.
> (Suberu 2001: 20)

26 Supporters of civic nationalism might respond that British (or other forms of) civic nationalism were not neutral between the United Kingdom's diverse peoples, and that a more genuinely inclusive version of civic nationalism might have worked. This is indeed part of the weakness of civic nationalism. It often reflects the values and interests of the state's dominant national community.

27 The Kosovo rebellion of 1997 was a response, albeit delayed, to the Milosevic's regime's removal of Kosovo's autonomy in 1989 (Hechter 2000: 76–7).

28 They might also have avoided secession.

29 Interestingly, Czechoslovakia is absent from Snyder's account of the relationship between ethnofederalism and violence.

30 A cautionary argument for those who maintain that cross-cutting republican and ethnic boundaries have conflict-reducing effects.

31 Just as violence cannot be fairly attributed to ethnofederalism, nor can ethnic

unmixing (i.e. the large movements of population that accompanied the break-up of Yugoslavia and the Soviet Union) – see Brubaker 1996. Unmixing flowed partly from the lack of congruency between ethnic groups and federal boundaries, and the nationalizing policies of the successor states (i.e. their unwillingness to consider ethnofederal principles).

32 As Watts claims: 'it is not so much because they are federations that countries have been difficult to govern but that it is because they were difficult to govern in the first place that they adopted federation as a form of government' (Watts 1999: 110).

33 But see note 19. India's success is explained away by Snyder because of the unwillingness of its civic central authorities to recognize ethnicity (2000: 287–96). But the internal boundaries of India's provinces were reconstructed along linguistic lines after 1956. It is true that Indian governments have refused to recognize religiosity as the basis of provincial formation.

34 For a contrasting, and interesting, explanation of Russia's stability, see the arguments of Hale (2004, 2005).

35 'Federalism reduces conflict by allowing those political forces excluded from power at the top the opportunity to exercise regional power' (Hanf 1991: 43).

36 The Ibo coup led by Major-General Aguiyi-Ironsi in January 1966 was followed by a 'Unification Decree' which moved Nigeria towards a unitary state. The regional and federal public services were combined, to the considerable advantage of the better-educated southerners and the disadvantage of the Hausa. This move, and the loss of many northern military leaders in the January coup, set off anti-Ibo violence in the north, and contributed to Ironsi's assassination in July (Suberu 2001: 31).

37 Nigeria is equally divided between Muslim and Christian and between north and south, all but four military governments in the 1984–99 era were headed by northern Muslims. After General Abacha's rise to power in 1993, not only the head of state was a Muslim, but also the Chief of Defence staff, Inspector-General of Police, Minister of Internal Affairs, National Security Adviser and Chief Justice. This sectionalism, in Suberu and Diamond's words, provoked 'much alarm, alienation, and even paranoia' (Suberu and Diamond 2002: 13). Abacha's northern and Muslim-dominated government trampled on the rights of the minorities in the oil-rich Niger Delta, and executed their leaders, including the novelist Ken Saro-Wiwa.

38 This is particularly important where, as in Nigeria, the lion's share of power is allocated to the centre (Diamond 2001: xvi). An obstacle to consociation in Nigeria is its presidential system of government, which does not lend itself as well to broad-based representative government as parliamentary (cabinet-style) executives (Watts 1999: 88).

As federal regions are also usually ethnically heterogeneous, it is helpful to have consociational practices at the intra-regional level. This device not only addresses the criticism that giving self-government to national minorities will lead to an abuse of their powers against local minorities, but promotes good inter-regional and regional-centre relations. Particularly when a regional minority is part of a state majority, abuse of its position by the regional majority can have serious and negative effects on centre-regional and inter-regional relations.

One of the weaknesses of the Canadian federation is that while the francophone minority has been reasonably accommodated at the federal level through (partly informal) consociational practices, there has been no commensurate accommodation of minorities at the provincial level, except, arguably, in New Brunswick. Measures taken by Quebec against its anglophone minority in the late 1980s helped to produce an anti-Quebec backlash in the rest of the country that undermined constitutional negotiations aimed at accommodating Quebec. One result was that, by 1990, support for separation in Quebec had soared to its highest levels ever. The Canadian federation may have been saved by the fact that separatists were not in power at the time and were unable to capitalise on the divisions by calling a referendum on separation. When they were able to call such a referendum, five years later, when the atmosphere was calmer, they still managed to win 49.4 per cent of the vote.

39 From 1885, elections in the UK were based on a universal male franchise, and from 1918, a universal franchise.

40 The Canadian Federation's birth was in fact a hybrid of 'coming together' and 'holding together' processes: on the one hand, it involved the joining together of a number of previously separate British North American colonies; on the other hand, it involved the division of the unitary colony of the 'Two Canadas' into the separate federal units of Ontario and Quebec.

41 The importance of voluntary origins for the legitimacy and stability of states, whether federations or union states, is often recognized in the rival historiographies of federalists/unionists and separatists. The former arguing that the federation/union arose voluntarily while the latter argue it was imposed. In Canada, Quebecois nationalists point to the conquest of 1759 as Canada's starting point, or argue that the confederation agreement of 1867 was not 'really' voluntary. Federalists, on the other hand, point to the key role that francophone elites had in shaping the federal agreement. Similar debates take place between unionists in Britain and Scottish nationalists.

References

Adeney, K. 2002 'Constitutional Centring: Nation Formation and Consociational Federalism in India and Pakistan', *Journal of Commonwealth and Comparative Politics*, Vol. 40, No. 3: 8–33.

Arora, B. and D.V. Verney. 1995. *Multiple Identities in a Single State: Indian Federalism in Comparative Perspective*. New Delhi: Konark Publishers PVT Ltd.

Bauer, O. 2000. *The Question of Nationalities and Social Democracy* (translation of *Nationalitätenfrage und die Sozialdemokratie* by J. O'Donnell). Minneapolis, MN: University of Minnesota Press.

Bosco, A. ed. 1992. *The Federal Idea: the History of Federalism since 1945*. London: Lothian Foundation Press.

Brass, P. 1990. *The Politics of India Since Independence*. New Delhi: Cambridge University Press.

Brubaker, R. 1996. *Nationalism Reframed*. Cambridge: Cambridge University Press.

Bunce, V. 1999. *Subversive Institutions: The Design and the Destruction of Socialism and the State*. Cambridge: Cambridge University Press.

Connor, W. 1984. *The National Question in Marxist-Leninist Theory and Strategy*. Princeton, NJ: Princeton University Press.

——— 1994. *Ethnonationalism: The Quest for Understanding*. Princeton, NJ: Princeton University Press.

Diamond, L. 2001. 'Foreword' in R. Suberu 2001 ed., *Federalism and Ethnic Conflict in Nigeria*. Washington DC: United States Institute of Peace.

Elazar, D. 1987. *Exploring Federalism*. Tuscaloosa, AL: University of Alabama.

——— 1994. *Federalism and the Way to Peace*. Kingston: Queen's Institute of Intergovernmental Relations.

Ferenczi, T. 2001. 'The Republic, a French Myth' (unpublished paper).

Forsyth, M. ed. 1989. *Federalism and Nationalism*. Leicester: Leicester University Press.

Gellner, E. 1983. *Nations and Nationalism*. Ithaca, NY: Cornell University Press.

Glazer, N. 1983. 'Federalism and Ethnicity: The American Solution' in N. Glazer ed., *Ethnic Dilemmas, 1964–82*. Cambridge, MA: Harvard University Press: 274–92.

Gordon, M. 1964. *Assimilation in American Life*. New York: Oxford University Press.

Hale, H. 2004. 'Divided We Stand: Institutional Sources of Ethnofederal State Survival and Collapse', *World Politics*, Vol. 56, No. 2: 165–93.

—— 2005. 'The Makeup and Breakup of Ethnofederal States: Why Russia Survives Where the USSR Fell', *Perspectives in Politics*, Vol. 3, No. 1: 55–70.

Hanf, T. 1991. 'Reducing Conflict Through Cultural Autonomy: Karl Renner's Contribution' in U. Ra'anan, M. Mesner, K. Armes and K. Martin eds, *State and Nation in Multi-Ethnic Societies: The Breakup of Multi-National States*. Manchester: Manchester University Press: 33–52.

Hayden, R.M. 1992. 'Constitutional Nationalism in the formerly Yugoslav Republics', *Slavic Review*, Vol. 51: 654–73.

Hayward, J. 1993. *After the French Revolution: Six Critics of Democracy and Nationalism*. New York: New York University Press.

Hechter. M. 2000. *Containing Nationalism*. Oxford: Oxford University Press.

Hooghe, L. 1993. 'Belgium: From Regionalism to Federalism' in J. Coakley ed., *The Territorial Management of Ethnic Conflict*. London: Frank Cass: 44–68.

Horowitz, D. 1985. *Ethnic Groups in Conflict*. Berkeley: University of California Press.

—— 1998. 'Self-Determination: Politics, Philosophy and Law' in M. Moore ed., *National Self-Determination and Secession*. Oxford: Oxford University Press: 181–214.

Keating, M. 2001. *Plurinational Democracy: Stateless Nations in a Post-Sovereignty Era*. Oxford: Oxford University Press.

—— 2002. 'Plurinational Democracy in a Post-Sovereign Order' (unpublished paper).

King, P. 1982. *Federalism and Federation*. London: Croom Helm.

Kymlicka, W. 1995. *Multicultural Citizenship*. Oxford. Oxford University Press.

—— 2001. *Politics in the Vernacular*. Oxford: Oxford University Press.

Leff, C.S. 1998. *The Czech and Slovak Republics: Nation Versus State*. Boulder, CO: Westview.

Lieven D. and J. McGarry. 1993. 'Ethnic Conflict in the Soviet Union and its Successor States' in J. McGarry and B. O'Leary eds, *The Politics of Ethnic Conflict Regulation*. London: Routledge: 62–83.

Lijphart, A. 1977. *Democracy in Plural Societies: A Comparative Exploration*. New Haven and London: Yale University Press.

—— 1979. 'Consociation and Federation: Conceptual and Political Links', *Canadian Journal of Political Science*, Vol. XII, No. 3: 499–515.

—— 1996. 'The Puzzle of Indian Democracy: A Consociational Interpretation', *American Political Science Review*, Vol. 65: 682–93.

Linz, J. 1997. 'Democracy, Multinationalism and Federalism' Working Paper, 1997/103.

Linz, J. and A. Stepan. 1992. 'Political Identities and Electoral Sequences: Spain, The Soviet Union, and Yugoslavia' *Daedalus*, Vol. 121, No. 2, Spring: 123–39.

Lipset, S.M. 1960. *Political Man: The Social Bases of Politics*. Garden City, New York: Doubleday.

—— 1985. 'The Revolt against Modernity' in S.M. Lipset, *Consensus and Conflict: Essays in Political Sociology*. New Brunswick: Transaction: 253–93.

McGarry, J. 2001. 'Northern Ireland and the Shortcomings of Civic Nationalism' in J. McGarry ed., *Northern Ireland and the Divided World*. Oxford: Oxford University Press: 109–36.

McGarry, J. and B. O'Leary. 1993. 'The Macro-Political Regulation of Ethnic Conflict' in J. McGarry and B. O'Leary eds, *The Politics of Ethnic Conflict Regulation*. London: Routledge: 1–40.

Madison, J., A. Hamilton and J. Jay. 1788/1987. *The Federalist Papers*, edited and with an introduction by Isaac Kramnick. Harmondsworth: Penguin.

Majocchi, L.V. 1991. 'Nationalism and Federalism in 19th Century Europe' in A. Bosco ed., *The Federal Idea: The History of Federalism from Enlightenment to 1945*. London: Lothian Press: 155–65.

Mathew, G. 2005. 'India' in A. Griffiths ed., *Handbook of Federal Countries 2005*. Montreal: McGill-Queen's University Press: 166–82.

Moore, M. 2001. *The Ethics of Nationalism*. Oxford: Oxford University Press.

Nasr, V. 2001. 'The Negotiable State: Borders and Power-Struggles in Pakistan' in B. O'Leary, I.S. Lustick and T. Callaghy eds, *Right-Sizing the State: The Politics of Moving Borders*. Oxford: Oxford University Press: 168–200.

Noel, S. 1993. 'Canadian Responses to Ethnic Conflict: Consociationalism, Federalism and Control' in J. McGarry and B. O'Leary eds, *The Politics of Ethnic Conflict-Regulation: Case Studies of Protracted Ethnic Conflicts*. London: Routledge: 41–61.

Nordlinger, E. 1972. *Conflict Regulation in Divided Societies*. Harvard: Center for International Affairs.

O'Leary, B. 2001. 'An Iron Law of Nationalism and Federation? A (Neo-Diceyian) Theory of the Necessity of a Federal Staatsvolk, and of Consociational Rescue', *Nations and Nationalism*, Vol. 7, No. 3: 273–96.

—— 2002. 'In Praise of Empires Past', *New Left Review* 2nd series Vol. 18: 106–30.

—— 2005. 'Debating Consociational Politics: Explanatory and Normative Arguments' in S. Noel ed., *From Power-Sharing to Democracy: Post-Conflict Institutions in Ethnically Divided Societies*. Montreal: McGill-Queen's University Press: 3–43.

O'Leary, B. and McGarry, J. 1996. *The Politics of Antagonism: Understanding Northern Ireland*, 2nd edition. London: Athlone Press.

O'Leary, B., J. McGarry and K. Salih eds, 2005. *The Future of Kurdistan in Iraq*. Philadelphia: University of Pennsylvania Press.

Pfabigan, A. 1991. 'The Political Feasibility of the Austro-Marxist proposal for the Solution of the Nationality Problem of the Danubian Monarchy' in U. Ra'anan, M. Mesner, K. Armes and K. Martin eds, *State and Nation in Multi-Ethnic Societies: The Breakup of Multi-National States*. Manchester: Manchester University Press: 53–63.

Premdas, R.R. 1998. *Secession and Self-Determination in the Caribbean: Nevis and Tobago*. St. Augustine, Trinidad: The University of the West Indies.

Riker, W.H. 1964. *Federalism: Origin, Operation, Significance*. Boston: Little, Brown & Company.

Roeder, P. 1991. 'Soviet Federalism and Ethnic Mobilization', *World Politics*, Vol. 43, January: 196–232.

Snyder, J. 2000. *From Voting to Violence: Democratization and Nationalist Conflict*. New York: Norton.

Steiner, J. 1989. 'Power-Sharing: Another Swiss Export Product?' in J. Montville ed., *Conflict and Peacemaking in Multiethnic Societies*. Lexington, MA: Lexington Books: 107–114.

Stepan, A. 1999. 'Federalism and Democracy: Beyond the U.S. Model', *Journal of Democracy*, Vol. 10, No. 4, October: 19–34.

—— 2001. *Arguing Comparative Politics*. Oxford: Oxford University Press.

Suberu, R. 2001. *Federalism and Ethnic Conflict in Nigeria*. Washington DC: United States Institute of Peace.

Suberu, R. and L. Diamond. 2002. 'Institutional Design, Ethnic Conflict Management, and Democracy in Nigeria' in A. Reynolds ed., *The Architecture of Democracy: Institutional Design, Conflict Management and Democracy*. Oxford: Oxford University Press: 400–28.

Tarlton, C. 1965. 'Symmetry and Asymmetry as Elements of Federalism: A Theoretical Speculation', *Journal of Politics*, Vol. 27, No. 4: 861–74.

Trudeau, P. 1968 (1965). 'Federalism, Nationalism and Reason' in P. Trudeau ed., *Federalism and the French Canadians*. Toronto: University of Toronto Press: 182–203.

von Beyme, K. 1985. *Political Parties in Western Democracies*. Aldershot: Gower.

Watts, R. 1987. 'Federalism' in *The Blackwell Encyclopaedia of Political Institutions*, edited by Vernon Bogdanor. Oxford: Basil Blackwell: 228–30.

—— 1998. 'Federalism, Federal Political Systems, and Federations', *Annual Review of Political Science*, Vol. 1: 117–37.

Watts, R.L. 1999. *Comparing Federal Systems*. London: Queen's University Press.

—— 2001. 'Models of Federal Power-sharing', *International Social Science Journal*, Vol. 53, No. 167, March: 23–32.

Weller, M. 1992. 'The International Response to the Dissolution of the Socialist Federal Republic of Yugoslavia', *American Journal of International Law* 86: 569–607.

Woodward, S. 1995. *Balkan Tragedy*. New York: Brookings Institution.

11 India and Switzerland as multinational federations

Harihar Bhattacharyya

> In a world in which the national state is the overwhelming norm, all of this means that nations can now be imagined without linguistic communality – not in the naive spirit of nosotros los Americanos, but out of a general awareness of what modern history has demonstrated to be possible.
>
> Benedict Anderson (1983)[1]

Introduction: the problem

The basic question that I seek to raise in the discussion in this chapter relates to relative political stability and unity in multinational countries. In this age of what Hobsbawm calls 'nation-splitting',[2] the unity and integrity of Switzerland and India, and their ability to hold themselves together in the face of a number challenges are remarkable indeed. Generally, India and Switzerland do not seem to be comparable. In terms of size, population, levels of development, culture and history, they are simply incomparable. Comparing the two would mean to compare, as if, the rich with the poor, which is not usually done. In that case, the more appropriate word to be used is 'contrast', not 'comparison'. Switzerland, a very small country in central Europe, population estimated to be around seven million, is one of the top richest countries in the West and the world. India, by contrast, the second most populous country after China in the world (population over a billion now), is a very vast yet poor, developing post-colonial country in Asia marked by mass poverty, a high degree of unemployment, massive illiteracy, regional imbalances in development and marked social and economic inequalities. Switzerland's democracy is the oldest in the world, and its confederal experience was more than 600 years old before it was transformed into a federation in 1848. Both democracy and federalism in India, by contrast, are of a relatively recent origin beginning in the 1950s after two centuries of British colonial rule.

And yet, Switzerland and India are comparable. Both have complex social and cultural diversities, and both are more or less stable, democratic and federal countries. Switzerland's political stability is more than a century and a half old while India's is half a century old. Although India is the most diverse country in the world, Switzerland's diversity is no less intriguing. Switzerland is a multilingual and multi-religious country in which the combination of either or both of them with region(s) cuts across each other in ways that has made the country's diversity baffling. India's diversity is proverbial: it is a multilingual, multi-religious, multi-communal, multiracial, multi-tribal country in which the various ethnic markers in combination with region(s) have given it a complex character (see Chapter 4 on India). Ethnically, both are multinational countries although constitutionally, not designated as such. Both are fragmented societies with potential and manifest conflicts, yet have maintained unity and integrity.

If India was a nation state in the classical sense of the term, this multinational country would have disintegrated long ago. The Preamble of the Constitution of India begins with 'We, the People of India' which resonates with the notion of the nation state. Interestingly enough, the paradigmatic and ideological sway of the nation state in India has remained far removed from the growing political reality which has experienced a specific state formation, itself the result of ethno-national pressures from below. What took shape in India is a multilayered and democratic federal polity as political expressions of the multinational society. In both India and Switzerland, federalism backed by democracy has thus limited the nation state, ethnically speaking. To the extent that India and Switzerland are federations, they are certainly not nation states.

The basic reason as to why India and Switzerland should nonetheless be compared consists mainly in the following reason: an identification of the specific elements of the political models responsible for managing conflicts with different degrees of success in complex multinational contexts. Both are fragmented societies with bases of potential conflicts. Historically, both have experienced (India still does!) violent conflicts manifested in religious, ethnic and subnational demands, and riots and pogroms. Since the founding of the Swiss federation in 1848, Switzerland has maintained remarkable ethnic peace except for the secession (internal) of the Jura, the French-speaking and Catholic area, which separated itself from the predominantly Protestant and German-speaking Canton of Berne in 1978, and formed the twenty-sixth canton of the Swiss federation. In India, such internal secession in order to rightsize the territory for establishing the correspondence between the ethno-national boundary and the political boundary, as far as possible, has marked the federation's most challenging task. Indeed, as recently as 2000, three new *states*, as constituent units of the federation, were added to the list of 25 states.[3] In both, specific notions of federalism with their respective traits have been found to be instrumental in resolving, politically, many of the conflicts, and ensuring political order and legitimacy. In both, federalism has enabled the democratic process to deal effectively with ethno-national conflicts and to maintain political order.

The basic argument that I seek to advance in this chapter is based on a distinction between what I would call 'thick' and 'thin' nations. The thick nations are nations in the ethnic sense defined by such terms as language and tribal ethnicity, and are usually deeply rooted in history, culture and tradition (see Chapter 4 on India). The thin nation is mostly the nation as originally imagined by the elites, and subsequently created; it has an artificial character. Its most distinctive character is that it is imagined to be a political community in which a sharing of certain common political values is emphasized. This distinction has special relevance in multicultural, diverse countries whose nationalizing quest (politically speaking), as a legitimate basis of the state, is alone possible in the political realm. Compared to the ethnic character of the thick nations, the distinctive character of the thin nation, which is not associated with any particular ethnic marker, is political and secular. In this chapter, I take federalism as a dynamic political equilibrium which, when backed by democracy, better accommodates nations in culturally diverse countries, and serves as an effective tool of resolving ethnic conflicts.

Multinational Switzerland: demographic

Switzerland is a small country both in size and population. It has an area of $41,293 \text{ km}^2$, which is about half the size of the Indian state of West Bengal, and comparable to the small Indian state of Haryana (44,202 square kilometres). A landlocked territory with no natural frontiers, this very hilly state has also very limited land available for use: 4.3 per cent for residential/industrial, 28.3 per cent for meadow/arable, 20.6 per cent for pasture, 25.5 per cent for forestry and 21.3 per cent wasteland, rivers and lakes.[4] Its 7.09 million (1997) population again is comparable to the population of such small Indian states as Nagaland (6.9 million), one of the Christian majority states in India's north-east, but less than the population of Delhi (9.4 million) (1991), India's capital. Switzerland's small population lives in as many as 26 cantons and half-cantons. Switzerland's population is about 2 per cent of the population of Western Europe.

Linguistic diversity

Like India, Switzerland is also a diverse country in terms of languages, religions and identities. There are four languages in Switzerland (Table 11.1): Swiss German, Swiss French, Swiss Italian and Romansh. In 1990, the distribution of linguistic population was like this: Swiss German (63.6 per cent), Swiss French (19.2 per cent), Swiss Italian (7.6 per cent) and Romansh (0.6 per cent). Linguistic diversity in Switzerland is more complex than it appears. The good majority of the German-speaking people in the population of Switzerland (around 65 per cent today)[5] has not resulted, as it would have otherwise elsewhere, in the domination of the German linguistic community in the Swiss political system. But thanks to the canton-based Swiss federal system, this has not happened. Also, the linguistic situation in

Table 11.1 Linguistic distribution of population (by mother tongue) of Switzerland (1950–90) (%)[34]

Year	Swiss German	French	Italian	Romansh	Others
1950	72.1	20.3	5.9	1.0	0.7
1960	69.3	18.9	9.5	0.9	1.4
1970	64.9	18.1	11.9	0.8	4.3
1980	65.0	18.4	9.8	0.8	6.0
1990	63.6	19.2	7.6	0.6	8.9

Source: *Statistisches Jahrbuch der Schweiz 1995*, quoted in Steinberg (1996), p. 131.

Note
The fluctuations in the population in this table is to be understood in terms of two things: first, the Swiss population contains 18 per cent foreigners of different languages and religions, and second, migration to Switzerland has fluctuated due to a host of socio-political factors in the countries from which people have migrated. For instance, from the beginning of the century up to about 1960, the German speakers constituted a very high percentages of all foreigners (53.2 per cent in 1930, 49.1 per cent in 1941, 40.1 per cent in 1950 and 27.5 per cent in 1960). *Statistisches Jahrbuch der Schweiz 1999*, p. 408.

Switzerland in so far as the Swiss German, Swiss French and Swiss Italian are concerned is very complex. Except the French, which has a regional basis, to some extent, these actually refer to a plurality of dialects rather than single homogeneous languages like those across the borders. However, the key to understanding the linguistic situation in Switzerland lies at the level of the cantons.

The data in Table 11.2 show that in Switzerland, there are 19 German, six French and one Italian majority cantons and half-cantons. However, this has not led to the dominance of the German-speakers in the Swiss political process. The other distinctive feature, from the point of view of the minorities in Switzerland, is that the cantonal boundaries today correspond mostly, though not entirely, to the linguistic ones. Except Graubunden (a trilingual canton) where the German-speakers are 65.3 per cent of the total population with 11 per cent Italian and 17.1 per cent Romansh minorities (the rest, others), in the rest of the 18 cantons and half-cantons, the German-speakers range from 78.6 per cent to 93.1 per cent. Except Valais (59.7 per cent) and Fribourg (61.0 per cent), the French majority is quite high in the rest of the French majority cantons (ranging from 70.5 per cent to 87.8 per cent). In the lone Italian Canton of Ticino, the Italian-speakers are also a very high (82.8 per cent) proportion of the population. The German-speakers are minorities most significantly in Fribourg (29.7 per cent) and Valais (29.4 per cent), but constitute an important element of the population in some cantons and half-cantons (9.8 per cent in Ticino, 9 per cent in Vaud, 5.5 per cent in Geneva, 5.2 per cent in Neuchatel and 4.8 per cent in Jura). But the French-speakers are minorities of importance only in Berne (7.8 per cent), and in others, they constitute a very small proportion of the population (1.5 per cent and below). The Italian-speakers, however, are significant minorities in many cantons and

Table 11.2 Linguistic distribution of population in cantons and half-cantons (1990) (%)

Canton	German	French	Italian	Romansh	Others
Zurich	82.5	1.5	5.9	0.3	9.9
Bern	83.8	7.8	2.8	0.1	5.6
Luzern	88.6	0.6	2.8	0.1	7.8
Uri	93.2	0.2	1.9	0.2	4.5
Schwyz	89.4	0.4	3.1	0.2	6.9
Obwald-En*	92.8	0.4	1.4	0.1	5.3
Nidwald-En*	93.1	0.5	1.7	0.2	4.6
Glarus	83.6	0.3	6.8	0.2	9.1
Zug	85.0	1.1	3.7	0.3	10.0
Fribourg	29.7	61.0	1.9	0.1	7.5
Solothur-N	87.1	1.1	4.7	0.1	6.9
Basel-City*	78.6	2.7	6.4	0.1	12.1
Basel-Region*	86.0	1.7	4.6	0.1	7.5
Schaffh-Housen	86.7	0.6	4.0	0.1	8.6
Appenz-Ell (OR)*	88.6	0.3	2.9	0.2	8.0
Appenz-Ell (IR)*	91.7	0.2	1.7	0.1	6.3
St-Gallen	87.2	0.5	3.6	0.3	8.6
Graubuen-Den	65.3	0.5	11.0	17.1	6.1
Aargau	85.7	0.9	4.9	0.2	8.4
Thurgau	86.2	0.4	4.4	0.2	8.8
Ticino	9.8	1.9	82.8	0.1	5.4
Vaud	9.0	77.1	4.4	0.1	12.5
Valais	29.4	59.7	3.0	0.1	7.9
Neucha-Tel	5.2	80.2	4.8	0.1	9.7
Geneva	5.5	70.5	5.3	0.1	18.7
Jura	4.8	87.8	2.5	0.1	4.9

Source: *Statistisches Jahrbuch der Schweiz 1999*, p. 407.

Note
* Indicates half-cantons.

half-cantons (11 per cent in Graubunden, 6.8 per cent in Glarus, 6.4 per cent in Basel-City, 5.3 per cent in Geneva and so on) (Table 11.2).

Religion

Religions, like languages, have divided and united the Swiss. Table 11.3 provides data on the total population of Switzerland. Since all those who live in Switzerland as residents are not Swiss *citizens*, the proportions of the religious composition of the Swiss need to be shown particularly because this makes the Protestants the single largest religious group. Thus, of the Swiss citizens, the following figures indicate the religious composition of the federation: Protestants (47.3 per cent), Roman Catholics (43.3 per cent), and

Table 11.3 Religious composition of the population (1990)

Religions	Persons	Percentage
Roman Catholic	3,172,321	46.1
Protestant	2,747,821	40.0
Christcatholic*	11,748	0.2
East Church (Orthodox)	71,501	1.0
Other Christians	58,501	0.9
Israelists	17,577	0.3
Muslims	152,217	2.2
Other religions	29,175	0.4
Not belonging to any religions	510,927	7.4
Religion not stated	101,899	1.5
Total	6,873,687	100.0

Source: *Statistisches Jahrbuch der Schweiz 1999*, p. 408.

Note
* Refers to traditional Catholics.

others (9.94 per cent). Switzerland nonetheless is a multi-religious country because apart from the two major religious groups, there are significant proportions of other faiths (Table 11.3). Since religions informed (and continue to inform) cultures and identities, religious conflicts visited Switzerland, historically, very much like elsewhere in Europe. However, given the different historical trajectories of social and political development in Switzerland, religious conflicts there did not take the same dramatic forms, such as the great European divide, throughout the late middle and the early modern ages, between the church and the state. Up to the middle, or to be precise, the late nineteenth century, the ancient religious cleavages in Switzerland had, Anderson argues, more political salience than linguistic ones.[6] Therefore, the great secularism debates of Europe of the time were not revisited in Switzerland in the same manner. Steinberg (1996) has offered an excellent analytical discussion of the religious conflicts in Switzerland, and has shown how the Swiss effectively handled the religious issues for a 'lasting religious peace' in the country since the nineteenth century.[7] He has shown the virulence and complexities of the religious conflicts in the cantons, and their impact in shaping the identity and the contours of politics of many of the cantons.

'Religious denomination', says Steinberg, 'is part of the geography of Swiss identity'.[8] The Swiss rejected the French imposed secular, uniform centralized state, in the early nineteenth century, but did not re-establish theocracies in its stead. Political power in Switzerland never derived either from the church or from an absolute monarchy based on the divine right theory of kings, as in the rest of Europe. This was to give a different paradigm to the state–religion relations in Switzerland. In a country where all power derived democratically from the people, the religious conflicts had to have different resolutions. The Swiss typically had their (decentralized) institutional solutions to religious problems. The solutions got enmeshed with the power balance and political processes.

Several historical forces facilitated the decline of what Linder has called 'confessional schism': the impact of modern liberal democracy (1874 Federal Constitution), which reduced the direct religious influence on the state, the process of modernization which overcame the separation between Catholic and Protestant societies (this migration across regions inside the country led to desegregation), and the changes in the role of political Catholicism (in the 1970s, for instance, the Catholic Conservative Party renamed itself the Christian Democratic Party). Swiss federalism also played an important political role in the same way by providing for genuine autonomy to the cantons, and thus confined the religious issues to the paradigm of cantonal autonomy. Therefore, although the Swiss confederal authority is modern and 'secular', the same cannot be said to be true for the cantonal authorities where the relation between the state and the church varies from canton to canton, and is yet to be settled. Linder's view is instructive: 'Usually, there is no complete separation of state and church: the Protestant, Roman Catholic and the small Christ-Catholic churches are acknowledged as public institutions, called *Landeskirchen*.'[9]

Nation-accommodating institutional measures: India and Switzerland

Demographically, as we have seen above, both India and Switzerland contain many 'thick' nations (ethnically speaking). Many regionally-based linguistic, tribal or ethno-religious communities in India are not only significant in number, but also have a distinct history, culture and tradition. In Switzerland, it is not accurate simply to characterize the four linguistic groups (German, French, Italian and Romansh) as 'nations' because they live in 26 cantons and half-cantons. This is so in spite of the fact that the current Swiss Constitution has recognized them to be 'national' languages. In India, by comparison, Bengalis, a distinct nationality, are the overwhelming majority in two Indian states (West Bengal and Tripura), and the Hindi speakers, India's single largest linguistic group, are in the majority in Uttar Pradesh, Madhya Pradesh, Rajasthan and Bihar (the Hindi heartland of India).

In Switzerland, salience of religion was reduced after the Civil War of 1847 and the foundation of the federation in 1848. In India, after the major conflicts between the Muslims and the Hindus, and the Partition in 1947, religion as a factor of nationality was de-recognized. The question is: how have these two federations institutionally accommodated many 'thick' nations in their respective federations.

Switzerland: nation-accommodating territorial measures

The Swiss federation is based on the sovereignty of the cantons. According to Thomas Fleiner, the leading constitutional lawyer on the Swiss federation, 'The Swiss Confederation exists through and by the will of the Cantons.'[10] Article 3 of the current Constitution states 'The Cantons are sovereign insofar as their sovereignty is not limited by the federal Constitution; they shall exercise all rights which are not transferred to the Confederation.' Further, Article 47 states, 'The Confederation shall respect the autonomy of the Cantons.' The Swiss federation was the product of the cantons, that is, of the compact of the cantons. Although new cantons have been added to the federation subsequently by bifurcating the existing ones, or even by internal secession (Jura from Berne), the constitutive role of the cantons is retained. The Preamble of the present Constitution starts with the following words 'In the name of God Almighty, We, the Swiss People and Cantons . . . adopt the following constitution'. Article 1 of the current Constitution defines what constitutes the Confederation which means the 'Swiss People' and all the 26 cantons and half-cantons. Like the states in India, it is in the cantons that language and religious communities live out their lives in Switzerland. The Swiss Constitution has left the matter of state–church relationships to the authority and autonomy of the cantons. And it is cantonal autonomy that provides the major territorial institutional terrain for the accommodation of linguistic identity. All the cantons and half-cantons have in each a dominant linguistic group and the language of the majority in the cantons is also the official language of the canton concerned. Article 70 of the current Swiss Constitution declares: 'The Cantons shall designate their official languages. In order to preserve harmony between linguistic communities, they shall respect the traditional territorial distribution of languages, and take into account the indigenous linguistic minorities.'

The Swiss cantons are distinct historical entities, socially, culturally and politically speaking. They have an identity of their own which is akin to nationhood. When nations were being built in surrounding Europe, they maintained their separate cantonal identity. Thomas Fleiner (2002) has aptly described their identity as follows:

> Each of the cantonal democratic communities could thus live and develop according to its own culture, history, language, and religion. Each Canton acknowledged the legal culture of its neighbours but established its own perception of the state, law, democracy, and even state–church relations. They retained their own perception of a cantonal nationhood and state legitimacy.[11]

Wolf Linder and Adrian Vatter have also pointed out the deeper basis of cantonal identity: 'When founding the federation in 1848, the 25 cantons kept their own statehood, their own constitutions and most of their political autonomy'.[12]

Canton making

The 'sacredness' of the boundary of the Swiss cantons, recognized as such by both the constitutions of 1848 and 1874 for the sake of inter-cantonal peace,[13] has been as advantageous to the majority 'nation' (linguistically speaking) as it has been disadvantageous to the territorially rooted minorities within the canton concerned. The Swiss Constitution does not contain any provision for the formation of a new canton. Unlike India, where the aggrieved minority nations that are territorially rooted within a state may be accommodated politically in the form of a new state or a substate within the existing state, the Swiss attempt to resolve this problem in a similar fashion is very difficult, if not impossible, and depends primarily upon the affected cantonal constitution. The resolution of the right of self-determination of the Jura people out of the canton of Berne in 1978 was possible only because the canton, empowered by its residual powers, decided to grant such a right.[14] However, the constitutional procedures, followed by first allowing the secession of Jura from Berne and then reintegrating the new canton of Jura as a new federal and constitutional unit within the confederation, were multi-staged and complex.[15]

Non-territorial measures

The current Swiss Constitution, like its predecessor, is particularly sensitive about protecting Swiss diversity, especially its linguistic diversity. The Preamble of the Constitution is one example where it is written that the 'Swiss People and Cantons' are 'determined to live our diversity in unity respecting one another'. As we have already noted above, promoting the 'cultural diversity of the country' is stated to be one of the four purposes of the Confederation (Article 2) while Article 4 of the Constitution states that German, French, Italian and Romansh are the 'national languages' of the Confederation. Moreover, 'Freedom of language' is now a fundamental right of the Swiss people (Article 18).[16]

   The current Swiss Constitution recognizes all four languages of the country: German, French and Italian as official languages of the Confederation, and Romansh as the official language for communicating with persons of Romansh language (Article 70). It is stated in the same Article that it is the job of the Confederation and the cantons to 'encourage understanding and exchange between the linguistic communities'. The Confederation, it is further stated, 'shall support the plurilingual cantons in the fulfillment of their particular tasks'. Taken together, the points outlined above give us more than enough formal evidence about the various ways the Swiss Constitution has sought to accommodate and to protect the linguistic diversity of the country.

Thin nations as political communities

Over and above the so-called 'thick' nations, as we have just described above, there has developed in both India and Switzerland another level of 'nation-ness', which is political, and not particularly associated with any ethnic marker such as language and religion. And yet, it is broadly based on and draws sustenance from many thick nations in both cases. Benedict Anderson (1983), the famous British scholar on nationalism, defines the nation as 'an imagined political community, imagined as both inherently limited and sovereign'.[17] Here the nation is defined as a political community, a secular one, in which members of the nation (citizens), irrespective of their ethnic origins, share, or expect to share, a set of common political values and norms within the over-arching political systems. This nation is socially and culturally based yet politically formulated.

In the political history of nations, this notion of nation came late to Switzerland. According Benedict Anderson, this was a late nineteenth century development when the nation was becoming an international norm, and when it was possible to 'model' a nation in a much more complex way than hitherto.[18] He states that 'in a world in which the nation-state is the overwhelming norm, nations now can be imagined without linguistic commonality, but out of a general awareness of what modern history has demonstrated to be possible.'[19]

According to Anderson, the Swiss national awareness or nation-ness arose only in the late nineteenth century.[20] To be sure, Swiss national awareness was rooted in its pre-modern political institutions (non-dynastic, non-monarchical, republican and democratic) which served to prevent any excess of official nationalism as typically occurred elsewhere in Europe. Anderson's conclusion is that it was possible to 'represent' the Swiss nation-ness as an imagined community without requiring linguistic uniformity due to its rise on the eve of the communications revolution of the twentieth century when nation was becoming an international norm.[21] The Swiss nationhood, dating from 1891, arose in the 'last wave' of nationalism when nationalism was also being fashioned in complex ways in countries in Asia and Africa.[22] In this sense, Swiss nationhood is a later development than the Indian comparison in 1885.

Swiss scholarship has also grappled with the issue of the Swiss as a nation in conditions of four languages, many religions and 26 cantons. Steinberg wrote: 'It is true that Switzerland is not a multinational state but it is not a conventional national state either.'[23] And what Thomas Fleiner remarked about the issue corroborates Anderson's thesis: that the Swiss cantons 'were not integrated into the nation-building process of Europe in the eighteenth and nineteenth centuries'.[24] Elsewhere he noted: 'But as the nation is not ethnically homogenous, the only factor that does unify the country is a shared commitment to the same political values.'[25] Consider further his following observation:

Switzerland is by self-definition a 'non-nation state'. The only legitimacy for the unity of the Swiss Confederation is a political concept of direct democracy, federalism, a specific system of government, liberty of religion and equal rights of the three official languages German, French and Italian. With the exception of the United States, Switzerland is actually and probably the only country which does base its identity not on language, religion or nation, but a specific political concept.[26]

Lidija R. Basta (1996) in attempting to offer an 'outsider's perception' of the Swiss model believes that 'the Swiss nation is a political entity based on commonly shared political values'.[27] She calls it a *communal civism*,[28] a *Willensnation*, that is, nation by will.[29] Linder terms it 'an artificial multicultural nation'.[30] The so-called 'artificiality' is the political construction of a nation out of so many diversities. But then it was never imposed from the top down on the people. The political will involved in this construction was genuine and firmly rooted.[31]

To add further grist to the mill of Anderson (1983), following the 1848 Swiss Constitution, Article 1 of the 1874 Swiss Constitution stated: 'Together, *the peoples of 23 Cantons* of Switzerland by the present alliance . . . form the Swiss Confederation' (emphasis added). Linder and Vatter argued that around 1848, a Swiss society barely existed, and hence the 1848 Constitution spoke of the 'peoples of the cantons'.[32] Since the Swiss nationhood (politically speaking) was a post-1874 development, it is only the current Constitution of 2000 that for the first time recognized the Swiss people. In the Preamble of the Constitution, it is stated '*We, the Swiss People and the Cantons*' adopt the constitution (emphasis added). Article 1 of the present Constitution states: '*The Swiss People and the Cantons* of Zurich, Berne . . . Geneva and Jura form the Swiss Confederation' (emphasis added). The above are not mere constitutional niceties, but symptomatic of the larger changes in the political system. The Preamble of the current Constitution of Switzerland proclaims that the Swiss people are 'determined to live our diversity in unity respecting one another'. The Swiss 'diversity in unity' has been possible, to my mind, because of the political concept of the Swiss nation rather than one based on any single ethnic group or community. There is a remarkable similarity between the Swiss 'diversity-in-unity' and the Indian emphasis on 'unity-in-diversity'. Both of them are inherently federal.

Comparison and conclusion

In conclusion, I would reiterate that in both Switzerland and India, federalism backed by democracy has performed a double task. It has, first, satiated the ethnic, (i.e. thick) nations by providing for institutional arrangements within which thick nations, often combinations of language, religion and region, have been able to maintain and to celebrate their identity. Second, relatively satiated thick nations have facilitated the development of the thin nations, that is, nations as political communities. In Switzerland, federalism, has allowed *cantonal societies*, and Linder and Vatter argue the following: genuine autonomy of their government; ample opportunities to live differently; and the maintenance of their regional traditions and cultures.[33] In India, statehood – as well as the non-territorial measures for the protection of identity – has served as a basis of unity at the political level, and facilitated the development of the political nation. However, in India, it must be pointed out again, when the nation as a political community was always going to be a post-colonial experience, it was federalism coupled with democracy that facilitated the institutional expression of thick nations more or less successfully. The political history of post-independence India is replete with examples of when centralization and the corresponding weakening of the federal polity has encouraged and often hastened the process of 'nationalist' separation in parts of India, and vice versa. Consequently, we can conclude that federalism in India and Switzerland, rather than defeating national self-determination, has served effectively to promote the internal self-determination of many thick nations.

Notes

1 Benedict Anderson, *Imagined Communities: Reflections on the Origin of and the Spread of Nationalism* (London: Verso, 1983), p. 123.
2 Eric Hobsbawm, *Nations and Nationalism Since 1780* (Cambridge: Cambridge University Press, 1991), especially last chapter 'Nationalism in the late 20th century'.
3 For details, Harihar Bhattacharyya, 'India Creates Three New States', in *Federations: What's New in Federalism Worldwide* (Ottawa, Canada) 1 (3), 2001.
4 W. Linder, *Swiss Democracy: Possible Solution to Conflict in Multiethnic Societies* (London: Macmillan, 1994), p. 2.
5 Linder (1994), p. 2.
6 Anderson (1983), p. 125.
7 See for details, Steinberg, J. *Why Switzerland?* (Cambridge and New York: Cambridge University Press, 1996), Chapter 6 'Religion', pp. 206–33. The revision of the Federal Constitution in 1873–74 was undertaken in the backdrop of the so-called 'cultural struggles' between the Catholics and the Protestants, and thus the 1874 Constitution was the culmination, and the successful resolution, of those conflicts.
8 Ibid., p. 206.
9 Ibid., p. 20.
10 Thomas Fleiner, 'Recent Developments of Swiss Federalism', in *Publius: The Journal of Federalism*, 32 (2), Spring, 2002, p. 99.
11 Fleiner (2002), p. 99.
12 Wolf Linder and Adrian Vatter, 'Institutions and Outcomes of Swiss Federalism: The Role of the Cantons in Swiss Politics', in *West European Politics*, Vol. 24, No. 2, April 2001, Special Issue on *The Swiss Labyrinth* edited by Jan-Erik Lane, p. 95
13 Fleiner (2002), p. 106.
14 For further details, see Fleiner (2002), pp. 105–7, and Lidija R. Basta, 'Minority and Legitimacy of a Federal State: An Outsider Perception of the Swiss Model', in L.R. Basta and T. Fleiner (eds), *Federalism and Multiethnic States: The Case of Switzerland* (Fribourg: Institute of Federalism, 1996), pp. 41–69.

15 Fleiner (2002), p. 107.
16 Article 116 of the 1874 Swiss Constitution provided for the national and official languages. It said:

> German, French, Italian and Romansh are the national languages of Switzerland.
> The Confederation and the Cantons shall encourage mutual understanding and exchanges among the linguistic communities.
> The Confederation shall support the measures taken by the Cantons of the Grisons (i.e., Graubuenden) and Ticino to preserve and promote the Romansh and Italian languages.
> German, French and Italian shall be the official languages of the Confederation. Romansh shall serve as an official language for the relations between the Confederation and its Romansh-speaking citizens.

17 Anderson (1983), p. 15.
18 Ibid., p. 126.
19 Ibid., p. 122.
20 Ibid., p. 126.
21 Ibid., p. 127.
22 Ibid., pp. 126–7.
23 Steinberg (1996), p. 251.
24 Fleiner (2002), p. 98.
25 Fleiner (2002), p. 101.
26 Thomas Fleiner, 'Legal Instruments and Procedures to Prevent and Solve Ethnic Conflicts: Experiences of the Swiss Constitution', in T. Fleiner and Lidija R. Basta (eds), *Federalism and Multiethnic States: The Case of Switzerland* (Fribourg: Institute of Federalism, 1996), p. 115.
27 Basta (1996), p. 44.
28 Ibid., pp. 41–67.
29 Ibid., p. 45.
30 Linder (1994), op. cit., Introduction, p. xvi.
31 Fleiner (1996), op. cit., p. 115.
32 Linder and Vatter (2001), p. 100.
33 Linder and Vatter (2001), p. 109.

12 Multinational federations in comparative perspective

Ronald L. Watts

Introduction

Previous chapters of this volume have dealt with the broad conceptual issues related to the notion of multinational federations, with the examination of a range of specific examples, with federation as a method of conflict regulation, and some comparisons between Switzerland and India and with the European Union (EU). The introduction considering the concept of multinational federations and the chapter on federation as a means of conflict regulation have dealt mainly with the general issues, conditions and features common to federations in a multinational context. The focus of this chapter, however, is upon a comparison of the variations in the institutional design and political processes exhibited by multinational federations and how these variations have influenced their relative effectiveness. This will involve references mainly to the examples referred to in the earlier chapters on specific multinational federations, but also to some other examples including both successful cases and the pathology of those that have experienced difficulties or have failed.

Since federation involves a combination of elements of 'self-rule' for the constituent units for certain purposes and 'shared rule' through common institutions for certain other purposes, it will be the contention of this chapter that the form which each of these two aspects takes in an individual multinational federation has a crucial bearing on its relative effectiveness. Thus, the mere adoption of federation or not does not give the full picture. The organization of 'self-rule' for the constituent units may take a variety of forms, and the particular form has a direct effect upon the effective operation of a multinational federation. Similarly, 'shared rule' in the common institutions may take a variety of institutional forms and processes, and these too significantly affect the operation of a multinational federation.

Federalism, federal political systems, federations and multinationalism

To provide a definitional context for the comparison of multinational federations, I start with definitions of 'federalism', 'federal political systems', 'federations' and 'nationalism'. I have elsewhere previously distinguished the terms 'federalism', 'federal political system' and 'federation' (Watts 1998:119–22; 1999:6–14). Following the lead of Preston King (1982) I treat 'federalism' as a normative and philosophical concept involving the advocacy of federal principles, i.e. the combining of joint action and self-government. The terms 'federal political system' and 'federation' are by contrast descriptive terms, and here I follow a distinction made by Daniel Elazar (1987) and use the former term to refer to the broad genus that encompasses a variety of species including constitutionally decentralized unions, federations, confederations, federacies, associated states, condominiums, leagues, joint functional authorities. And I would add to Elazar's list hybrids of these species such as the confederal-federal EU (Watts 1999:9) which Murray Forsyth in Chapter 9 has described as a 'Federal Union'.

The term 'federation' in this threefold distinction refers to a specific species within the broad genus of 'federal political systems'. A 'federation' is a compound polity combining constituent units of government and a general government, each possessing specific powers delegated to it by the citizens through a constitution. As the Supreme Court of Canada has put it, it is a form of government in which territorial self-government is distributed in such a way that citizens 'participate concurrently in different collectivities' (2SCR217 (1998), para. 66). A number of authors, most notably Elazar (1987), have emphasized as distinctive the covenantal character of federations with the authority of each government derived from the constitution rather than from another government. In a federation each government is empowered to deal directly with its citizens in the exercise of a significant portion of its legislative, administrative and taxing powers, and a significant component of each government is directly elected by its citizens. Common characteristics of federations therefore are: the existence of two or more orders of government each acting directly on their citizens; a formal constitutional distribution of legislative and executive authority and allocation of revenue resources to the different orders of government; a supreme written constitution not unilaterally amendable by either order of government and requiring a measure of consent from each order; an umpire, usually in the form of courts, to adjudicate disputes between governments; processes and institutions to facilitate intergovernmental collaboration for those areas where governmental responsibilities are shared or inevitably overlap; and provision for the designated representation of distinct regional views within the federal policy-making institutions, usually including some form of federal second legislative chamber. While these basic features are generally common to federations, federations do vary widely, however, in the number and character of their constituent units, in the form and scope of the distribution of legislative and executive powers and financial resources, in the specific processes for constitutional amendment and flexibility, in the scope and role of the courts (or in the case of Switzerland of referendums) as constitutional umpires, in the character of their intergovernmental relations, and in the structure and processes of the shared representative institutions. Indeed, the relative effectiveness of a federation may depend as much upon the particular variations of these features that it incorporates as upon the general decision to adopt federation as a form of government. Since the focus of this book is primarily upon multinational federations, the analysis in this chapter will be limited to federations rather than to other forms of federal political systems which may also be multinational.

Turning, then, to the definition of 'multinational', I start with the definition offered by my colleague at Queen's University, Will Kymlicka (1995: 11) in which he defines a 'nation' as a 'historical community, more or less institutionally complete, occupying a given territory or homeland, sharing a distinct language and culture'. 'Nationalism', then, is 'a political philosophy that the nation should be collectively and freely institutionally expressed and ruled by its co-nationals' (O'Leary 2001:277–8). Furthermore, I would follow Will Kymlicka's lead (1995:10–16) in distinguishing two broad patterns of cultural diversity within states: 'multination' states and 'polyethnic' states. The former refers to states which contain more than one national group which see themselves as distinct societies and demand various forms of autonomy or self-government to ensure their survival as distinct societies. The latter refers to states which contain a variety of ethnic groups (usually as a result of immigration) which, while seeking greater recognition of their ethnic identity, have as their primary aim not to become separate self-governing communities, but to modify the laws and institutions of the mainstream society to make them more accommodating of cultural differences. While most federations encompass considerable cultural diversity, many of them, such as the United States, Australia, Austria, Germany and Brazil, belong primarily in the category of polyethnic rather than multinational states. Despite their internal cultural diversity, these federations are essentially mono-national in character. Nevertheless, there have been federations, notably the cases selected for consideration in this book – Belgium, Canada, Spain, Russia, Malaysia, Cyprus and India[1] – which encompass or attempt to encompass more than one national group. These multinational federations have sought to express, institutionalize and protect at least two or more national communities, usually on a permanent basis. Multinational federalists explicitly reject the strongly integrationist and assimilationist objectives of mono-national federalists, and indeed they believe that dual or multiple national loyalties are not only possible but indeed are desirable. This chapter will consider in what ways the institutional design and political processes in these federations have been similar or different and how effective these have been in accommodating their multinational character.

'Federation' as an institutional design was not originally developed specifically to deal with multinational situations. Indeed its origins in its modern form lie in the polyethnic but essentially mono-national United States in the eighteenth century, and it has since been applied in other basically mono-national societies such as Australia, Austria and Germany. But the logic on which 'federation' as a form of government is based, i.e. that territorially concentrated minorities are enabled to exercise autonomy or self-rule on matters crucial to their identity without fear of being overridden by a majority within the polity, and at the same time they retain the economic, social, diplomatic, security and other benefits of participating in a larger group, has a particular appeal in multinational situations (Simeon and Conway 2001:339–40). Federation in such cases provides an opportunity for self-rule and self-fulfilment of a specific nation through the institutions of self-government that it controls, while at the same time providing the opportunity to pursue common goals with other closely related nations.

Can multinational federations work?

But it is one thing to advocate the possibility or the desirability of multinational federations. There remains the question: can multinational federations work in practice? This issue has already been raised in Chapter 10 by John McGarry and Brendan O'Leary. This question also raises the further question: what does it mean to ask whether multinational federations can work in practice? How is success to be defined? Persistence and longevity of the federation is one obvious criterion. Avoidance of internal instability, violence, chaos and stalemates are among indicators most would accept (Simeon and Conway 2001:340). Secession and disintegration would clearly indicate failure. But other criteria are also relevant and significant. Have the constituent national groups been able to maintain their distinctiveness or has that been eroded or undermined? Have democratic processes and values been facilitated? Has economic performance been enhanced or hindered? These criteria will all need to be borne in mind in considering whether multinational federations have in practice worked.

Many multinational federations, as well as a number that are not multinational, have experienced difficulties or have even failed. There is a considerable body of literature examining the pathology of federations (Franck 1968; Watts 1977; Hicks 1978; Elazar 1987:240–4; Elazar 1993; Watts 1999:109–15; Ghai 2000:14–25; O'Leary 2001:283–4; Watts 2003). These indicate that where there have been failures these failures have had multiple causes. These examples also give ample evidence that multinational federations have generally experienced greater difficulties than mono-national federations. This has led some analysts, such as Daniel Elazar, to scepticism about the efficacy of multinational federations. Elazar often maintained that in a world marked by fragmentation, ethnic conflict and heightened nationalism, various forms of federal political arrangements combining self-rule and shared rule might provide a key to peace (Elazar 1994). At the same time, however, he saw ethnic nationalism as one of the strongest forces arrayed against federalism (Elazar 1994:167–8). Indeed, noting that multinational federations had in practice been among the most difficult to sustain and least likely to survive, he was inclined to suggest that confederations rather than federations of ethnic states would have a better chance of success.

A study of the pathology of federations confirms that Elazar was right to suggest that multinational federations have been among the most difficult to sustain and that federation is not a panacea for those seeking to reconcile conflicting nations. But the evidence is not as one-sided as Elazar was inclined to suggest. Note has to be taken of the persistence and longevity of such federations as Switzerland and Canada (despite its problems) both of which have survived and progressed for well over a century. Furthermore, despite early forecasts at the time of their independence that neither India nor Malaysia as federations would last a decade, the Indian federation has survived now for half a century and has been relatively successful in dealing with its ethno-nationalist challenges through democratic processes. Malaysia has survived for four decades and has been one of the most prosperous among the South-east Asian regimes. More recently there are the examples in Europe of the evolution of Belgium and Spain from unitary systems towards multinational federations. These examples taken together suggest that Elazar may perhaps have underestimated the extent to which, under certain conditions and with appropriate institutional arrangements and political processes, multinational federations can be sustained and may be considered preferable to confederations which tend to be more fragile. Indeed, the sparsity of long-standing multinational confederations which might serve as examples of effectiveness over the long term, and the fact that the European Union has already had to convert itself progressively into a hybrid of confederal and federal institutions raises doubts about the preferability of confederal solutions for reconciling sharp national divisions. While no doubt in some situations a confederal framework may be the only solution possible, confederal solutions have some inherent problems of their own for establishing long-term stability and legitimacy. Thus while experience confirms that multinational federations, both old and new, have often been particularly difficult polities to govern, these difficulties have usually been the very reason that it was necessary in the first place to establish some form of federal political system rather than some other alternative. Despite the fears often expressed that autonomy for national minorities is a one-way path to conflict and state disintegration, in fact autonomy and federation have often had an opposite and positive effect (McGarry 2002:433–6; Ghai 2000:23–4).

In relation to the other criteria referred to above, it is clear that within a number of multinational federations constituent groups have for more than a century been able to maintain a vigorous distinctiveness, as illustrated by Quebec and New Brunswick in Canada and by the linguistically and religiously distinct cantons of Switzerland. In terms of facilitating democratic political processes, it is noteworthy that Arend Lijphart (1999:5) included among the 36 democratic countries he analysed Switzerland, Canada, Belgium, Spain and India, all federations with a multinational character (see also Wachendorfer-Schmidt 2000:243). Indeed, Lijphart (1999:51) cites Larry Diamond who by the end of the 1980s judged India to be 'the most surprising and important case of democratic endurance in the developing world'. While the degree to which federal structures have contributed to or limited economic development and prosperity is difficult to determine conclusively, at least one study has suggested that empirically federations, including some multinational examples, have done at least as well or better than comparable unitary countries (Wachendorfer-Schmidt 2000:223,243).

My response, then, to the question 'can multinational federation work?' is that such multinational federations have generally been more difficult than most other forms of federation to sustain, but that in practice under certain conditions they have worked, a conclusion with which the chapter by John McGarry and Brendan O'Leary in this book is also in agreement. We need, therefore, to identify from a review of the successes and failures of multinational federations what factors have been necessary to sustain multinational federations. Chapter 10 by John McGarry and Brendan O'Leary suggests five general conditions contributing to the effectiveness of multinational federations. In this chapter rather than focusing on broad general conditions, we shall focus specifically on the significance of federal institutional design and political processes.

The significance of institutional design and political processes

As noted earlier in the section of this chapter devoted to distinguishing 'federalism', 'federal political systems' and 'federations', although federations have certain basic features in common, there has been considerable variation in their institutional design: in the number and character of their constituent units, in the form and scope of the distribution of legislative and executive powers, in the allocation and redistribution of financial resources, in the procedures required for constitutional amendment, in the scope and role of the courts as constitutional umpires, in the character of their intergovernmental relations, and in the form and character of their shared representative institutions, including their federal second chambers. These differences in the particular institutional design and the resultant political processes that have developed have had a direct bearing on the effectiveness of individual multinational federations that may be as significant as the adoption or not of federation as a general form of government.

The importance of both effective self-rule and effective shared rule

In considering the significance of institutional design and political processes for the effectiveness of a federation, whether multinational or not, it must be emphasized that the elements of self-rule and shared rule are both essential.

Sometimes debates have arisen over these as alternatives. An example was the debate in Canada in the 1980s over the relative importance of 'intrastate federalism' versus 'interstate federalism' (Smiley and Watts 1985). But in fact *both* are key elements in the federal idea and are therefore fundamental to the effective application of a federal solution (Watts 1999:7), and this is particularly so in the case of multinational federations. The importance of effective national autonomy within such federations has been emphasized by a number of authors (Kymlicka 1995:27–30; Ghai 2000:14–25). But effective autonomous 'self-rule' by itself is insufficient. Institutions and processes for effective 'shared rule' have been equally essential in order to provide the glue to hold the different national groups within a federation together (Kymlicka 1995:31–3). Consequently, in each case we need to look at the extent to which the particular form of the institutions established and the particular political processes encouraged by the electoral system, the character of the political parties, organized groups, bureaucracies and informal elites, have contributed either to the moderation or accentuation of political conflict.

Features of institutional design and political processes facilitating self-rule

Careful design of institutional structures has been essential for the success of autonomy within multinational federations (Ghai 2000:21–3). Among the institutional features affecting autonomy or *self-rule* for the constituent national groups within a multinational federation are: (1) how congruent the constituent territorial units of government are with the distribution of national groups; (2) the number of constituent units of government; (3) the form and scope of the distribution of legislative and executive authority; (4) the allocation of financial resources; (5) the degree of symmetry or asymmetry in the relationship of the constituent units to the federation; (6) the effectiveness of the guarantees of autonomy; and (7) effective dispute settlement mechanisms.

The congruence of constituent units with the distribution of national groups

There have been two approaches to attempting to harmonize nationalisms within a multinational federation. One is to enable each nation to have a measure of autonomous self-rule by having the territorial units of the constituent governments coincide with the distribution of national groups. The other, as advocated by Horowitz (1985), is that of weakening potentially competing ethno-nationalisms by deliberately creating constituent units of government that do not coincide with the distribution of national groups.

The clearest examples of the latter strategy were the initial delineation of states within India in 1950 and more recently the establishment of the nine new provinces in South Africa. Empirical evidence suggests, however, that generally the approach of making constituent units of government congruent with the national groups has been preferred. Indeed this has often proved irresistible under the insistence of national groups pressing for their own self-governance. Broadly speaking, Canada in relation especially to Quebec, Switzerland in respect of its majority of unilingual cantons and Belgium with its three communities, have followed this path. Moreover in both India and Nigeria national pressures have proved irresistible leading to the progressive reorganization of internal state borders along largely linguistic lines, a development undertaken in the case of India despite Nehru's initial reluctance. The most extreme example of this approach is the 'ethnic federalism' approach in Ethiopia, although that example has not been analysed in depth in this volume.

Nevertheless, even where the national social segmentation is relatively clearly concentrated and differentiated territorially, populations rarely in practice have been distributed into neat and completely watertight territorial national units. In Canada there is the significant English-speaking minority in Quebec and the French-speaking minorities in the other provinces, especially New Brunswick and Ontario. In Switzerland there are three bilingual cantons and one trilingual canton. In Belgium there is the particular case of Brussels. Malaysia provides a fairly extensive example of overlapping populations. Consequently, in most federations some intra-unit minorities have existed. In such cases one or a combination of two or three types of solution has been adopted (Watts 1999:104–7). The first has been to redraw the boundaries of the constituent units to coincide better with the distribution of linguistic and ethnic groups. Major examples have been the creation of the new Jura canton in Switzerland, the recent establishment of the new Nunavut Territory in Canada, the reorganization of states in India along linguistic lines during the 1950s and 1960s and the more recent revisions particularly in the north-east, and in Nigeria the progressive increase from three regions to 36 states. A second approach has been to assign a special responsibility to the federal government as guardian of intra-regional minorities against possible oppression by a regional majority. Canada and India have provided examples of such constitutional arrangements, although in the case of Canada the federal government has never actually exercised this authority. A third and the most widespread approach has been to protect intra-regional minorities through embodying a set of fundamental citizens' rights in the federal constitution. Examples in multinational federations are the constitutions of India, Malaysia, Spain, Canada (added in 1982), Belgium and the new Swiss Constitution of 1999.

The number of constituent units and the special problems of binational federations

While most multinational federations have found that permitting national groupings to express their distinctiveness through their own autonomous political units has in fact contributed to the easing of tensions rather than reinforcing them (Ghai 2000:23–4), this recognition has not necessarily followed a rigorous formula of 'one nation – one province'. Indeed, in the cases of Switzerland, Canada and India, it is significant that while distinct national minorities have been differentiated in the constituent units, larger national groups have been distributed over a number of constituent units so that no one single constituent unit represents a majority or unduly large portion of the federal population. These examples suggest that while a statistical 'Staatsvolk' may be identified in some of these federations (O'Leary 2001:286), in terms of political reality the multiple units into which the majority is divided limits the applicability of this concept (ibid.: 287–8). Indeed, the multiple German-speaking cantons in Switzerland, some Roman Catholic and some Protestant, and similarly of French-speaking Roman Catholic and Protestant cantons, has provided classic examples of cross-cutting cleavages moderating national divisions. One further benefit of a larger number of constituent units within a federation is that it is less likely that individual units will be tempted to adopt intransigent positions. On the other hand, an excessive number of constituent units, such as the 89 in Russia, has created problems of coherence in intergovernmental relations and has led to recent presidential efforts in Russia to group them for purposes of coordination.

One particular situation worthy of special examination is that of federal systems composed of only two constituent units. The particular problems of dyadic federations, whether binational or not, have been generally recognized (Duchacek 1988:5–31; Watts 1999:113–14). Chapter 8 by Michael Burgess on Cyprus and Chapter 3 by Patrick Peeters on Belgium draw attention to these issues. The experience of Pakistan prior to the secession of Bangladesh in 1971 and of Czechoslovakia prior to the segregation of its two parts in 1992 have provided eminent examples of the difficulties that have arisen in federations organized along binational lines. St Kitts-Nevis currently illustrates the difficulties that arise in two-unit federations even when the division is not based on conflicting nationalisms. Among cases considered in this volume, Cyprus exemplifies most sharply the difficulties of trying to establish a binational federation.

The problem with two-unit federations generally has been the inevitable tendency to insist upon parity between the two units in all matters. This has usually produced impasses and deadlocks. These occur because there is no opportunity for shifting alliances and coalitions among the constituent units or their representatives varying with different issues, processes which are among the ways issues are often resolved in multi-unit federations. Instead in a two-unit federation every policy issue becomes a zero-sum game in which one of the units is seen as the winner and the other as the loser. Furthermore, since invariably one of the units is less populous than the other, e.g. West Pakistan before 1971, Slovakia before 1992 and the Turkish community in Cyprus, that unit has usually been particularly conscious of the need to insist upon equality of influence in policy making, while the larger unit has usually developed a sense of grievance over the apparently undemocratic constraints imposed upon it in order to accommodate the smaller unit. When this is reinforced by competing nationalisms, the resulting cumulative bipolarity has usually led to terminal instability.

Canada and Belgium represent two other federations where their societies have a fundamentally binational character. In each of these cases, however, the federation has been designed to consist of more than two constituent units. Although their national minorities have their own autonomous units of self-government, Canada is organized as ten provinces and three territories and Belgium as three communities and three regions (although the Flemish community and region have combined their institutions, producing in effect five constituent units). Thus, in these two federations the fundamental binational character of their federal societies has been moderated by the political dynamics of a federation consisting of more than two units. Even though tempered in this way, nevertheless, as the chapters in this volume make clear, the predominant bipolar character has been a source of stress in both Canada and Belgium.

The issue of how to apply federal principles to a binational society is particularly salient today given the difficult negotiations in Cyprus, Sri Lanka and Serbia-Montenegro (Montenegro decided to secede from the short-lived union in 2006) that have recently been under way with the avowed aim of establishing some sort of federal solution. Some innovative institutional arrangements will undoubtedly be required in order to avoid the consistent past record of the frequent failure of binational federations (Ghai 2000:17–18).

The distribution of legislative and executive competence

Of particular importance to the character of national autonomy within a multinational federation is the form and scope of the distribution of legislative and executive competences. But the distribution of powers has taken different forms (Watts 1999:36–41). Some multinational federations, like Canada, and Belgium, have tended to emphasize the predominantly exclusive jurisdictions of each order of government by comparison with the large areas of concurrent jurisdiction more prevalent within mono-national federations such as the United States, Australia and Germany. In some federations, most notably those in Europe, and also in India in relation to areas of concurrent jurisdiction, the constituent units have been assigned executive responsibility for much of the federal legislation. But where these arrangements have required the federal government to issue directives to state governments, and even more where the federal government has been assigned power to suspend state governments for prescribed reasons, as in India and Pakistan, these provisions have often soured federal–state relations. Particularly important in the distribution of powers within multinational federations has been the allocation of responsibility over those matters of especially cultural, religious or linguistic significance, such as education and social services. In multinational federations these have usually been assigned to the constituent units of government. Generally it may be said that where over-centralization has undermined the confidence of national minorities in their autonomy over matters crucial to the expression of their distinctiveness, this has become a major source of stress. It is not surprising therefore that Switzerland and Canada should in fact be among the most decentralized federations in the world, especially by comparison with such mono-national federations as the United States, Australia, Austria and Germany (Watts 1999:79), and that Spain and particularly Belgium have experienced progressive decentralization.

The allocation of financial resources and fiscal equalization

The allocation of financial resources is particularly significant because these enable or constrain governments in the exercise of their constitutionally assigned legislative and executive responsibilities. A crucial factor here is the degree to which 'own-source' revenues form a significant portion of the finances of the constituent units and the degree to which the constituent units are dependent upon transfers from the federal government, especially discretionary transfers. Here it is significant that in the degree of decentralization of own-source revenues, Switzerland and Canada are the two most decentralized federations in the world, and that India is more decentralized than either the United States or Australia (Watts 1999:46). As Chapter 3 on Belgium by Patrick Peeters notes, this also explains the significance of the fifth stage of state reform in Belgium in 2001. In Spain such issues have led also to the different fiscal regimes for the Basque country and Navarre. Furthermore, federal conditional grants as a percentage of total provincial or state revenues have tended to be lower in multinational federations such as Canada (0.9 per cent), Malaysia (12.2 per cent), Switzerland (15 per cent) and Spain (18.2 per cent) than in the mono-national federations such as the United States (29.6 per cent) and Australia (21.6 per cent), although Germany (9.8 per cent) is an outlier in this pattern (Watts 1999:50).

Virtually all federations, mono-national or multinational, have found some form of systematic financial equalization desirable to assist the less wealthy constituent units, the notable exception being the USA (Watts 2000a). Equalization transfers have been considered necessary not simply to correct horizontal imbalances in revenue capacity among constituent units, but also to moderate the corrosive impact upon political cohesion within a federation arising from disparities of wealth among different regions or national groups (Watts 2000a:380–2). But in comparative terms it is notable that in such mono-national federations as Australia and Germany the emphasis upon financial equalization and uniform benefits throughout the federation has been much stronger than in Switzerland and Canada.

In the latter the pressures for equalization have been moderated considerably by a political culture emphasizing the importance of not sacrificing the autonomous decision making of the constituent units of government (Watts 2000a:386).

Symmetry and asymmetry in the relationship of constituent units to the federation

Although symmetry in the relationship of constituent units to the federation is the most common pattern in mono-national federations, a number of multinational federations have adopted some degree of asymmetry, either transitional or permanent, in order to accommodate sharply differing degrees of intensity in the pressure for autonomy among different national groups (Agranoff 1999). Among notable examples of asymmetry in federations have been Canada, Malaysia, India, Belgium, Spain and Russia (Watts 2000b). These cases of asymmetry have all exhibited some degree of success in accommodating the differing internal pressures for autonomy. In some other cases, however, notably the disintegration of the USSR (1991) and Yugoslavia (1991) and the expulsion of Singapore from Malaysia in 1965, the existence of sharp asymmetries was a major contributing factor. One must also note the Canadian, Spanish and Russian experience, where asymmetrical arrangements or their advocacy provoked in turn counter-pressures for symmetry, and therefore became a source for greater rather than reduced political conflict. These examples suggest that asymmetry may often be helpful but is not a panacea, and that there may be limits beyond which *de jure* asymmetry among constituent units may prove dysfunctional (Watts, 2000b).

The guarantee of autonomy arrangements by constitutional entrenchment

In a multinational context, the guarantee of the autonomy arrangements for constituent national groups is a crucial factor in reducing tensions (Ghai 2000:21–2). The constitutional entrenchment of national autonomy has been important in order to provide a sense of security for each national group. Most federal constitutions require for their amendment the assent of the federal government and of a specified majority of the constituent units (whether by referendum or by their legislatures). Furthermore, in the case of Malaysia, major amendments affecting the Borneo states specifically require the concurrence of those states. Belgium and Spain depart from this pattern. The Belgian procedure for constitutional amendment (Article 131) is somewhat different. It does not involve the regions or communities as such, but does require a complex process requiring a special election, special majorities in each federal house, and in many aspects special legislation supported by a majority of each of the two major linguistic groups in Parliament. In Spain the formal role of the autonomous communities in constitutional amendments is also relatively limited, although there is provision for an Autonomous Community Assembly to propose constitutional amendments. Ratification of constitutional amendments, however, requires only special majorities in each federal chamber and in certain circumstances also a referendum.

Dispute settlement mechanisms

An independent dispute settlement mechanism is essential for the long-term effectiveness of the autonomy arrangements in a multinational federation. While this is true of all federations where the common form of dispute resolution is judicial review with either a Supreme Court or a Constitutional Court as the ultimate body for resolving constitutional disputes, it is a particularly important feature where the governments concerned may represent different national groups. A unique alternative to reliance upon judicial review is the arrangement in Switzerland. There federal legislation is not subject to judicial review, but if challenged may be subject to a ratifying referendum. This has in practice reinforced the consensus character of federal politics in Switzerland since the threat of a referendum has induced a practice of seeking maximum support (not just a bare majority) in the Parliament for federal legislation. The usual passage there of legislation by much more than a narrow majority reduces the potential vulnerability of legislation to a subsequent referendum challenge.

While in most federations the courts may provide the ultimate dispute settlement mechanism, in all of them the political settlement of disputes as an alternative has also been particularly important. Given the inevitable interdependence of the different governments that constitute a federal partnership, a vital feature in practice in all federations, and multinational federations are no exception, has been the development of mechanisms and processes for effective intergovernmental collaboration and dispute resolution (Watts 1999:57–61). There are some kinds of disputes such as those relating to the allocation of financial resources or those relating to intergovernmental cooperation, which are in fact better handled by political bargaining and negotiation than by judicial review. But it is important that these intergovernmental processes are genuinely cooperative, and that they do not smother the autonomy or initiative of governments at each level. Where one level of government tends to dominate these processes, as in South Africa, the result has been an undermining of genuine self-government within the provinces.

Features of institutional design and political processes facilitating shared rule

While the particular institutional arrangements and political processes for providing and securing genuine self-government for national groups participating in multinational federations have had a major effect upon the moderation of political conflict and thus the sustainability of these federations, equally important have been the institutions and processes facilitating *shared rule* (Smiley and Watts 1985:1–5). Here we need to look at how the design of the institutions and the development of political processes have contributed to cohesion within multinational federations. A particularly important feature is the extent to which the institutions of federal government have contributed to what Lijphart has labelled the consensus model of democracy as opposed to the majoritarian model of democracy (Lijphart 1999:9–47). Generally, successful multinational federations have exhibited the characteristics of consensus democracy, although the extent to which that has been the case has varied considerably. Of the multinational federations considered in this book, Switzerland and Belgium have gone furthest in developing institutions and political processes of consensus democracy. India, although its parliamentary institutions have some of the majoritarian characteristics of the Westminster model has, with the reliance in recent decades upon wide coalitions of regional parties at the federal level, developed political processes involving the characteristics of consensus democracy. Malaysia too, while retaining predominately majoritarian parliamentary institutional structures, has exhibited interracial coalition politics of a more consensual character. Other multinational federations such as Canada and Spain are primarily majoritarian in the character of their institutions of federal government, but have tempered these with some political processes more typical of the consensus model of democracy.

Among the different institutional arrangements that will be noted here in terms of how they have contributed to consensus processes and power-sharing are: (1) the form of federal government executive–legislative relationships; (2) arrangements for cross-community executive power-sharing; (3) the proportional representation of different major national groups in the institutions of federal government; (4) bicameralism; (5) minority veto rights regarding decision making at the federal level; (6) the electoral system; (7) the operation of political parties; (8) the constitutional entrenchment of individual and group rights; and (9) conceptions of citizenship.

Executive–legislative relations in the institutions of federal government

A major factor facilitating or constraining the development of consensus politics has been the character of the relationships between federal executive and legislative institutions. Among federations we can identify two broad categories in the legislative–executive relationships in their representative institutions of federal government: (1) those embodying the separation of executive and legislative powers as in the presidential–congressional institutions of the United States and of the Latin American federations and in the fixed term collegial executive of Switzerland, and (2) those embodying the fusion of legislative and executive powers in a parliamentary executive responsible to the popularly elected house of the federal legislature. This second pattern may itself take two different forms. One is that following the majoritarian Westminster model as originally adopted in Canada, Australia, India and Malaysia. The other follows European traditions of responsible cabinet government generally based on coalitions and therefore emphasizing power-sharing and consensus politics as generally found in Austria, Germany, Belgium and Spain.

Each of these forms has a different democratic premise and each has a significant impact upon the dynamics of power-sharing within the institutions of federal governments. The separation of executive and legislative powers with fixed terms for each is directed at limiting the abuse of power by a majority. It does this through diffusing authority and thereby requiring compromises that take the views of minority groups into account. In theory it aims at limiting majoritarian dominance. In practice the presidential–congressional form, especially in its Latin American manifestations, because of the dominant position of the President in practice has, however, been prone frequently to authoritarianism. The Swiss variant, because of the collegial character of the executive and the annual rotation of the presidency among its members, has been much more effective in encouraging the meaningful representation of nearly all the major groups within the decision-making processes of the federal executive and legislature. It provides an example of a fully consensual model of democracy.

The contrasting democratic premise of parliamentary executive institutions is that by placing the executive in the legislature and making it continuously responsible to the legislature, which is itself democratically controlled by the electorate, coherent but controlled and accountable federal policies will be possible. This form, like the Swiss, enables the representation of different groups within the executive. But in those examples modelled on Westminster, especially with single member plurality electoral systems, the tendency for party discipline to prevail and for prime ministerial dominance to result, has in practice led to a much more majoritarian character than in the Swiss institutions and processes. A clear example is the operation of the Canadian federal institutions. This majoritarian tendency is somewhat moderated, however, in the European examples of parliamentary government by the prevalence of coalition governments. This has resulted from the tendency to multiparty situations induced by their reliance on proportional representation in their electoral systems. In the Belgian case, this tendency to consensus rather than majoritarian decision making is strongly reinforced by a number of institutional arrangements requiring balanced representation in the cabinet and legislative processes in order to ensure support by both major linguistic groups for particularly contentious policies.

There is a third category which might be described as a hybrid presidential–parliamentary form of government. Russia and most recently Pakistan are examples within multinational federations of this form in which a directly elected President holds some significant executive powers combined with a parliamentary cabinet responsible to the federal legislature. An earlier non-federal example of this form of executive–legislature relationship is provided by France. From the point of view of power-sharing amongst different national groups in a multinational federation this hybrid would appear, however, to combine the defects of both the presidential and the parliamentary forms of institutions.

Cross-community executive power-sharing

Cross-community executive power-sharing has been a common feature in most effective multinational federations. It has been most marked in Switzerland in the operation of the collegial Federal Council based for so long until recently on the traditional 'magic formula' for the representation of the four major political parties (generally representing over three-quarters of the seats held in the federal Parliament), on the constitutional requirement that no canton may be represented by more than one Councillor, and on the tradition of representation of the major language groups. This has been further reinforced by two features. One is the tradition of extensive consultation with cantonal governments on major issues, now under the new constitution, adopted in 1999, including even some aspects of foreign policy. The other is the way in which, as already noted, in order to reduce the vulnerability of ordinary federal legislation to referendum challenges, the widest possible (not merely majoritarian) support for federal legislation in the Parliament has been regularly sought.

The parliamentary federations have also been marked by extensive representation of different communities and interests in their executives, and in addition have developed an extensive variety of intergovernmental executive relations between the federal and constituent unit governments. In Canada, although single party majorities have prevailed most of the time, the balanced representation of different groups within the cabinet has become a firm tradition. Furthermore 'executive federalism', as the predominant mode of intergovernmental relations, has become a distinctive characteristic of the Canadian federation (Watts 1999:85–90). India in recent years has, because of the fragmenting of federation-wide parties, by contrast, developed a tradition of multiparty coalitions in Parliament and the federal cabinet. These have required power-sharing among the different interests represented by the variety of state parties participating in the federal coalitions. As is typical of parliamentary federations, India has also relied heavily on federal–state intergovernmental executive consultation and negotiation. Belgium has developed explicit constitutional rules about the balanced composition of the federal executive giving strictly equal representation to the two major linguistic communities (not counting the Prime Minister). There are also constitutional rules requiring support from both linguistic communities in the processes for establishing certain policies. In addition there are explicit arrangements to ensure intergovernmental consultation and negotiation including the coordination of the activities of the federal and constituent unit governments in foreign affairs. Of these multinational federations, Switzerland and Belgium have incorporated the most specific legal requirements for cross-community executive power-sharing, whereas in Canada, India and Spain such arrangements are extensive but have rested more on convention and pragmatic practice.

Proportional representation of national groups

Representation of all major national groups proportionally within the institutions of federal government has been typical of effective multinational federations. These have related not simply to representation in the federal executive, as already noted above, but to the composition of the federal public services, agencies and commissions, and the courts. In relation to the courts, for instance, in Belgium strict legal requirements are laid down for linguistic balance in the Court of Arbitration, and in Canada Quebec's distinct civil law tradition is recognized by the arrangement that three of the nine judges of the Supreme Court are chosen from Quebec. Thus, through the operation of a 'proportionality syndrome' members of different national communities have participated in various sectors of federal policy making. In some cases, provision for distinct national and cultural groups within federal government institutions has been entrenched in laws or constitutional documents, particularly in Switzerland and Belgium. In most multinational federations, however, these requirements have been informal, the result of political conventions or sometimes of general election results that have left particular national groups holding the balance of power in the federal legislature (as during the period when in Spain the ruling Conservatives governed with the support of the Catalan nationalists).

Bicameralism

Lijphart (1999:205–15) distinguishes between strong and weak bicameralism arguing that the former is an important element in democracies based on the consensus model and in federal as opposed to unitary systems. Federal legislative second chambers provide a means of moderating or counteracting the usually majoritarian tendency of the first chambers, where representation is based on population. Minority national groups are assured an effective voice in federal policy making through a second chamber based on a different principle of representation. Bicameralism has been a feature of most multinational federations, but the degree to which bicameralism has had a strong influence has varied (Watts 1999:92–7). The Council of States of Switzerland, with equal powers to the other chamber in the federal legislature and with full cantons each equally represented, provides a clear example of strong bicameralism. However, in the multinational federations with parliamentary institutions, whether of the Westminster or of the European type, bicameralism has been considerably weaker. A major factor is that the relative influence of the second chamber has been limited by the predominant role occupied by the federal legislative chamber to which the executive is responsible. In addition, most parliamentary second chambers have been granted only limited veto powers. Furthermore, their role in representing state or minority national views has in a number of cases been weakened by the composition of the federal second chamber or the method of selection of their members. In the case of India representatives in the federal second chamber are elected by the state legislatures. But this is only partially the case in Malaysia, Belgium and Spain. In Canada and Malaysia, where all or a majority of members of the federal second chamber are in fact appointed by the federal government, their legitimacy as representatives of national or regional minorities is clearly seriously undermined. Thus, with the exception of Switzerland, the multinational federations examined in this volume have in fact relied only to a modest degree upon bicameralism as an element of federal power-sharing.

The significance of the electoral system

Electoral systems have affected the way in which national groups have been represented within federal policy-making institutions (Watts 1999:96). The single member plurality system in Canada, for instance, has often exaggerated national differences by turning what is merely a plurality opinion within a particular constituency or province into virtually an overwhelming majority or an apparently 'only' opinion. Canada's federal elections during the past three decades have often exaggerated the radical nationalist and secessionist support in Quebec and the anti-Quebec support in western Canada, in both cases penalizing more moderate parties whose votes are spread more evenly across the different provinces. By contrast, in the European federations, the use of proportional representation electoral systems has represented the different national groups more accurately, and in the case of those with parliamentary institutions has moderated the majoritarian tendencies by leading regularly to the need for coalition governments at the federal level. Generally speaking proportional representation electoral systems have tended to encourage multiparty systems. As a result multiparty coalitions have been the norm, rather than the exception, for federal governments in both parliamentary federations such as Belgium and non-parliamentary federations such as Switzerland.

The role of political parties

An important factor in the dynamics of power-sharing in any federation has been the character and role of its political parties (Riker 1975; Watts 1999:90–2). These tend to be influenced by the institutional framework, particularly the executive–legislative relationship and the electoral system, and by the diversity in the underlying society.

In terms of party organization, in non-parliamentary federations such as Switzerland, federal political parties have tended to be loose confederations of cantonal and local party organizations. This has contributed to the maintenance of non-centralized government and the prominence of cantonal interests within federal policy debates. In the parliamentary federations based on the Westminster model, by contrast, the prevalence of stronger party discipline has tended to sharpen the differences between federal and provincial party organizations, most notably in Canada, and to place some limits upon the open expression of different interests within each political party at the federal level.

Given the importance of power-sharing among national groups within the federal institutions of multinational federations, a significant contrasting pattern is that between those federations in which at the federal level, coalition building between different national groups is predominantly *within* political parties, and those in which coalition building is predominantly *between* political parties. The federal Liberal Party in Canada, the ANC in South Africa and the Indian National Congress in India (during the Nehru era) have represented efforts to build a consensus among various national groups and interests within a single party in order to achieve a majority government within the federal parliament. Switzerland, Belgium and more recently India provide a variety of examples where in a multiparty situation the aggregation of different national groups and interests at the federal level has had instead to be achieved by inter-party coalitions.

Minority veto rights

One way of assuring minority national groups a sense of security for their participation in federal policy making is by incorporating in the federal institutional design a right of veto over federal policies or constitutional amendments that might threaten their distinctiveness. Indeed Lijphart (1977) includes among the four essential features of consociational political regimes the operation of formal or informal minority veto rights. In terms of formal national minority veto rights, a particularly clear example is the Belgian 'alarm bell' procedure within the federal parliament which calls into operation certain specified procedures to accommodate minority concerns. Another example of a formal minority veto right is that incorporated in the Malaysian constitution relating to constitutional amendments that affect the Borneo states. But even where minority veto rights are not formally specified in the constitution, the widespread informal acceptance of national minority veto rights in relation to certain federal policies has been a significant feature in most multinational federations, and most of all in Switzerland. It is noteworthy that while giving real weight to national minority views in policy making at the federal level has played an important role in accommodating national minorities in the Belgian, Swiss and Canadian federations, the undermining of such arrangements can have extremely divisive effects. One reason for the strains in the relationship between the Québécois and the rest of Canada after 1982 was the non-inclusion in the Constitution Act, 1982, of what the Québécois had previously regarded as a traditional informal right to veto major constitutional changes (McGarry 2002:437). Significantly some of this resentment was placated in the late 1990s by a resolution in the Canadian Parliament that it would not in future amend the Constitution without the approval of the Quebec National Assembly (and of each of the four other major regional groupings of provinces). Nevertheless, this veto is not constitutionally entrenched and therefore remains dependant upon the federal Parliament to honour it.

Constitutionally entrenched group and individual rights

Most of the multinational federations examined in this book have embodied in their constitutions a set of fundamental citizens' rights. Examples are India, Malaysia, Spain, Canada (added in 1982), Belgium and the new Swiss Constitution (1999). Earlier, we noted that one function of such entrenched group and individual rights has been to provide assurances to minorities within minorities. But constitutionally entrenched fundamental group and individual rights have also been advocated as a way of providing overarching values shared by all the different groups within the federation, thus serving to foster and strengthen a sense of common loyalty and identity among the different national groups within a multinational federation (Simeon and Conway 2001:361,363).

Conceptions of citizenship

One factor that may affect cohesion in a multinational federation is the degree to which the majority community accepts the multinational character of the federation by recognizing and supporting the minority national communities as nations. Contributing to the tensions within Canada in the four decades after 1960 was a situation in which many Québécois tended to think of Canada as composed of two national communities, Quebec and English-speaking Canada, while many English Canadians tended to think instead in terms of a national federation in which there was only one national community based on Canada as a whole but containing multicultural and polyethnic elements (McGarry 2002:437). As Alain Gagnon (1993, and his Chapter 2 in this volume) has suggested, this conflict between two perspectives of nation, in ethnic or in civic terms, might be better resolved if the distinction between nation and citizenship were to be drawn more clearly. The multinational character of Canada might then be recognized as relating to national components which share a common citizenship within a multinational federation.

In Chapter 6 on Spain Luis Moreno refers to a 'nation of nations' and draws our attention to the distinction between the constituent nations and the 'composed' character of a multinational federation. Harihar Bhattacharrya in his comparison of India and Switzerland in Chapter 11 makes a similar point about both federations as 'composed states'. He suggests a distinction between 'thick' and 'thin' nations and identities. This metaphor is an interesting one, but it may be open to misinterpretation, however, if it leads readers to infer varying strengths of nationalism. What he clearly intends, however, is to indicate different kinds, not strengths, of nationalism, i.e. ethnic nationalism and civic nationalism. In Switzerland, India, Spain, Malaysia and Canada these two kinds of nationalism are significant. What is important to the cohesion of these multinational federations is to avoid the sense of conflict between the two kinds of nationalisms: the constituent ethnic nations and an overriding federal civic nationalism. The accommodation of multiple identities within a multinational federation is more likely to be facilitated if the distinct constituent nations are recognized as elements within the federation which is itself characterized not as a nation but as a polity in which the constituent nations share a common federal citizenship.

Conclusion

Multinational federations have in practice tended to be more difficult to work, but there have been a number of examples of stable liberal democratic multinational federations. A full picture of the ways in which multinational federations have been sustained requires an examination of the variety of ways in which the self-government of the constituent national groups has been implemented and safeguarded, and of the variety of institutions and processes within the common institutions of shared rule that have facilitated power-sharing.

Five further concluding points should be emphasized. First, federal political systems *do* provide a practical way of achieving through democratic representative institutions the management of conflict in multinational societies. They are *not*, however, a panacea for all humanity's political ills.

Second, the extent to which a federal system can accommodate multinational realities depends not just on the adoption of federation, but upon whether the particular form or variant of federal institutions established gives adequate expression to the specific needs and characteristics of that particular society. Third, institutional arrangements and political processes that ensure effective autonomy and self-rule for constituent national groups are essential for accommodating their desire to maintain their identities, distinctiveness and self-fulfilment. Fourth, institutional arrangements and political processes that involve genuine power-sharing within the federal level of government are also essential for generating a continuing consensus required for holding the federation together. Finally, federal arrangements are more likely to succeed where there are established traditions of democracy, rule of law and compromise. In practice the degree to which a multinational federation is effective has depended not just on its constitutional and institutional structure, but even more on the degree to which there has been a broad public acceptance of the political culture and values of federalism, of the need to cherish diversity and to develop mutual respect, of a sense of shared rule and community, of respect for constitutional norms, and a prevailing spirit of tolerance and compromise.

Note

1 For a fuller discussion of their multinational character see Chapter 1. Also considered in this volume are Switzerland and the European Union. Switzerland is clearly not a mono-national federation, but rather a 'composed federation' although its constituent units are not distinct nations (as noted in Chapter 11). The European Union is clearly multinational, but rather than a federation it is an evolving federal union which includes some elements of an intergovernmental confederation and some of a federation (as noted in Chapter 9).

References

Agranoff, R. ed. 1999. *Accommodating Diversity: Asymmetry in Federal States.* Baden-Baden: Nomos Verlagageselschaft.

Duchacek, I. ed. 1988. 'Bicommuinal societies and politics', *Publius: the Journal of Federalism*, Special issue 18(2).

Elazar, Daniel J. 1987. *Exploring Federalism.* Tuscaloosa, AL: University of Alabama.

Elazar, Daniel J. 1993. 'International and Comparative Federalism', *PS: Political Science and Politics*, 26(2):190–5.

Elazar, Daniel J. 1994. *Federalism and the Way to Peace: Essays by Daniel J. Elazar.* Kingston: Institute of Intergovernmental Relations.

Franck, Thomas M. 1968. *Why Federations Fail: An Inquiry into the Requisites for Successful Federation.* New York: New York University Press.

Gagnon, A.-G. 1993. 'The Political Uses of Federalism' in M. Burgess and A.-G. Gagnon, eds. *Comparative Federalism and Federation: Competing Traditions and Future Directions.* Hemel Hempstead: Harvester Wheatsheaf:15–44.

Ghai, Yash. ed. 2000. *Autonomy and Ethnicity: Negotiating Competing Claims in Multiethnic States.* Cambridge and Oakleigh: Cambridge University Press.

Hicks, Ursula K. 1978. *Federalism, Failure and Success: a Comparative Study.* London: Macmillan.

Horowitz, D.L. 1985. *Ethnic Groups in Conflict.* Berkeley, CA: University of California Press.

King, Preston. 1982. *Federalism and Federation.* London: Croom Helm.

Kymlicka, Will. 1995. *Multicultural Citizenship.* Oxford: Clarendon Press.

Lijphart, Arend. 1977. *Democracy in Plural Societies: A Comparative Exploration.* New Haven, CT and London: Yale University Press.

Lijphart, Arend. 1999. *Patterns of Democracy: Government Forms and Performance in Thirty-Six Countries.* New Haven and London: Yale University Press.

McGarry, J. 2002. 'Federal Political Systems and the Accommodation of National

Minorities' in A. Griffiths, ed. *Handbook of Federal Countries*. Montreal and Kingston: McGill-Queen's University Press for the Forum of Ederations:416–47.

O'Leary, Brendan. 2001. 'An Iron Law of Nationalism and Federation? A (Neo-Diceyian) Theory of the Necessity of a Federal *Staatsvolk* and of Consociational Rescue', *Nations and Nationalism*, 7(3):273–96.

Riker, W.H. 1975. 'Federalism' in F.I. Greenstein and N.W. Polsby, eds. *Handbook of Political Science: Governmental Institutions and Processes*. Vol. 5. Reading, MA: Addison-Wesley:93–172.

Simeon, Richard and Conway, D.-P. 2001. 'Federalism and Management of Conflict in Multinational Societies' in Alain-G. Gagnon and James Tully, eds. *Multinational Democracies*. Cambridge: Cambridge University Press:338–65.

Smiley, D.V. and Watts, R.L. 1985. *Intrastate Federalism in Canada*. Toronto: University of Toronto Press.

Supreme Court of Canada. 1998. *Reference on Secession of Quebec*. 25CR217.

Wachendorfer-Schmidt, U. ed. 2000. *Federalism and Political Performance*. London and New York: Routledge.

Watts, R.L. 1977. 'The Survival and Disintegration of Federations' in R. Simeon, ed. *Must Canada Fail?* Montreal: McGill-Queen's University Press:42–62.

Watts, R.L. 1998. 'Federalism, Federal Political Systems and Federations', *Annual Review of Political Science*, 1:117–37.

Watts, R.L. 1999. *Comparing Federal Systems*. 2nd edn. Montreal and Kingston: McGill-Queen's University Press.

Watts, R.L. 2000a. 'Federal Financial Relations: A Comparative Perspective' in H. Lazar, ed. *Canada: The State of the Federation: Toward A New Mission Statement for Canadian Fiscal Federalism*. Montreal and Kingston: McGill-Queen's University Press:371–88.

Watts, R.L. 2000b. *Asymmetical Decentralization: Functional or Dysfunctional?* Ottawa: Forum of Federations.

Watts, R.L. 2003 'Lessons from the Pathology of Multicultural Federations' in Peter Hanni, ed. *Mensch und Staat; L'homme et l'Etat: Festschrift in Honour of Thomas Fleiner*. Fribourg: Editions Universitaires Fribourg Swisse:221–36.

Index

Tables are indicated by italic page numbers and illustrations by bold numbers.